Knowing Nothing
Staying Stupid

MW00834584

Knowing Nothing, Staying Stupid draws on recent research to provide a thorough and illuminating evaluation of the status of knowledge and truth in psychoanalysis. Adopting a Lacanian framework, Dany Nobus and Malcolm Quinn question the basic assumption that knowledge is universally good and describe how psychoanalysis is in a position to place forms of knowledge in a dialectical relationship with non-knowledge, blindness, ignorance and stupidity. The book draws out the implications of a psychoanalytic theory of knowledge for the practices of knowledge construction, acquisition and transmission across the humanities and social sciences.

The book is divided into two sections. The first section addresses the foundations of a psychoanalytic approach to knowledge as it emerges from clinical practice, whilst the second section considers the problems and issues of applied psychoanalysis, and the ambiguous position of the analyst in the public sphere. Subjects covered include:

- The logic of psychoanalytic discovery.
- Creative knowledge production and institutionalized doctrine.
- The desire to know versus the fall of knowledge.
- Epistemological regression and the problem of applied psychoanalysis.

This provocative discussion of the dialectics of knowing and not knowing will be welcomed by practising psychoanalysts and students of psychoanalytic studies, but also by everyone working in the fields of social science, philosophy and cultural studies.

Dany Nobus is Senior Lecturer in Psychology and Psychoanalytic Studies at Brunel University. He is the author of *Jacques Lacan and the Freudian Practice of Psychoanalysis* and the Editor-in-Chief of *Journal for Lacanian Studies.*

Malcolm Quinn is Senior Lecturer and Research Co-ordinator at Wimbledon School of Art. He has published work on the fascist spectacle, art and cultural politics. He is an Editor of *Journal for Lacanian Studies.*

Knowing Nothing, Staying Stupid

Elements for a psychoanalytic epistemology

Dany Nobus and Malcolm Quinn

Routledge
Taylor & Francis Group

LONDON AND NEW YORK

First published 2005
by Routledge
27 Church Road, Hove, East Sussex BN3 2FA

Simultaneously published in the USA and Canada
by Routledge
270 Madison Avenue, New York NY 10016

Routledge is an imprint of the Taylor & Francis Group

Copyright © 2005 Dany Nobus & Malcolm Quinn

Typeset in Times by RefineCatch Ltd., Bungay, Suffolk
Printed and bound in Great Britain by
MPG Books, Bodmin, Cornwall
Paperback cover design by Bob Rowinski
Paperback cover image: 'Blockhead' by Paul McCarthy, 2003.
Inflatable sculpture, courtesy the artist and Hauser & Wirth Zürich
London; © Paul McCarthy Photographic; © Tate, London 2005.

This publication has been produced with paper manufactured
to strict environmental standards and with pulp derived from
sustainable forests.

British Library Cataloguing in Publication Data
A catalogue record for this book is available from the British Library

Library of Congress Cataloging-in-Publication Data
Nobus, Dany.
    Knowing nothing, staying stupid : elements for a psychoanalytic
epistemology / Dany Nobus and Malcolm Quinn.–1st ed.
        p. cm
    Includes bibliographical references and index.
    ISBN 1-58391-867-1 (hbk) – ISBN 1-58391-868-X (pbk.)
    1. Psychoanalysis and philosophy.   I. Quinn, Malcolm,
    1963–   II. Title.
    BF175.4.P45N63 2005
    150.19'5–dc22   2005002571

ISBN 1-58391-867-1 (hbk)
ISBN 1-58391-868-X (pbk)

Contents

Acknowledgements

Chapter 2 is based on D. Nobus (2002) 'A Matter of Cause: Reflections on Lacan's "Science and Truth"', in J. Glynos and Y. Stavrakakis (eds) *Lacan and Science*, London–New York: Karnac Books, pp. 89–118.

A preliminary version of Chapter 3 was published as D. Nobus (2004) 'The Punning of Reason: On the Strange Case of Dr Jacques L. . . .', *Angelaki*, 9(1), pp. 189–201 (www.tandf.co.uk).

Chapter 4 is based on D. Nobus (2004) 'Knowledge in Failure: On the Crises of Legitimacy within Lacanian Psychoanalysis', in A. Casement (ed.) *Who Owns Psychoanalysis?*, London–New York: Karnac Books, pp. 203–225.

Introduction

Education and culture tell us that knowledge is good and that shared knowledge is even better. This assumption should not pass unquestioned. A psychoanalytic approach to knowledge offers a different view, which is that knowledge exchange is one of the things that sustains 'the good' as a zone of work, intersubjective communication and deferred desire. What is now called the 'knowledge economy' is but another name for a form of dependency in which we are all potential knowledge specialists, and therefore perpetually in debt to someone else's knowledge. Rather than establishing a commonality of understanding, this situation consolidates the rule of the individual knowledge ego, from the car mechanic to the nuclear scientist. Under this rule, any criticism of the 'knowledge is good' thesis can only appear uncalled-for, frivolous, even antisocial. Yet it is our contention in this book that psychoanalysis offers a rational, systematic and thorough means of questioning the good of knowledge, as well as the value of knowledge goods.

The necessary first step towards this end is to clarify the epistemological status of psychoanalysis itself. Scholars investigating the question of a specifically psychoanalytic epistemology have generally attempted to seek answers by examining which established forms of knowledge Freud's intervention most closely resembles. The best-known example of this approach is to question whether psychoanalysis is an art, a science or a religion, prompting numerous researchers to evaluate the origin and function of psychoanalytic knowledge. The issue as to what kind of knowledge psychoanalysis epitomizes has also emerged in controversial debates on the 'veracity' or 'fabrication' of evidence in the psychoanalytic setting (Borch-Jacobsen 2000). These debates, which also employ the technique of comparison across discourses and forms of knowledge,

[handwritten left margin: ...uualizations in English depts]

[handwritten bottom: epistemology (noun) the philosophical theory of knowledge.]

generally occlude the specificity of psychoanalytic knowledge and the particular ways in which psychoanalysis aligns knowledge and truth.

This book avoids establishing the 'truth' of psychoanalysis in relation to other disciplines. Instead, it proceeds to show how the specificity of a psychoanalytic approach to the relationship between knowledge and truth has significant implications for other disciplines, and for the social conditions of knowledge production, acquisition and accumulation. In this respect, our book does not share the assumption that psychoanalysis can be readily assimilated within interdisciplinary frameworks combining (for example) literary theory, anthropology and cultural studies. Yet our argument also carries implications for the psychoanalytic community, since the ill-considered 'application' of psychoanalytic terms and concepts by analysts or analyst academics to political, social and cultural phenomena, may ignore fundamental epistemological issues in much the same way as does the social contextualization of psychoanalytic knowledge by the human sciences. Our book therefore occupies the hitherto unexplored territory between the free-for-all postmodern rhetoric of much applied psychoanalysis, and the current reaction in favour of quantitative and evidence-based methods in the human sciences. It accomplishes its aim through a return to the function of knowledge in the clinical situation, using this strategy to re-examine the relationship between knowledge, public discourse and the service of goods.

The Baconian aphorism 'knowledge is power' was the defining truism of the second half of the last century and it has also cast its shadow over the new one. It is the basis of the public fantasy that knowledge is something that should be acquired, and that access to the right kind of knowledge is the key to success. The other side of this fantasy is the threatening spectre of the knowledge that we have not acquired, and which we suspect that our partners, colleagues or leaders may be withholding from us. In this book, we offer another way to read the phrase 'knowledge is power'; notably that 'knowledge is not what it seems', a reworking that is entirely consistent with Bacon's own rejection of the impotent scholasticism that was identified as knowledge in his own era. But the challenge we discern in the works of Freud and Lacan is much more radical than the Baconian manoeuvre, which merely exchanges one kind of knowledge (scholasticism) for another (empiricism). Psychoanalysis offers a more comprehensive refutation of the notion that knowledge is something acquired by means of comparison and choice between competing discourses and positions. We argue that Lacan's 'return to Freud' posits knowledge as something *worth losing*, a proposition heralded in the title of our book. *Eternal Sunshine of the Spotless*

mind

In our everyday lives, the experience of traumatic knowledge loss is already gaining pace on the value of knowledge acquisition; we constantly encounter situations where the knowledge we have so painstakingly acquired is seen to deliver less and less 'power' in the form of personal and social agency. Our allegedly refined ethnographic consciousness does not make us any better at reading other cultures, or even our own; our knowledge of the inner workings of capital or the machinations of government 'spin' does not seem to connect us to the levers of power. The erudite are humbled and the lowbrow destined for high office. If our contemporary situation is one in which the getting of knowledge produces agency without consequence, then 'the fall of knowledge' in psychoanalysis introduces us to the dimension of the unconscious, in which there is consequence without agency. The unconscious is not *the* knowledge, the secret undercurrent of discourse, but *a* knowledge, the intractable Other of knowledge itself. Paradoxically, all the clarity required for the exposition of psychoanalytic vocabulary and technique is devoted to exposing this point of irreducible obscurity within the demand to know. Whereas ordinary discourse separates the victorious moment of acquiring knowledge from the trauma of being unable to lay hold of it, psychoanalysis sees this very moment of triumphant acquisition as being marked by the inexorability of the epistemological fall.

Culturally speaking, there are knowledge winners, knowledge losers and knowledge providers. There are people whose epistemic capital is growing through careful investing and regular visits to the institutional banks of knowledge, and people whose poverty of thought is deemed to have reduced their chances of self-empowerment so much that they urgently require a new boost of knowledge fused with the transferable skills to employ it profitably. From a psychoanalytic point of view, this distinction no longer applies. Whereas cultural discourses oppose the usefulness of clear knowledge to the uselessness of obscurantist beliefs and ignorance, the analytic discourse supersedes this antagonism and exposes the radical inconsistencies underpinning the epistemic structures of reason. This is, at least, what the psychoanalytic enterprise is geared towards in the clinical applications of Freudo-Lacanian theory. Instead of *(noun) a person undergoing psychoanalysis*

regarding the analysand as someone whose quality of life is disturbed because of a pervasive lack of knowledge, we should see the analysand as the only player in the analytic game who is considered to harbour the true 'supposed subject of knowing', despite the fact that he may invest the analyst with the ability to know and bring to light all the unknowns. When the analyst eventually falls from knowledge and the analysand comes to recognize that the attribution of the 'supposed subject of knowing' was but an avatar of her own fantasmatic belief in the power of knowledge, this event coincides with a reorganization of knowledge around the gaps and fissures that animate it. If there is any kind of end (aim, goal) to the psychoanalytic process, it thus entails the analysand's acknowledgement of the dimension of not-knowing on which every epistemic discourse is based, the more so as it attempts to suture the cracks of ignorance with the totalizing and universalizing ideals of academic science.

Lacan was adamant that the analysand's attribution of the 'supposed subject of knowing' to the analyst should never be an excuse for the latter's identification with knowledge, even less for his employment of knowledge as a therapeutic tool. If the analytic discourse, by virtue of the rule of free association, clears the path for the emergence of the analysand's stupidities, as epitomized in the 'formations of the unconscious', then the analyst's profession of knowledge would effectively transform the process of analysis into an educational practice. Rather than reintegrating the analysand's stupidities within a consistent body of knowledge, or replacing them with a more adequate, adapted and competent knowledge whose market value is recognized by the authoritative discursive ideologies, the analyst fully exposes the formations of the unconscious as headless pieces of knowledge, disruptive eruptions of meaninglessness against the comfortable backdrop of established reason. Sometimes this exposure will take place through the analyst's 'wise' use of ignorance, through his pretending not to know, not to understand, not to have a clue about what the analysand is talking about. Sometimes it will occur through the analyst's intentional employment of puns, mishearings, misreadings and associated rhetorical devices designed to overturn the analysand's 'common' discourse and reveal the degree of nonsense which traverses the surface of sense.

If the analyst's attempts at reintegrating the analysand's stupidities within a regulated discursive practice imperil the survival of the analytic discourse, then the same is true for the recuperation of stupidity into a new form of cleverness, for this would inevitably entail the possibility of the meaningless eruptions, the headless knowledge and the fissures of learning being 'positivized' as the material contents of a new instructional paradigm. For this reason, the reader should not interpret our elements for a psychoanalytic epistemology as the written outcome of our desire to glamorize the qualities of non-reason. Although we argue against the antagonism of cleverness and stupidity, and the culturally endorsed belief in the superiority of the former, our discourse does not intend to expound the virtues of stupidity and contribute to a new radical 'pedagogy of ignorance'. Such a project would no doubt elevate stupidity to the dignity of an ontological state and thus annihilate its fundamental aspect of non-relationality. Contrary to Avital Ronell, who claimed in her book *Stupidity* that 'stupidity consists . . . in the absence of a relation to knowing' (Ronell 2002: 5), we believe that stupidity is not so much defined by the absence of a relationship to knowing, as, more radically, by *a knowledge that is no longer relational*, that essentially disrupts the relational quality of any discursive structure. Stupidity is a modality of knowledge which evacuates the inter-subjective relations that structure the epistemic field. This is why stupidity is not a new, fashionable way of being clever. By replacing an established discourse on knowledge with an alternative discourse on stupidity, the latter would acquire a new form of sense within the context of social practice, which would no doubt enlighten the threatening darkness of the stupid world but would also eradicate its elusive, inchoate nature. For precisely this reason, psychoanalysis does not make someone stupid, but allows someone to stay stupid, inasmuch as it allows one to experience and acknowledge the non-relational character of stupidity again, and again.

Adopting a Lacanian framework of reference, our book opens with the epistemological issues that are raised by the interface between psychoanalytic theory and clinical practice. The epistemo-logical economy of psychoanalytic clinical practice, which is neither accumulative nor sacrificial, differs radically from that of even the most progressive and liberal of academic disciplines. This singularity of psychoanalytic practice establishes a distinct relationship to theory and knowledge, which are not so much applied as encountered anew in each clinical situation. Following Freud, Lacan argued that psy-choanalysts should not employ a ready-made knowledge, but should always approach each new clinical encounter as if they had never seen a patient before, thus avoiding anyone's becoming a psycho-analytic 'case'. The key argument, here, is that psychoanalysis allows us to separate the vexed question of the relationship between truth and knowledge in new and radical ways. To establish and reinforce this argument, the book addresses the foundations of psychoanalysis' clinical epistemology, whilst considering the problems and issues of applied psychoanalysis, and the ambiguous position of the analyst and the analytically trained academic in the public sphere.

Chapter 1 focuses on the logic of psychoanalytic discovery and introduces the reader to the thorny issue of the status of knowledge within psychoanalytic practice. Drawing on Freud's peculiar desire to associate psychoanalysis with the scientific *Weltanschauung*, precisely because the latter does not constitute a total and totalizing body of knowledge, we argue that the analyst can never aspire to a state of full knowledge, either in himself or in the analysand, and is rather driven by the passion of ignorance and the logic of abduction. The result is that the analyst does not concern himself with any of the traditional criteria for establishing the truth of a knowledge product, but situates truth within the inherent limitations of knowledge itself. In Chapter 2, we probe deeper into the relationship between knowledge and truth, and the scientificity of psychoanalysis, through a re-examination of Lacan's seminal paper 'Science and Truth'. Here we explain that psychoanalysis should not measure itself against the ideal of modern science, because modern science has lost its Cartesian roots in its complete rejection of 'truth as cause'. In this chapter we also demonstrate how Lacan initially entertained the possibility of endowing psychoanalysis with an alternative scientificity through the paradigm of structuralism, but subsequently distanced himself from its exclusive reliance on the power of formal language systems, in order to reconceptualize the relationships between meaning and nonsensicality, without therefore adopting a hermeneuticist framework. Meaning is the central focus of Chapter 3, in which we zoom in on Lacan's own allegedly unfathomable discourse with the purpose of showing how his original (structuralist) thesis that the unconscious is structured like a language gradually complicated itself into a more encompassing perspective on the unconscious as a structured amalgamation of language and *jouissance*. After this, we round off the first part of our book with some reflections on the difficulty the psychoanalytic community, especially the Lacanian one, has in guaranteeing its own knowledge domain. In this chapter, we highlight the nature and origin of the legitimacy crises which have affected (Lacanian) psychoanalysis, briefly chart the epistemological challenges with which the (Lacanian) psychoanalytic community is currently confronted, and open a perspective on Lacan's discourse theory, which creates a bridge to the next section of the book.

Our second part focuses on how a Lacanian epistemology identifies various key divisions of the field of knowledge and how these divisions are at work under the conditions of modernity in which psychoanalysis has developed. In order to grasp the epistemological specificity of psychoanalysis, we believe that it must be considered in its contradictory relationships with, *inter alia*, academic knowledge, the knowledge economy and the free market of ideas. In Chapter 5, this task is undertaken with reference to Lacan's *Seminar XVII* (Lacan 1991 [1969–70]), and its startling contention that 'truth is a fall of knowledge'. The difficulty of sustaining the rigour of an epistemology that aligns certainty with a fall of knowledge is tackled here through a discussion of Lacan's 'four discourses' of the master, the university, the hysteric and the analyst. We argue that the four discourses are not interpretive tools or templates, but are instead designed to intervene at particular points within a field of knowledge, in order to expose a primary distinction between communicative acts and unconscious thought processes. Chapter 6 elaborates this theme on the basis of Lacan's discussion of the 'prisoner's sophism', in which intervention takes the form of a moment of concluding the speculation on the nature of truth. We argue that the collective certainty introduced by this moment of concluding provides thought with an ethical dimension, and we subsequently contrast this collective cum ethical dimension of thought with the difficulty of sustaining the search for significant truth in the free market of ideas. The chapter that follows demonstrates how a Lacanian notion of an unconscious 'game beneath the game' and a Freudian approach to the analytic construction offer a set of directions for connecting interpretive moves to ethical, critical and collective effects. Chapter 7 also introduces the problem of sustaining a psychoanalytic ethic in applied psychoanalysis, via a discussion of the critical effect of the hoax. This issue is the starting point for Chapter 8, in which we return to Freud's famous 'archaeological metaphor' in order to claim that, far from being a mode of comparison, Freud's move on archaeological knowledge may offer a way out of the deadlock of applied psychoanalysis, notably through a systematic approach to 'epistemological regression' and that which is 'less than knowledge'.

This book is not another primer of Lacanian theory, nor a general exposition of applied psychoanalysis in its various forms. Instead, it resituates epistemological debates on the difference between truth (reality, objectivity) and fabrication (fantasy, fallacy) within the framework of the Lacanian subject, where these distinctions become inevitably blurred and fundamentally irrelevant. This approach constitutes both the specificity of psychoanalysis as a form of knowledge, and its central methodological significance for the analysis of other epistemologies. Those branches of psychoanalysis which have been most fully engaged with the consequences of Freud's work, such as Lacanian discourse, have indeed proceeded on the assumption that the centralization of the subject in psychoanalytic discourse weakens rather than strengthens its claims to knowledge. This implies that the constitutive impossibility or failure of psychoanalytic knowledge, as a discourse on knowledge, may be used to reveal the unacknowledged yet highly specific impossibilities of other epistemologies, on their own terms. Rather than simply being one of the products available in a knowledge economy, psychoanalysis is in a position to place regimes of knowledge in a dialectical relationship with non-knowledge, blindness, ignorance and stupidity. What Lacan called 'the sublimity of stupidity' is discernible only within the terms of a discourse which knows how, when and where to relinquish its fascination with knowledge as control and mastery.

Part I

The subject of psychoanalysis: knowledge, truth and meaning

Chapter I

Midwives of the whys and wherefores: on the logic of psychoanalytic discovery

It is far, far better and much safer to have a firm anchor in nonsense than to put out on the troubled seas of thought.

John K. Galbraith, *The Affluent Society*, 131

The mad Hatter ↑

Science is the belief in the ignorance of the experts.

Richard P. Feynman, attributed

Psychoanalytic knowledge

How did Freud arrive at the complex body of ideas that is known to us as psychoanalysis? If it seems ludicrous to proclaim that it suddenly emerged from his head, like Athena from Zeus, or that he quite simply discovered it through focused research and a smidgeon of serendipity, like a fully formed diamond waiting to be found by one fortunate soul, can we honestly say that he invented it, if not entirely *ex nihilo*, perhaps from the soft clay of his own creative thought processes? More than one hundred years after the birth of Freud's 'talking cure' and in the aftermath of a plethora of scholarly studies on the epistemology of psychoanalysis, these questions may appear as totally superfluous, because their hackneyed, if often antithetical answers do not bear a renewed challenging. Freud came to psychoanalysis, it is being peddled, after engaging in the heroic enterprise of his 'self-analysis', after failing to find a neurophysiological explanation for the experiences reported by his hysterical and obsessional patients, after relentlessly pursuing his ardent ambition to give birth to a new revolutionary science, quite independently from established scientific traditions yet resolutely geared to resolving the mysteries of the human condition on the basis of reason, and reason alone.

In this chapter it is not our intention to reopen the debate concerning the value of the various 'origin myths' that have been formulated, sometimes quite persuasively, over the past fifty years or so in order to account for the birth of psychoanalysis. Nor do we wish to study, in typical structuralist fashion, the symbolic rules of transformation governing the intellectual replacement of Jones's popular portrait of Freud the hero (Jones 1953–57) with Sulloway's controversial picture of Freud the cryptobiologist (Sulloway 1992). Instead we wish to examine how Freud described and explained the knowledge underpinning the theoretical models and therapeutic techniques within the general doctrine of psychoanalysis. What type of knowledge does psychoanalysis contain? Where does this knowledge come from? How does the psychoanalyst operate with it in his clinical work and beyond the walls of the consultation room? Does this knowledge meet the rigorous requirements of scientific *episteme* or is it doomed to remain stuck in the *doxa* of beliefs and opinions?

It is common knowledge that Freud always considered himself a child of the Enlightenment, putting all his trust in the power of scientific reason, yet it is equally accepted that his allegiance to the ideology of 'illumination through knowledge' did not suffice as a guarantee for the scientificity of his work. Interestingly, the scientific status of psychoanalytic knowledge has been disputed not only by its most ardent detractors, but also by some of its most loyal adherents, amongst which it would surely be wrong not to include Professor Freud himself. In an oft-quoted passage from his case history of Elisabeth von R, Freud deplored the fact that he had not been able to maintain his own intellectual standards: '[I]t still strikes me myself as strange that the case histories I write should read like short stories and that, as one might say, they lack the serious stamp of science. I must console myself with the reflection that the nature of the subject is evidently responsible for this, rather than any preference of my own' (Freud and Breuer 1895d: 160). In terms of Lyotard's distinction between scientific knowledge and narrative knowledge (Lyotard 1984 [1979]: 25–27), Freud clearly admits to operate in the realm of the latter, although very much despite himself and owing to 'the nature of the subject'. Many case studies later, at the very end of his career, it did not stop him from saying that psychoanalysis should be regarded as a 'natural science like any other' (Freud 1940a [1938]: 158). Some critics will no doubt argue here that the alternatives of science and belief are spurious in themselves, since psychoanalytic knowledge is just a load of codswallop ingeniously disguised as profound wisdom. Yet if the critics are right, this still leaves the question as to where the hogwash comes from and why so many people, including patients and practitioners, produce and consume it.

One probably does not need to ascertain the feats of Freud the hero in order to accept that, unlike many founding figures in the history of ideas, or most mainstream scientists for that matter, Freud never really wrote up the results of a finished empirical and/or intellectual research process. Although it cannot be denied that he preferred knowledge over ignorance, rational clarity over irrational obscurantism, and that he was deeply driven by a strong sense of *Wahrhaftigkeit* (truthfulness) (Freud 1915a [1914]: 164) and *Wahrheitsliebe* (love of truth) (Freud 1937c: 248), Freud rarely presented a set of definitive truths with a view to eradicating manifest falsities. Although any postgraduate student would be berated for presenting her work not as a retrospective account of a completed research project but as a reflection, in real time, of the actual research process, Freud seems to have done exactly that, expressing his views on things he was still very much in the process of investigating. He announced, postponed and eventually aborted the idea of completing a 'general methodology of psychoanalysis' (Freud 1910d: 142), settling instead for a series of technical papers which contain little or no practical advice, numerous thorny questions and few solid answers. Purportedly expository volumes such as the *Introductory Lectures on Psycho-Analysis* (Freud 1916–17a [1915–17]) and the posthumously published *Outline of Psycho-Analysis* (Freud 1940a [1938]) invariably offer new perspectives on relatively well-known psychoanalytic issues which challenge the outsider and defamiliarize the insider. Reading Freud gives one the idea that at the end of his life he still had not succeeded in finishing the project he initially set out to research.

From these initial observations it can already be concluded that Freud did much more than introducing the ear into the reigning clinical establishment of his time. For he also stubbornly pursued a research practice based on the vicissitudes of speech and language, speaking and listening, reading and writing, which contravened his scientific aspirations, affected the status of psychoanalytic knowledge, and informed an unusual epistemological economy. The position adopted by Freud, which cannot be disjointed from the body of knowledge he produced, was unlike any other recognizable scientific, philosophical or professional position, although, as we shall see later on in this chapter, we have to acknowledge certain similarities between the Freudian analyst, Socrates' 'atopic' position, the detective, the archaeologist and the Zen master. In releasing the whys and wherefores sustaining the symptomatic straitjackets in his patients' minds, and accounting theoretically for the dynamic relationships between the agencies of the 'psychical personality', Freud wanted to be a scientist, yet at the same time his epistemology was miles removed from the hypothetico-deductive method pervading scientific practice. Apart from exploring the way in which Freud developed the knowledge which supports the psychoanalytic edifice, this chapter will demonstrate why psychoanalysis cannot constitute a *Weltanschauung*, how it differs from closed systems of knowledge, and, perhaps most importantly, why Freud was right in proving himself to be continuously wrong.

In search of psychoanalytic research

Let us consider the possibility that psychoanalysis is included as an acknowledged discipline within an academic curriculum leading to a degree in social sciences. It is extremely likely that the lecturer responsible for the psychoanalysis module(s) will at some point be asked to consider or even to teach the research principles governing psychoanalytic practice, so that students gain insight into the nature of psychoanalytic research questions, are able to pursue a psychoanalytic research project in a psychoanalytically correct fashion, and are capable of interpreting research results in accordance with the psychoanalytic orientation of a project and psychoanalytic principles in general. The lecturer will probably be led to examine how psychoanalysis may be situated within or vis-à-vis the traditional distinction between quantitative and qualitative research methods in the social sciences, and he will probably decide that his discipline ranks amongst the qualitative approaches, sharing some of its central assumptions with content analysis, discourse analysis and grounded theory, although nonetheless sufficiently different from these methods to deserve further investigation. In addition he might recall Dilthey's classic dualism between *Naturwissenschaften* (natural sciences) and *Geisteswissenschaften* (sciences of the mind), whereby the former favour *Erklärung* (explanation) and the latter emphasize *Verstehen* (understanding), and he might even remember Windelband's equally classic opposition between nomothetic (universalizing) sciences and ideographic (individualizing) sciences. And he will presumably conclude that psychoanalysis is an ideographic science of the mind which operates in the realm of understanding. Adding a touch of

Weber, he might then proceed to the assertion that the type of understanding which comes closest to the research methodology employed within psychoanalysis is a rational, explanatory understanding, whereby someone's actions are understood through inferring the motives and intentions behind them, as opposed to a direct observational understanding, which merely relies on empathy or an awareness of situational rules. *methodology*

Relying on a set of contemporary and classical epistemological distinctions, the lecturer builds his case, and slowly the module on psychoanalytic research methods is starting to take shape. However, no matter how convincing the result may be, there are at least two problems with this approach. Firstly, and most importantly, the lecturer seeks to find answers to the question as to what constitutes psychoanalytic research (and, by extension, which epistemological status psychoanalysis has), by trying to situate Freud's invention within a series of known methodologies and accepted forms of knowledge. As such, he has recourse to a list of purportedly established concepts, trying to capture the specificity of psychoanalysis through one or more of these notions, yet unwittingly reducing the very specificity that he is supposed to account for. It may make sense to say that psychoanalysis is qualitative rather than quantitative, and few people will indeed doubt that Freud was not particularly concerned with trying to measure the size of the unconscious, yet this apparent convergence between psychoanalysis and qualitative methodologies in the social sciences does not preclude the fact that psychoanalysts would be very hard-pressed to admit that they practise a kind of (clinical) discourse analysis, if only because discourse theorists tend to attribute most meaning to central, recurrent themes, whereas psychoanalysts are much more attuned to marginal, isolated inconsistencies. This strategy of trying to situate psychoanalysis within accepted methodological and epistemological categories has also generated the (hitherto unresolved) debate on whether psychoanalysis is an art, a science or a religion, which, as we shall see, did not escape Freud either and which has prompted numerous researchers to evaluate the origin and function of psychoanalytic knowledge. Again, this debate obfuscates the specificity of psychoanalytic knowledge and generally occludes the particular ways in which psychoanalysis aligns knowledge and truth. Secondly, our conscientious lecturer assumes that it is possible (necessary, even) to restrict psychoanalytic research to one or the other of the opposing poles within the various dimensions of scientific practice, thus

p.a. is it an art a science or a religion?

excluding, for instance, its realm of action from the natural, explanatory, nomothetic sciences and the praxis of direct observational understanding. Yet if anything can be learnt from the way in which Freud practised and developed psychoanalysis, it is that his highly individualized clinical technique did not stop him from formulating universal laws, that his 'science of unconscious mental processes' (Freud 1925d [1924]: 70)—a science of the mind if there ever was one—did not prevent him from betting on the (past and future) achievements of the natural sciences, especially biology, and that his rational, explanatory understanding of a patient's symptoms did not preclude his having recourse to the method of empathy. One could of course use Freud's epistemological wobbliness, here, as yet another indication of his total lack of scientific rigour, yet it may be more accurate, and more in accordance with the epistemological specificity of psychoanalysis, to say that Freud refused to commit himself to one particular alternative. Transcending the split between C.P. Snow's famous 'two cultures' (Snow 1993 [1964]), Freud testified both to the artificiality of traditional epistemological distinctions when human intentionality is allowed to enter the research equation, and to the extraordinary status of knowledge in psychoanalysis.

Although throughout his life Freud remained very concerned about psychoanalysis being a respected and respectable discipline, and often complained about the resistance against it (Freud 1925e [1924]), despite its significance for a wide range of psychological and non-psychological sciences (Freud 1913j), he never bothered to try to identify it along one or more of the aforementioned epistemological lines. Dilthey, Windelband and Weber do not have the honour of figuring amongst Freud's intellectual sources; their distinctions do not appear as such in any of Freud's major contributions to psychoanalysis. The term 'research' does not feature in the subject index of the *Standard Edition*, and given James Strachey's tight control over the translation project and his pervasive desire to ensure the scientific respectability of psychoanalysis, it is difficult to blame this absence on the compiler's forgetfulness. Freud's only extensive comment on the nature of psychoanalytic knowledge, the type of research activity that contributes to it and the relation between psychoanalysis and other praxes is embedded in 'The Question of a *Weltanschauung*', Lecture 35 of the *New Introductory Lectures on Psycho-Analysis* (Freud 1933a [1932]: 158–182]). Yet even here, late in life and drawing on the benefits of professional hindsight, he seems better at exposing—in strict allegiance to Comte's famous law of the three stages—the epistemological dynamics of magic, religion, philosophy, art and science, than at clarifying the exact status of psychoanalysis.

Freud expresses his position on the matter in no uncertain words right at the beginning of the lecture and again at the very end, devoting the lion's share of his discussion to a psychoanalytic interpretation of various 'proper' *Weltanschauungen*. 'As a specialist science,' Freud says of psychoanalysis, 'it is quite unfit to construct a *Weltanschauung* of its own: it must accept the scientific one. But the *Weltanschauung* of science already departs noticeably from our definition ["a *Weltanschauung* is an intellectual construction which solves all the problems of our existence uniformly on the basis of one overriding hypothesis, which, accordingly, leaves no question unanswered and in which everything that interests us finds its fixed place"]' (ibid.: 158). We cannot fail to be struck by the strange, seemingly inconsistent argument that Freud is formulating here: 1. psychoanalysis is incapable of forming its own *Weltanschauung* (and this speaks in its favour, since *Weltanschauungen* are essentially idealistic and illusory); 2. psychoanalysis must conform to the scientific *Weltanschauung*, and thus give up its epistemological lack for a newly found, non-psychoanalytic completeness; 3. the scientific *Weltanschauung* is not a *Weltanschauung* in the first place, and this is why it fits psycho-analysis. After having said that psychoanalysis is unable to construct its own, Freud claims that it still needs one, yet the one it can embrace does not actually qualify!

Witness his explanation of how science 'departs noticeably' from the traditional *Weltanschauung*: 'It is true that it [science] too assumes the *uniformity* of the explanation of the universe; but it does so only as a programme, the fulfilment of which is relegated to the future. Apart from this it is marked by negative characteristics, by its limitation to what is at the moment knowable and by its sharp rejection of certain elements that are alien to it. It asserts that there are no sources of knowledge of the universe other than the intellectual working-over of carefully scrutinized observations—in other words, what we call research—and alongside of it no knowledge derived from revelation, intuition or divination' (ibid.: 158–159). It remains to be seen whether Freud's description of science here would meet with much approval from contemporary hard-nosed scientists, partly because they might doubt that their explanations should follow a uniform pattern but mainly because they might feel quite uncomfortable acknowledging the 'negative characteristics' of their

weltanschauung: refers to the framework of ideas and beliefs through which an individual interprets the world and interacts with it.
WORLD VIEWS

paradigm, and perhaps outright weary at the idea that there are serious limitations to knowledge. Freud's unflinching support for the scientific enterprise, here, has of course been used by noted Freud critics, such as Adolf Grünbaum (1984, 1993, 2004), and equally noted Freudian revisionists, such as Mark Solms (Kaplan-Solms and Solms 2002; Solms and Turnbull 2002), to underscore the unequivocal tenor of his intellectual aspirations and to define psychoanalysis respectively as a fundamentally flawed undertaking or a radically unfinished project. What most critics miss, however, is the fact that Freud is happy to align psychoanalysis with science precisely because science is *not* a *Weltanschauung*, because it does not claim to solve all the problems, because there exists a constitutive lack of knowledge at the heart of its intellectual body, because its knowledge is not all-encompassing but strictly limited in space and time. It is because the truth of science rests in its negative characteristic of an incomplete knowledge that Freud is confident that psychoanalysis' fundamental and characteristic inability to constitute a *Weltanschauung* will not be annihilated when it embraces the 'ideology' of science. Only by virtue of its central gap in knowledge can science provide psychoanalysis with an epistemological paradigm that does justice to its own field of enquiry; once the gap in knowledge is closed and science starts to operate with a uniform and universal knowledge base, fully realized in the here and now, it becomes a genuine *Weltanschauung* which psychoanalysis can no longer embrace. Hence, Freud's optimistic outlook on the solidarity between psychoanalysis and science takes its bearings from a very specific observation concerning the status of knowledge in both fields: psychoanalysis and science share the same truth, notably that their knowledge is limited and must reckon with an unknown, perhaps potentially unknowable element. As we shall see in the next chapter, when we critically reconstruct the argument put forward by Lacan in his paper 'Science and Truth' (Lacan 1989b [1965]), it is precisely at the point where knowledge fails and non-knowledge, nonsense and stupidity emerge that the unconscious subject, as the cardinal dimension of psychoanalysis, can be situated.

Apart from Freud's emphasis on the negative characteristics of science, it is also important not to miss the implications of his contention that science sharply repudiates the conditions that are alien to its practice, particularly the claims and suggestions that knowledge may be gained from 'revelation, intuition or divination' rather than 'the intellectual working-over of carefully scrutinized observations'. If Freud's assertion is true and science does indeed identify *non-scientific outside us, scientific inside* and reject, on epistemological grounds, everything that is not-science as mere religion, spirituality, metaphysics, pseudo-science or non-sense, then this demarcation between a non-scientific outside and a scientific inside puts science in a defensive position of epistemo-logical conflict which inhabits the scientist with a profound realiz-ation of what might entail the downfall of her practice as science. *conflict* For the serious scientist, this realization will probably entail her trying to safeguard at all costs the cherished principles of objectivity, neu-trality, standardization, reliability and validity, yet, as Jonathan Lear has pointed out so perceptively, 'a scientist should be perpetually asking herself whether she is shaping herself to pursue her inquiries in the right sort of ways' (Lear 2003: 43). As soon as a demarcation is drawn between science and not-science, the question emerges as to what constitutes science and the answer to this question remains forever inchoate, not because it cannot be formulated effectively and accurately—indeed, the above principles demonstrate that it can—but because it can never be fully realized. The scientist's knowledge of the necessity to be objective and neutral, to choose standardized methods and to employ reliable and valid instruments, does not suf-fice as a guarantee for the production of scientific knowledge. The latter may be achieved asymptotically only through the scientist's constant subjective reflection upon the nature of her practice and her continuous measurement of the distance between her ontological and ethical position and that of the abstract, de-subjectified scientist. Put differently, true scientific knowledge will emerge only if the sci-entist is able to gauge how much her 'stupidity' is affecting her know-ledge of the central prerequisites for engaging in scientific practice and if she completely succeeds in cancelling out the traumatic, dis-turbing infiltration of all nonsense. As we shall see in the next chap-ter, from a Lacanian perspective this kind of complete annihilation of 'noise' may be every scientist's wet dream, yet it can reach its full realization only within the extra-discursive, non-residual dynamics of psychosis.

If Freud believes in the conjunction between psychoanalysis and science, it is also by virtue of the perennial state of conflict that he recognizes in the latter's struggle to maintain itself against the non-scientific forces of magic and religion and, we may add, against the unconscious subjective forces that permeate the implementation of its principles. Reflecting upon the commitments a psychoanalyst should be able to make in the psychoanalytic treatment, Jonathan

Lear points out that the analyst must live with 'a lively sense of death', that is to say, he must be aware of what type of event would betray the continuation of the treatment as psychoanalytic, and he must be aware from the beginning that his actions cannot be geared to the installation of a new form of dependency but must facilitate, and perhaps even accelerate the occurrence of an end (Lear 2003: 54–58). For Lear, the analyst's 'lively sense of death' applies primarily to the way in which she directs the treatment, yet there is no reason why it should not apply also to her relationship with knowledge. For just as much as a psychoanalyst needs to ensure that his patient does not become dependent upon him, and vice versa, it makes sense to say that he needs to ensure that he does not become dependent upon his own knowledge, and vice versa. For this epistemological dependency would constitute in its own right a betrayal of the psychoanalytic process *qua* psychoanalysis (and *qua* science, Freud would probably add), owing to the subjective transformation of knowledge into a hypostatized, limitless tool for the uniform interpretation of the human condition.

Knowledge and ignorance in the analytic conjunction

As we pointed out above, the term 'research' does not feature in the index of the *Standard Edition* of Freud's complete works, from which it can be inferred that the definition of a psychoanalytic research methodology does not seem to have featured very highly on Freud's professional agenda. Nonetheless, there are some places in Freud's oeuvre where the term does appear and some of these mentions are actually very instructive. For example, in the first chapter of his Leonardo study, Freud took the Italian master's inexhaustible thirst for knowledge against the backdrop of his relatively uneventful life as a source of inspiration for launching a remarkable theoretical principle: 'The postponement of loving until full knowledge is acquired ends in a substitution of the latter for the former. A man who has won his way to a state of knowledge cannot properly be said to love and hate; he remains beyond love and hatred. He has investigated instead of loving [*Man hat geforscht, anstatt zu lieben*]' (Freud 1910c: 75).

   In defining the state of full knowledge (and the research process leading up to it) as the opposite of love, or as something for whose attainment an individual will eventually be forced to sacrifice his

passions, Freud distances himself again from traditional philosophical conceptions of knowledge and research, in which the
accumulative dimension tends to prevail. Against the progressivist, *scientific*
expansivist definition of research, Freud claims that an investigatory *objectivity*
process, whether grounded in an ostensibly insatiable desire to know
(more) or animated by a more casual and balanced inquisitiveness,
can reach its fulfilment only through the renunciation of love and
hate. One may, of course, regard Freud's assertion as a rather convoluted description of the cherished principle of scientific objectivity.
A researcher conducting a methodologically sound research project
needs to transform the 'passionate attachment' he experiences vis-à-
vis the object of study into a neutral, passionless interaction. The
scientific investigation of an object, especially when it involves human
participants, is predicated upon the researcher's ability to relinquish
whatever affects he may be experiencing with regard to this object.
However, Freud's portrayal of the 'research spirit' is not particularly
concerned with a methodological rule nor, for that matter, with a
deontological code to which the scientist needs to adhere if he wishes
to maintain the ethical standards of his practice. Much more than a
recommended code of conduct for good research practice, Freud is
explaining what could deservedly be called an 'ontological state', a
'way of being', an 'existential condition'. Achieving 'full knowledge',
reaching a 'state of knowledge', does not reflect the temporary
attitude of a researcher committed to the faithful execution of his
project, but epitomizes the ultimate coincidence of essence and existence, the particular and the universal, in the epistemological realization of human potential. And if full knowledge arises from the
desert of the passions, then love and hatred will not regain their
vivacity through the researcher's accomplishments. If one wants to
know more, one needs to stop loving (and hating); if one wants
to carry on loving (and hating), it is better not to want to know too
much.[1]   *1st principle*
   The first principle of psychoanalytic research emerging from
Freud's own research into the life and works of Leonardo da Vinci
can be formulated as follows: conducting research, as a practice
motivated by a desire to know, is predicated upon a relinquishment
of the passions. Given the way in which Freud conceived psychoanalysis, this principle evidently not only applies to extra-clinical
investigations, such as those carried out by Freud himself in the
Leonardo study, but also covers the direction of the psychoanalytic
treatment.[2] Yet the question remains whether the above principle has

any positive value for the implementation of psychoanalytic research. If we restrict ourselves to the psychoanalytic treatment for a moment, it is indeed questionable whether a psychoanalyst is analytically justified to employ 'full knowledge' as a clinical goal for the analysand, regardless of his power to induce it. For if Freud is right in opposing 'full knowledge' to 'love and hatred', then the analytic induction of the former will by definition take place at the expense of the analysand's passions, an effect which does not seem particularly beneficial. Needless to say, the analysand himself may lament the traumatic absence of knowledge about his condition, invest the analyst with epistemic superpower or what Lacan called the function of the 'supposed subject of knowing' (*sujet supposé savoir*) (Lacan 1961–62: session of 15 November 1961), and crave the acquisition of a new, fuller knowledge through the analytic treatment.[3] Someone who does not arrive at the analyst's doorstep owing to an unresolvable problem in living, but for reasons of 'personal development' or because he wants to train as an analyst himself may equally express a desire to embark on a journey of self-discovery, to follow the path of self-actualization, to learn to know himself more truthfully. Would a psychoanalyst feel comfortable in her position if she said to her (potential) analysands that 'full knowledge' can be obtained on condition that the passions are extinguished? More importantly, would a (potential) analysand feel comfortable in the pursuit of his analytic goal if he knew that this is the price he would have to pay for being successful? How much would an analysand need to suffer for him to hand in his passions in exchange for the knowledge of well-being?

As we shall argue in subsequent chapters of this book, 'a state of full knowledge' is not an item on the psychoanalytic menu. If anything, the first principle of psychoanalytic research defines clinical practice in a negative way: however much an analysand may be engaged in a search for knowledge, the analyst needs to avoid assisting him in the realization of this task and maintain the analysand 'on this side' of love and hatred. Rather than facilitating the accumulation of knowledge, the analytic position is geared towards the 'fall of knowledge', which implies that the search for (better, truthful) knowledge is turned against itself, in the direction of an emergent non-knowledge.[4] As such, the analyst is not concerned with fostering insight in places of blindness, nor with nurturing meaning in areas of nonsensicality and bringing intelligence to pockets of ignorance, and even less with the Franciscan project of replacing discord with harmony, error with truth, doubt with faith and despair with hope.[5]

If anything, the analyst attempts to exorcise the spectre of 'full knowledge' by pinpointing its fundamental inconsistency and clearing the ground for its dialectical counterpart—the subject-less, acephalic knowledge that goes by the name of the unconscious. If we accept that the aforementioned research principle can only be inscribed negatively within a psychoanalytic epistemology pertaining to the dynamics of knowledge on the side of the analysand, we may still consider its applicability on the side of the analyst. Indeed, it does not seem too far-fetched to ponder the possibility that Freud's characterization of the researcher as an individual who is renouncing love and hatred concerned not only Leonardo, or the abstract scientific investigator, but also (and perhaps primarily) himself. Isn't the psychoanalyst supposed to have acceded to an elevated state of theoretical and practical knowledge before she is able (and can be allowed) to conduct the treatment in a responsible fashion? Isn't it one of the tasks of psychoanalytic training organizations to guarantee that their candidates possess 'full knowledge' of psychoanalytic theory and practice, and have given evidence to this effect, before they are let loose on the sick people of the nation?[6] And if this 'state of knowledge' can be achieved only at the expense of the passions, this is no doubt a huge bonus, for it will prevent the analyst from falling into the trap of his own unconscious counter-transference and should help him maintain the famous Freudian principles of neutrality and abstinence (Freud 1915a [1914]: 164–166).

Endorsing the negative principle of 'full knowledge' for the analyst but not for the analysand may seem sensible, but, unfortunately, it gives rise to an insuperable problem. The main 'learning school' for becoming an analyst is the analytic setting, where the analyst *in spe* is an analysand working in the same way as any other analysand and, from a Lacanian perspective, engaging in proceedings that are identical to a 'regular' clinical treatment process.[7] In line with our agreement that acquiring 'full knowledge' is not an analytic aim, despite its regularly being on the analysand's agenda, the analyst could thus not have reached his 'state of knowledge' in the consultation room of his own analyst. But if he cannot acquire it there, where else would he be provided with it? Apart from this apparent contradiction, there is a more serious problem with the idea that the analyst should aspire to 'full knowledge': the analyst may inadvertently start to act with it and thereby transform the analytic setting into an educational establishment in which he, the expert, is the master-teacher and the analysand becomes the ignorant pupil. The danger

here is that what Lacan defined as the discourse of the analyst transforms itself into the discourse of the university, in which knowledge
occupies the master position (Lacan 1991 [1969–70]). Analysing is
not teaching, and being in analysis is not the same as being in
school.[8]

The state of total knowledge suits neither the analysand nor the
analyst. Freud does not depict the analyst as a latter-day Leonardo,
nor does he believe that the analysand has much to learn from the
analyst's interventions. If anything, matters are rather the other way
round. Consider the following passage from Freud's 'Postscript' to
'The Question of Lay Analysis': 'In psychoanalysis there has existed
from the very first an inseparable bond between cure and research.
Knowledge brought therapeutic success. It was impossible to treat a
patient without learning something new; it was impossible to gain
fresh insight without perceiving its beneficent results. Our analytic
procedure is the only one in which this precious conjunction is
assured' (Freud 1927a: 256).[9] Let it be understood that when Freud
talks about knowledge bringing therapeutic success, he does not
want to convey that the patient finds relief as a result of gaining
knowledge about himself and his condition. Therapeutic success is
not based on the analysand acquiring knowledge, but on the analyst
obtaining 'fresh insight'. It should also be understood, however, that
this does not imply that the analyst 'applies' his 'fresh' knowledge as
a doctrinal body of ideas within the analytic setting. Perhaps the
most striking part of the above paragraph is Freud's admission: 'It
was impossible to treat a patient without learning something new.'
Perhaps some analysts may still believe that it is impossible to treat a
patient without *teaching* something new, but clearly Freud was of the
opinion that the analytic treatment of a patient coincides with the
analyst's acquisition of a new piece of knowledge—not once, but
every single time, for as long as he treats patients psychoanalytically.

Putting the psychoanalyst in the position of a learner presupposes
a firm belief in the incompleteness of the knowledge of the analyst
and the epistemological lack that resides at the centre of psychoanalytic theory. From this vantage point, we can begin to understand
why Freud was keen to emphasize that an analyst always needs to
treat a patient as if it is the first one she has ever treated, thus avoiding the transformation of the patient's singularity into a diagnostic
category (a known case), and refusing to capitalize on the knowledge
goods she has acquired during her own training and under previous
treatment conditions (Freud 1912e: 114, 1933a [1932]: 173–175).

Instead of acting like an expert and banking on the effective thera-peutic value of her knowledge, the analyst needs to put the knowledge she has acquired into a state of risk, that is to say, she needs to act upon a willingness to put it on the line as a fundamentally flawed and intrinsically unfinished body of thought. Instead of *acting with* her knowledge, the analyst *acts upon* it, using knowledge itself as an object of research. Ideally, the same is supposed to happen on the side of the analysand, and the extent to which the analysand is cap-able of acting upon his knowledge (rather than using it as an already established system in order to further understanding) may count as a measure for his approximation of the analytic position. Hence, both the analyst and the analysand operate with a lack of knowledge, the only difference between them being that the analyst finds the 'lack of knowledge' adequate to his professional position, whereas the analy-sand experiences it as a heavy burden.[10] As we shall see in subsequent chapters of this book, the analyst's main task basically comes down to using her own 'lacking knowledge' as a tool for directing the treatment towards the analysand's epistemological fall, which does not coincide with the certainty of 'full', 'true' knowledge, but with the certainty of the rift that separates his desire to know from the unconscious 'stupidity' that precludes this desire's full satisfaction. By actively avoiding the road towards full knowledge, the analyst is thus entitled to keep his passions of love and hatred and he can even draw upon them to animate his analytic desire, which is evidently not a desire to harm the patient, nor a desire to fulfil the patient's wishes, but a desire to conduct the treatment in an analytically correct fashion.[11]

In accordance with Freud's portrayal of the analyst as a lifelong 'active learner', Lacan at one point added a third passion to the dualism of love and hatred, which he singled out as the passion 'which needs to give the whole of analytic training its direction' (Lacan 1966c [1955]: 358). Alongside love and hatred, the analyst is supposed to be endowed with the 'passion of ignorance', a con-stantly active commitment to keeping his own knowledge in a state of incompletion. In *Seminar I*, Lacan compared the analyst's passion of ignorance to Cusanus' famous principle of *docta ignorantia*—a wise (learned) ignorance, a knowledge about the limits of know-ledge, a profound awareness of the significance of not-knowing (Lacan 1988b [1953–54]: 278).[12] As is clear from these definitions, *docta ignorantia* is not synonymous with the absence of knowledge but rather epitomizes a 'higher wisdom', a 'learned sagacity' to

docta ignorantia

acknowledge the fundamental limits of knowledge and, by implication, to refrain from transmitting it as doctrinal learning. As Lacan
himself put it: 'The positive fruit of the revelation of ignorance is
non-knowledge [*non-savoir*], which is not a negation of knowledge,
but its most elaborated form' (Lacan 1966c [1955]: 358).[13]

However, beyond its direct effect on the status of knowledge, the
passion of ignorance also affects the analyst's being, insofar as it
should prevent the analyst from identifying with his position *qua*
analyst. The epistemological limits the analyst needs to recognize not
only involve his knowledge of the analysand, and of psychoanalytic
theory in general, but also crucially concern his knowledge of himself as a psychoanalyst. For a while, Lacan considered the possibility
of the analyst acting with his being (Lacan 2002d [1958]: 239–245),
yet he eventually settled on the much more radical idea that the
analyst should occupy a position of dis-being (*désêtre*) (Lacan 1968a
[1967]: 59). Following his passion of ignorance, the analyst may
know that he is in the analytic position, without therefore *knowing* it,
that is to say, without possessing sufficient knowledge about its
nature to be able to assimilate it and identify with it. As Serge André
has argued, 'psychoanalyst' is above all a function conditioned by
the discourse of the analysand, which one can only ever 'try to
become' if one is to remain truthful to the principles of psychoanalysis (André 2003). Analytic dis-being thus involves a certain way
of eternal becoming.

Drawing on the work of Hans Loewald, and arguing in favour of
the quintessential importance of self-reflexivity, Jonathan Lear has
recently made a similar point when stating that a psychoanalyst
'must always keep up her own activity of analysis as a way of continually coming back to herself as an analyst' (Lear 2003: 14). And
further: '[T]o *be* an analyst one must ever be in the process of *becoming* an analyst. For anyone for whom the process of becoming is over,
he or she has ceased to be an analyst. In that sense, being an analyst
is a constant process of re-creative repetition' (ibid.: 32). Just as
much as non-knowledge does not signal the absence of knowledge
for Lacan, self-reflexivity does not entail non-being in Lear's
account: '[T]he essential problem would be neither with being or not
being . . . but with thinking there was an answer' (ibid.: 25). The
latter assertion demonstrates again how the issue of being/becoming
is bound up with the perceived value of knowledge. The passion of
ignorance precludes a belief in the power of knowledge to provide
answers to the questions of life and therefore suspends any possible

recourse to a state of being. Put differently, the analyst's passion of ignorance radically undermines the state of knowledge about his being an analyst.

How to act with one's ignorance

If the analyst should not aspire to a state of full knowledge, either in the analysand or in himself, but cultivate the passion of ignorance, the question remains how he is supposed to proceed in order to facilitate the 'fall of knowledge' on the side of the analysand. At first sight, the answer might seem obvious: the analyst operates on the analysand's free associations with the technique of interpretation. But this answer just generates more questions: Which aspect of the analysand's associations does the analyst interpret?, What exactly is an interpretation?, How does the analyst avoid acting with his knowledge when formulating an interpretation?, How does an interpretation contribute to the 'fall of knowledge'?

It is well known that Freud always felt reluctant to delineate specific rules for interpreting analytically sensitive material. As he formulated it so eloquently in the opening paragraphs of 'On Beginning the Treatment', 'The extraordinary diversity of the psychical constellations concerned, the plasticity of all mental processes and the wealth of determining factors oppose any mechanization of the technique' (Freud 1913c: 123). For those who may still be considering plumbing the depths of Freud's *Interpretation of Dreams* (Freud 1900a) in search for some technical know-how and practical skills, it is worth knowing that the book in question has many things to offer, but no concrete rules-of-thumb for interpreting dreams. In this respect, the popular dream books in the equally popular 'self-help' section of the 'good bookshops' will be much more rewarding than any Freudian writing.

Figuring out how Freudian psychoanalytic technique works requires some effort, yet, as is the case with the principles of psychoanalytic research, Freud did leave some traces behind which can put us in the right direction. This time, the illuminating passage appears in Freud's study of another Italian master, written shortly before World War I, at the same time as his essays on psychoanalytic technique. After long and careful deliberation, Freud submitted an anonymous paper to the journal *Imago* on the marble statue of Moses by Michelangelo, in which he included the following comment, which deserves to be quoted at length:

Long before I had any opportunity of hearing about psycho-analysis, I learnt that a Russian art-connoisseur, Ivan Lermolieff, had caused a revolution in the art galleries of Europe by questioning the authorship of many pictures, showing how to distinguish copies from originals with certainty, and construct-ing hypothetical artists for those works whose former supposed authorship had been discredited. He achieved this by insisting that attention should be diverted from the general impression and main features of a picture, and by laying stress on the signi-ficance of minor details, of things like the drawing of the finger-nails, of the lobe of an ear, of halos and such unconsidered trifles which the copyist neglects to imitate and yet which every artist executes in his own characteristic way. I was then greatly interested to learn that the Russian pseudonym concealed the identity of an Italian physician called Morelli, who died in 1891 with the rank of Senator of the Kingdom of Italy. It seems to me that his method of inquiry is closely related to the technique of psycho-analysis. It, too, is accustomed to divine secret and concealed things from despised or unnoticed features, from the rubbish-heap, as it were, of our observations.

(Freud 1914b: 222)[14]

In order to discover what really matters, the psychoanalyst thus needs to focus on the marginal aspects of the analysand's discourse. If Morelli's success stemmed from his ability to 'look awry', the analyst's resolve originates in his capacity for 'hearing awry'. What-ever object the analyst researcher decides to investigate, whether the unconscious mechanisms conditioning the patient's life history or the implicit dynamics permeating a cultural phenomenon, the tiniest of apparently superfluous details is considered more revealing than the overt, central representation.[15]

The paramount importance of detail, especially those trifles that are normally regarded as redundant noise, within the process of psychoanalytic discovery is the main reason why the majority of so-called qualitative research methods have no direct bearing on the methodology of psychoanalysis. Many qualitative research methods assume that recurring thematic patterns in the main body of a dis-cursive structure can be grouped, classified and interpreted as the core features of the narrative. The Freudian approach, however, zooms in on the characteristics of the narrative's marginalia, the inconsistencies and incongruities appearing alongside the main text.

In its most radical form, psychoanalysis attributes more importance to what disturbs or what is absent from a body of knowledge than to the themes which give it consistency, coherence and cohesion. In the aforementioned passage, Freud dubs these features 'the rubbish-heap of our observations', yet we could also designate them as the 'stupidities of knowledge', those areas of our lives in which we are 'apparently thoughtless', 'seemingly absent-minded', 'temporarily distracted', 'clearly clueless'. For Freud, these potentially disturbing interferences of mental noise contained the most valuable analytic information, and this is precisely why he decided to investigate dreams, slips of the tongue, bungled actions, etc. These ostensibly negligible occurrences have in principle the same value as a clinical symptom: they escape our control, defy conscious reason, potentially disturb our daily actions and present themselves as 'meaningless, silly things'.[16] After singling out 'the stupidities of knowledge' for psychoanalytic research, Freud went on to demonstrate that they ought to be taken seriously as rational occurrences in their own right. In other words, Freud went on to show that the 'stupidities of knowledge' do not coincide with a loss of mind or an absence of thought, but follow their own rational logic beyond the constraints of everyday conscious reason, and this also implies that they are not to be regarded as sudden, random infiltrations of silliness but as structured emergences of thought with a specific history and a certain future.[17]

What does the analyst do, then, once the 'errors of reason' have been established as suitable objects for research? It is first of all important to note that he does not 'point out' the analysand's stupidities, because this practice would inevitably entail his occupying a position of 'cleverness'. Only from a position of intellectual authority and superior knowledge would it be possible to expose the stupidity of the Other. Rather than pinpointing the analysand's stupidities, the analyst 'punctuates' the analysand's knowledge as an inconsistent, obscure, paradoxical and self-contradictory thought process. As we shall see in subsequent chapters of this book, this strategy requires the analyst's 'playing dumb' rather than 'acting clever'. Subsequently, the analyst engages in a rather peculiar process of reasoning, which is quite different from the two classic methods of deduction and induction for the development of knowledge.

Much like the 'qualitative research methods', psychoanalysis has of course often been qualified as an inductive practice, especially in light of its purported idiographic nature (as opposed to the nomothetic character of the hypothetico-deductive, empirico-experimental tradition) and its strict reliance on case-study materials. More concretely, because Freud allegedly arrived at a general theory of obsessional neurosis on the basis of a limited number of case studies of obsessional patients, it has been argued that his is a theory of obsessional neurosis that moves from the particular/existential to the universal/essential and that is therefore emblematic of an inductive type of reasoning, with all its associated problems of external and ecological validity. However, it is our firm belief that this typification does not do justice to the intricacies of Freud's practice. If we continue Freud's comparison of psychoanalytic technique with Morelli's strategy for attributing the authorship of a painting, it is clear that 'induction' is not really the issue here. Morelli did not aspire to formulating a general theory of authorship attribution on the basis of one or several individual observations, nor did he claim to be capable of extrapolating the significance of a particular detail in one type of painting to all pictures with a similar content. Instead, Morelli produced a retroactive explanatory paradigm strictly within the boundaries of the specific object of research under consideration.

In a short essay on the principles of psychoanalytic detection, Michael Shepherd has linked Freud's research practice to the so-called 'Zadig method', named after the protagonist in a tale by Voltaire, who surprises everyone by his extraordinary ability to divine all the essential features of the horse that has passed through the woods by simply scrutinizing the trees and the marks on the ground (Shepherd 1985). Adopting the terminology of Thomas H. Huxley, Shepherd proposed to describe the 'Zadig method' (and Freudian research practice) as a technique of 'retrospective prophecy', yet it seems more appropriate to define it as an instance of 'logical abduction', if only because Huxley's notion of 'prophecy' has a strong religious connotation. The term 'abduction' was coined by Charles Sanders Peirce, who explained it in the following terms: 'Abduction is the process of forming an explanatory hypothesis. It is the only logical operation which introduces any new idea' (Peirce 1934 [1903]: 171). Abduction has often been vilified as a type of 'unsound reasoning' that comes close to mere guessing and that is as such unworthy of sitting next to deduction and induction, yet the fact that abduction is not governed by specific rules of inference was not a sufficient reason for Peirce to question the validity of abductive arguments. In his view, abductive reasoning is as 'secure' and 'productive' as its deductive and inductive counterparts.

The basic form of abductive reasoning is exceedingly simple:

1 A surprising event (E) is observed.
2 If hypothesis (H) were true, E would be obvious.
3 There is reason to believe that H is true.

It is easy to see how this type of reasoning operates in Freudian practice:

1 A surprising 'formation of the unconscious' (dream, slip of the tongue) occurs.
2 If our psychoanalytic explanatory hypothesis were true, this formation of the unconscious would be obvious.
3 We have reason to believe that our explanatory hypothesis is true.

Yet, apart from psychoanalysis, it also seems to play an important part in the work of police detectives: confronted with the crime scene characteristics, the inspector formulates a hypothesis which, if it were true, would explain all the circumstances of the crime. This is what scholars such as Shepherd (1985) and Ginzburg (1980) have dubbed the 'Sherlock Holmes paradigm', and it cannot be doubted that there is some connection between the way in which the famous fictional sleuth solved criminal mysteries and the way in which his real-life contemporary approached the formations of the unconscious. Freud himself, however, preferred the similarity with archaeological excavation and reconstruction, whereby he particularly modelled himself on the achievements of Heinrich Schliemann (Masson 1985: 353, 391–392).[18]

During the 1950s, Lacan seemingly rekindled the analogy between the psychoanalyst and the detective in his famour 'Seminar on "The Purloined Letter" '(Lacan 1972 [1956]), yet he was more keen to paint the analyst as a latter-day Zen master than as a super sleuth.[19] Much more than the detective—even when the latter is called C. Auguste Dupin and does not believe in the value of traditional investigative practices—the Zen master lives with the passion of ignorance, which underpins his radical refusal of any type of didacticism. In the very first sentence of his first public seminar, Lacan averred: 'The master breaks the silence with anything—with a sarcastic remark, with a kick-start. That is how a buddhist master conducts his search for meaning, according to the technique of *zen*' (Lacan 1988b [1953–54]: 1). Although Lacan himself occupied the position of a teacher here, and would increasingly be pushed into adopting the role of the *maître-à-penser*, he nonetheless insisted on the difference between analytic practice and the profession of knowledge. When the Zen master speaks, his voice is not intended to generate meaning (a psychological concept, the signified) but to transmit sound (the acoustic image, the signifier). When the Zen master produces a *koan* (a short riddle, but literally a 'public document'), he intends to occupy a space between meaning and non-meaning, between saying something meaningful and talking non-sense.[20] The practice of the Zen master also stands in sharp contrast to that of Socrates, whose technique of 'epistemological midwifery' has sometimes been compared to the clinical procedure of the psycho-analyst. Indeed, Lacan himself sometimes played with the idea of the analyst's occupying a Socratic position (Lacan 2001b [1960–61]: 203–217). But beyond Socrates' notorious 'atopia', and his constant admission of ignorance, there is little in the philosopher's attitude that could possibly be regarded as psychoanalytic. In his attempt to prove that the slave is endowed with tacit, 'endopsychic' know-ledge—a knowledge he knows nothing about—Socrates hardly ever lets his interlocutor say more than 'Yes', 'That is right', 'So it does', etc.[21] In delivering the slave of his knowledge, Socrates is the one who does the talking and the convincing, whereas the other does nothing but acquiesce. If the psychoanalyst operates as a midwife of the analysand's whys and wherefores, the least we can say is that the 'labour' occurs on the side of the analysand.

The comparison of the analyst and the Zen master of course reaches its limits at the level of the agency's desire and the dis-course's overall aim. Whereas the Zen master seeks to attain spiritual enlightenment, no matter how partial, through the knowledge of ignorance, the analyst's intentions are much more modest and do not reach out beyond the realization of the inherent limits of knowledge. The analyst is satisfied with acknowledging the certainty of the funda-mental instability of knowledge and uses her passion of ignorance in order to relieve the analysand from his relentless desire to under-stand, to rationalize, to know more. The analyst does not aim to cancel out all the 'stupidities of knowledge' with a view to installing a higher state of consciousness, but restricts herself to punctuating the epistemological gaps in the analysand's mental economy.

Perhaps this is why Lacan eventually forged a link between 'being a psychoanalyst' and 'being a saint' (Lacan 1990d [1974]: 15). In a highly instructive reading of this 'detail', Jacques-Alain Miller has pointed out that Lacan's ostensibly facetious analogy primary served the purpose of contrasting the position of the psychoanalyst (and the ethics of psychoanalysis) with the spirit of Western capitalism:

> [T]his civilization of growth was supposedly produced to *satisfy* needs. But, as a matter of fact, we *produce* needs, new needs, and never satisfy desire. Capitalism could be defined by Lacan as the intensive production of the want-to-enjoy: that is, the lack-of-enjoyment and at the same time, the desire-to-enjoy . . . Sainthood is certainly an attitude foreign to capitalism . . . I believe he [Lacan] is thinking of the patient saints, the saint for whom the work ethic is foreign; it is the saint who assumes the position of being useless and, in this very nonusefulness, finds his true usefulness to others . . . [A] saint is *not* a producer, but a *product of what remains* after production: that is, simple trash, refuse, reject.
>
> (Miller 1990b: 9–10)

The crucial point here is that the analyst steers away from any market economy in which the process of production is exclusively geared to the accumulation of capital. As such, the analyst does not produce new, different and better knowledge for and within the analysand. At most, the analyst aims at restructuring an already existing body of knowledge around its intrinsic fissures. In addition, Lacan's depiction of the analyst as a saint substantiates the idea that 'being an analyst' is indeed, as Freud (1925f, 1937c: 248) put it, 'an impossible profession'. Not one individual in the history of the Roman Catholic Church has ever 'been' a saint during his or her lifetime. 'Sainthood' is always recognized with hindsight, post-mortem, on the basis of a careful assessment of a person's 'life and works'. And if one does care to obtain the accolade, it is actually better not to try too hard, for self-confidence is not a good sign of sainthood. Instead of expressing one's ambitions, it is better to stay out of the picture, to work in silence with the unwanted, undesirable elements of society, and not to enjoy too much . . . *mother Thresea's work in Calcutta with the fringe of society a the height of humanity. depth*

Analytic truthfulness

If we are correct in defining the logic of psychoanalytic discovery as based on the Peircian principle of abduction, Freud's commitment to the scientificity of psychoanalysis appears as totally unwarranted.

Very few scientists have endorsed the value of abductive inferences for generating truthful scientific knowledge, partly because it remains unclear how else than through 'guessing', 'intuition' and 'insight' we can arrive at the explanatory hypothesis, partly because the reason to suspect that the hypothesis is true is unlikely to be anything else than common sense, plausibility or prejudice. Given these conditions, how would it be possible, then, for Freud ever to guarantee the scientificity of psychoanalysis? And how could he honestly claim to be driven by truthfulness and the love of truth?

Questions such as these invariably trigger endless discussions about the impossible validation of psychoanalytic knowledge and the strong 'confirmation bias' that contaminates clinical results. We do not feel that this is the place to reopen these debates and adjudicate between the warring factions occupying the intellectual battlefield. We shall restrict ourselves to pointing out how the psychoanalytic conception of truthfulness is radically different from any of the traditional criteria for establishing truth, and how this psychoanalytic truthfulness chimes with the 'fall of knowledge'.

Nowadays, philosophers of science distinguish between at least four major criteria for defining the veracity of propositions. The first criterion is the famous 'correspondence criterion', which defines truth as the convergence of essence (ideas, thought) and existence (things in the outside world). The second criterion, which is believed to be much weaker than the first, regards truth as a quality of coherent reasoning: propositions that are internally consistent and do not logically contradict one another can be regarded as true. Thirdly, truth can be defined in a pragmatic way: something is true simply because it works and the effects are visible. Finally, there is the 'consensus criterion' of truth, which suggests that something is true if a community of researchers agree to the validity of the knowledge product.

Needless to say, a brief glance at Freud's work and the history of psychoanalysis suffices to realize that psychoanalytic theory and practice do not meet any of these four criteria. Freud is by no means concerned with the correspondence between 'thought' and 'external reality'; if any 'correspondence of thought' is at stake in psychoanalysis, it refers to internal 'psychic' reality, regardless of the 'reality out there'. Our point could be disputed here on the grounds that Freud posited at the beginning of 'Instincts and Their Vicissitudes' that basic scientific concepts should not be 'arbitrarily chosen but determined by their having significant relations to the empirical material' (Freud 1915c: 117). Yet the whole question is: what constitutes 'empirical material' for the psychoanalyst? It is quite clear when reading through Freud's case studies that he does not work with 'factual realities', but with 'realities' as they emerge in the discourse of his patients without measuring their degree of congruence with 'how things really are'. As far as the coherence criterion of truth is concerned, any reader of Freud's work is able to tell that it is incoherent from beginning to end. Freud continually contradicts himself, constantly revises hypotheses, relentlessly changes his mind and incessantly replaces sophisticated theoretical models with new, supposedly better ones. Popper may have thought that psychoanalysis is not scientific because it cannot be refuted, but he clearly never paid much attention to the way in which Freud develops his ideas, for, if he had, Popper would have discovered that, however inhospitable the founder may have been to outsiders criticizing his work, he himself could not stop proving himself wrong. And the point is that he was entirely right to do so, for this is exactly what the logic of psychoanalytic discovery and the passion of ignorance dictate. If neither the correspondence nor the coherence criterion makes a strong case for the truth value of psychoanalytic knowledge, then the same is true for the pragmatic and the consensus criteria. Freud's case studies are primarily designed to prove that something in the clinical implementation of psychoanalytic theory does not work, and so are the majority of his papers on psychoanalytic technique. And if Freud cannot be brought to agree with himself, how could one ever have expected the community of psychoanalysts to agree with one another?

In keeping with his extraordinary claim that psychoanalysis may very well adopt the scientific *Weltanschauung* precisely because science is not a closed system of knowledge, Freud regarded 'truthfulness' as the particular quality of a fundamentally limited, intrinsically divided reason. 'Being truthful' has nothing to do with succeeding in one's efforts to represent things as they 'really are', but concerns the acknowledgement that any effort at representation is doomed to fail owing to the essential limits of representability. In the next chapter, we will examine this relationship between knowledge and truth more extensively through a detailed reading of Lacan's seminal paper on 'Science and Truth' (Lacan 1989b [1965]).

Chapter 2

A matter of cause: knowledge and truth in the practice of psychoanalysis

[*Crossed out*: All communication among men is rich with garbage. It is natural to want to avoid filth, garbage, ordinary trash. But a little simplicity reveals that a foul smell also marks the presence of life.]

Georges Bataille, *Socratic College*, 5

In seeking wisdom, thou art wise; in imagining that thou hast attained it thou art a fool.

Rabbi Ben-Azai, attributed

Analysing the knowledge of the text

This chapter charts Lacan's ideas on the status of psychoanalytic knowledge and the epistemology of psychoanalysis in the aftermath of his excommunication by the International Psychoanalytic Association (IPA) in autumn 1963 (Miller 1977). As such, it concentrates on Lacan's work from the mid-1960s, which roughly coincides with the period between his single-handed creation (in June 1964) of the École freudienne de Paris, Lacan's first institutional initiative, and his introduction of the procedure of the pass for the regulation of psychoanalytic training within his own school. During these years, Lacan progressively distanced himself from the letter of Freud's works, choosing to conduct his seminars on less clinical topics with wider implications for theory and practice, further elaborating his own doctrine of psychoanalysis, and raising crucial epistemological issues, which often reveal a strong allegiance to the then flourishing structuralist paradigm. This shift of perspective can be gauged already from the tenor of Lacan's programmatic *Seminar XI* of 1964, *The Foundations of Psychoanalysis*, which was subsequently renamed *The Four Fundamental Concepts of Psychoanalysis* (Lacan

1994a [1964]). This was the first seminar Lacan conducted after his 'excommunication' by the IPA, the first seminar to be published as a book-length series of lectures (in French as well as in English), and the first to generate massive appeal amongst psychoanalytic and non-psychoanalytic scholars alike. Instead of focusing on clinico-technical debates and their (Freudian) resolution, Lacan started off with a barrage of seemingly philosophical questions—'What constitutes a praxis?', 'What is the object of psychoanalysis?', 'What is the nature of the subject in psychoanalysis?', 'Which practice deserves to be called scientific?'—which all revolve around the perennially returning issue, 'What is psychoanalysis?'

[handwritten margin note: Lacan's question]

Lacan's intellectual trajectory during these years culminated in the 1965 paper 'Science and Truth' (Lacan 1989b [1965]), in which he posited that the subject of psychoanalysis is the same subject as the subject of science, whilst simultaneously maintaining that psychoanalysis can never be a science because science 'forecloses' the subject. These assertions crystallized through a re-examination of the place of the *cogito* within psychoanalysis, combined with a general exploration of the function of thought, reasoning and rationality for a psychoanalytic epistemology. As we shall see in this chapter, Lacan's claims in this text not only constituted a certain departure from his previous (Freudian) belief in a possible solidarity between psychoanalysis and modern scientific practice, but also paved the way for a radically new conception of what characterizes psychoanalytic knowledge, an innovative outlook on how the 'discourse of the analyst' integrates this dimension of knowledge, and a more sophisticated view on how the knowledge of the analyst operates within the psychoanalytic treatment.[1]

In this chapter we are not concerned with the way in which Lacan's stance towards science developed during the forty-odd years of his engagement with psychoanalysis, nor with how his ideas have been received within the various psychoanalytic schools, and even less with the value of his assertions for judging the scientific status of contemporary psychoanalytic theory and practice. We do not intend to construct a definitive Lacanian response to the endless stream of criticisms formulated by Cioffi (1998), Crews (1997), Grünbaum (1984, 1993, 2004) and others, which intend to show how the theory, practice and methodology of psychoanalysis are built on the shakiest of epistemological foundations. Over the past fifteen years, numerous writings on Lacan's changing conceptions of science and their significance for the interface between the psychoanalytic and the scientific discourses have been produced (Regnault 1985; Milner 1991, 1997, 2000; Miller 1994; Strauss 1994; Verhaeghe 1994, 2002; Laurent 1995 [1994]; Fink 1995b, 2002; Grigg 1999), and it would be quite futile, perhaps irrelevant even, to add further swathes of knowledge to this vast body of work. In addition, working psycho-analytically with an established body of knowledge can never entail adding supplementary bits and pieces of knowledge, let alone replacing its purportedly flawed, inferior aspects with more accurate, superior 'facts'. Working psychoanalytically with knowledge is not a question of finding out the truth (and nothing but the truth) about knowledge, even less of discovering and formulating 'true know-ledge', but of coming to terms with the fissures in our knowledge about truth, notably with the knowledge that truth can only ever be half-known or, as Lacan would have it, can only ever be half-said (Lacan 1971–72: session of 1 June 1972). In this spirit, the identifica-tion of certain 'elements for a psychoanalytic epistemology' through an assessment of Lacan's formulations on science must no doubt proceed from a systematic reconstruction and critique of the know-ledge within which these formulations are embedded, not with a view to establishing a new, better body of knowledge, but with the pur-pose of identifying a grid through which this knowledge can be critically evaluated.

In embarking on this task of reconstruction and critique, we evi-dently imply that this is what Lacan's knowledge requires, its struc-ture being neither accessible nor transparent, and its contents being neither clear nor comprehensible in themselves. This assumption contradicts a position defended by Milner (1995: 7), who claims that Lacan is a crystalline author whose mystifications evaporate if only his works are approached with sufficient care and attention. This may be a valid outlook for all those who, like Milner himself, have had the privilege of accompanying Lacan on his intellectual itinerary, but it does not apply to the majority of contemporary readers, no matter how sophisticated their reading procedures are. Apart from the difficulty of Lacan's grammar, his texts are littered with implicit borrowings from a warehouse of sources, punctuated with often cynical allusions to socio-historical circumstances and crammed with ingenious wordplay on names and titles. When Lacan told his audience in 1965, '*La chose, ce mot n'est pas joli, m'a-t-on dit textuellement, est-ce qu'il ne nous la gâche pas tout simplement, cette aventure des fins du fin de l'unité de la psychologie . . .*' (Lacan 1966g [1965]: 867), he cunningly conjured up the image of his former companion Daniel Lagache ('*la gâche*') and his book *L'Unité de la psychologie* (Lagache 1949). Those present at the time may have been capable of fathoming these references instantly, but the non-Lacanian, non-French and non-intellectual party is hardly in the position to grasp them. Lacan also assumed that his audience was immersed in the same readings as he himself was, relieving him from the task of having to give chapter and verse, but simultaneously increasing the esoteric character of his works. In addition, he frequently spoke through the mouth of others, integrating into his discourse terms and concepts completely alien to it, a fact which makes it extremely difficult to decide whether a proposition ought to be taken at face value. These problems are only exacerbated by Lacan's constant recourse to irony and other rhetorical and stylistic figures, which, as we shall see in the next chapter, actually reflects his constant desire to render the epistemological intricacies of the unconscious. Yet more importantly, Milner's conception of the Lacanian text also crucially dismisses the need for engaging in any psychoanalytic work whatsoever, since it implies that the truth of Lacan's knowledge is readily accessible, that his knowledge does not pose any limits to the reader's understanding, that it is some kind of 'full-knowing' which has succeeded in cancelling out the principle of 'half-knowing' and thus, by extension, the infiltration of nonsense. In other words, Milner no longer recognizes the principles of 'half-knowing' and 'half-saying' within the Lacanian text itself, but elevates it to a level of knowledge beyond 'half-knowing', from which the latter can be diagnosed in a perfectly knowable and knowledgeable fashion. There is no reason to assume, however, that Lacan's knowledge about the inevitability of 'half-knowing' would not itself be permeated by the very principle it is trying to transmit, and thus be crucially affected by a core of non-knowledge.

It bears repeating, then, that if Lacan's text does not present itself as a transparent, crystalline set of ideas, and may even be all Greek to many a reader, our reconstruction and critique should not be regarded as the revelation of its true meaning. In no way do we want to claim that this chapter represents the truth about 'Science and Truth'. On the contrary, it rather represents an attempt at demonstrating how, from a psychoanalytic perspective, truth (as the meaning of knowledge, the adequacy of concepts, and the strict convergence of thought and reality) continues to escape, and how knowledge therefore inevitably incorporates a core of stupidity (a dimension of nonsense) which cannot be cancelled out. Should truth be regarded in accordance with the consensus criterion to which we referred in Chapter 1, as a shared set of ideas within an established research community, our rendering will also be everything but true, since it differs significantly from accepted doctrine within the Lacanian psychoanalytic arena. We do not even want to pretend that we understand every twist and turn of Lacan's text, and that most references and allusions are clear. Many truths in 'Science and Truth' escape our knowledge, but, as will hopefully become clear from this chapter, from the vantage of a psychoanalytic epistemology it can never be otherwise.

Psychoanalysis is not a human science

Lacan's 'Science and Truth' constitutes the transcript of the opening session of his seminar *The Object of Psychoanalysis* (Lacan 1965–66). The text was originally published in the first issue of the journal *Cahiers pour l'analyse* (Lacan 1966f [1965]), a new initiative of a group of young enthusiastic students, who called themselves 'Le Cercle d'épistémologie' (the epistemological circle) at the École Normale Supérieure where Lacan was lecturing. When *Écrits* appeared in autumn 1966, 'Science and Truth' was included as its tailpiece (Lacan 1966g [1965]), and as such it was meant to convey the intellectual apogee of the long and arduous journey Lacan had followed through the 850 pages of text preceding it.

Many themes and ideas in 'Science and Truth', including the vexed issue of the scientificity of psychoanalysis, emanate directly from the contents of Lacan's 1964 seminar *The Four Fundamental Concepts of Psychoanalysis* (Lacan 1994a [1964]), the main thrust of which he had also summarized in the paper 'Position of the Unconscious' (Lacan 1995a [1964]). One of the key issues emerging from these texts concerns the question of how the idea that the unconscious is structured like a language, which goes all the way back to Lacan's work from the mid-1950s (Lacan 1993 [1955–56]: 11), may form the basis for the promotion of psychoanalysis as a scientific discipline. In addition, 'Science and Truth' builds on the results of an enquiry concerning the status of the subject in psychoanalysis, which Lacan had already been conducting for a number of years, and it clears the ground for epistemological reflections on the origin of psychoanalytic knowledge and the nature of the psychoanalytic act. Since January 1964, Lacan had effectively treated his audience at the École Normale Supérieure to a progressive delineation of the

unconscious structured like a language

psychoanalytic subject, and he now felt confident enough to use this work as a theoretical cornerstone for further elaborations. In light of these antecedents, and despite the title of the seminar for which 'Science and Truth' set the tone (*The Object of Psychoanalysis*), it is thus not surprising that Lacan commenced his lecture with a discussion of the *subject* in/of psychoanalysis.

How does this subject appear within psychoanalysis? The psychoanalytic subject is characterized by a 'state of splitting or *Spaltung*' (Lacan 1989b [1965]: 4), which means that it does not amount to an integrated, unitary, transparent and self-conscious being. *Spaltung* is a Freudian term designating the mental process through which a oneness becomes twofold. The term can already be found in 'The Neuro-Psychoses of Defence' (Freud 1894a) and the *Studies on Hysteria* (Freud and Breuer 1895d: 11–12). In these early texts, Freud maintains that a 'splitting of consciousness' (*Spaltung des Bewußtseins*) constitutes the basic, albeit non-primary phenomenon in many cases of hysteria, insofar as they bear witness to 'dream-like states' in which ideas are cut off from the regular content of consciousness, akin to what can occur under the influence of hypnosis. Subsequently, Freud introduces the term again in his 1927 paper 'Fetishism' (Freud 1927e), but this time to explain the mental condition of the fetishist, whose ego is supposed to incorporate and sustain two contradictory reactions to the problem of castration. When confronted with the mother's lack of a penis, the fetishist erects an object that he both worships and despises, due to the fact that it at once symbolizes his victory over castration and constantly reminds him of it. *Spaltung* resurfaces with the same meaning in the posthumous texts *An Outline of Psycho-Analysis* (Freud 1940a [1938]: 202–204) and 'Splitting of the Ego in the Process of Defence' (Freud 1940e [1938]), although Freud now generalizes the process to the broad field of neurosis. Apart from these widely quoted and well-known sources for Freud's notion of *Spaltung*, the term also appears with a different meaning in Lecture 31 of the *New Introductory Lectures on Psycho-Analysis* (Freud 1933a [1932]: 58). Here, Freud insists upon the temporary splitting of a unitary ego into an object and a subject part, whereby the latter takes the former as an object of study. Hence, the splitting represents the division of a subject and an object within the ego, the ego object becoming relatively independent from the ego subject as a source of knowledge about the ego itself.

When Lacan defines the subject in psychoanalysis as characterized by a state of *Spaltung*, he essentially claims that psychoanalysts, by virtue of their 'recognition of the unconscious' (Lacan 1989b [1965]: 4), must concede that human beings are inhabited and controlled by thoughts of which they are unaware. The unified subject, defined as an individual, a literally undivided character, may be useful (and, as we shall see, quite necessary) within psychology for pursuing empirical research (Lacan 2002f [1960]: 282–283), but it is completely alien to the way in which psychoanalysts conceive and conduct their practice. Psychoanalysts cannot fail to recognize the effects of this split between conscious and unconscious representations on a daily basis in their clinical work whenever they are faced with neurotic symptoms, dreams, bungled actions, strangely recurring patterns of behaviour, etc. All of these 'formations of the unconscious' are seen as evidence of Freud's thesis that human beings are preoccupied by 'thoughts without knowing anything about them' (Freud 1909d: 164).

However, Lacan is adamant that the empirical observation of the split subject does not suffice as a criterion for defining and safeguarding the status of psychoanalysis as a 'praxis'. In order to complete this task, 'a certain reduction is necessary . . . which is always decisive in the birth of a science . . . [and which] truly constitutes its object' (Lacan 1989b [1965]: 4). In this statement, as indeed throughout 'Science and Truth', Lacan employs the terms 'praxis' and 'reduction' with reference to Lévi-Strauss's terminology in, for example, *The Savage Mind*. 'Praxis' denotes the conceptual foundations, the invariable constitutive units on whose basis practices can unfold. Characterized by an endless empirical diversity, practices must be subjected to systematic reduction if the structural invariants are to be discovered (Lévi-Strauss 1966 [1962]: 130–131, 247).[2] Hence, only after the multifarious manifestations of the split subject have been shown to derive from a series of 'elementary structures' (Lévi-Strauss 1969 [1949]) will it be possible to institute psychoanalysis as a distinguished praxis, on the basis of these structural units. To justify and sustain their praxis, psychoanalysts ought to reduce the empirical chaos of the formations of the unconscious to an intelligible order, and this reduction should be their prime object, the latter term to be understood here as 'objective, goal, aim' rather than 'topic of research'. Lacan's idea that the reduction of empirical diversity to intelligible conceptual structures is a sufficient condition for qualifying an approach as scientific also echoes Lévi-Strauss's argument in the first chapter of *The Savage Mind*, entitled 'The Science of the Concrete', in which the anthropologist demonstrates that there is no difference between neolithic and contemporary classifications of nature as far as mental operations are concerned. From the latter perspective both attitudes deserve to be called scientific (Lévi-Strauss 1966 [1962]: 1–33).

Although defining the invariants that govern empirical diversity, with a view of validating a praxis as a scientific enterprise, seems to be a pre-set task for epistemology (and Lacan was notably addressing himself, *inter alia*, to the 'Cercle d'épistémologie'), epistemological projects are, in Lacan's opinion, unlikely to bring much enlightenment because they have the propensity to focus on research methods and objects to the detriment of the subjects involved (Lacan 1989b [1965]: 4). Epistemological investigations have insufficiently appreciated the crucial change in the subject position underpinning the decisive mutation from an ancient intuitive to a modern rational science during the seventeenth century. In this matter, Lacan acknowledges his debt to Alexandre Koyré, who argued that 'The birth of modern science is concomitant with a transformation—mutation—of the philosophical attitude, with a reversal of the value attributed to intellectual knowledge [*connaissance*] compared to sensible experience, with the discovery of the positive character of the notion of infinity' (Koyré 1971 [1955]: 261–262). Lacan equally supports Koyré's conviction that 'it is not Galileo, in any case, nor Bruno, but Descartes who clearly and distinctly formulated the principles of the new science' (Koyré 1957: 99), whereby the 'transformation of the philosophical attitude' is attributed to the Cartesian *cogito* because it epitomizes the first radical affirmation of human rationality, an uncompromising belief in the powers of the human mind, and the certainty of a thought experience in confrontation with the doubtful value of accumulated knowledge. 'For science,' Lacan states, 'the *cogito* marks . . . the break with every assurance conditioned by intuition' (Lacan 1995a [1964]: 261).[3] And since modern science relies crucially on the assumption that human beings are endowed with the capacity of reasoning, the *cogito* can be dubbed the 'subject of science'.

The expression 'subject of science' around which the entire argument of 'Science and Truth' hinges, is of course extremely ambiguous, as it may simultaneously refer to the scientist, the topics of study within scientific practice, science itself, the subjective element within science and the objects subjugated to scientific investigation. Yet it seems that Lacan's juxtaposition of the *cogito* and the subject of science indicates that the latter notion is a synonym for human rationality, mental power and the certainty of a continuous experience of thought. This would also explain why Lacan noted that modern science is concerned with the modification of our subject position in two ways (*au double sens*): the modification is an inaugural moment for modern science, and modern science invigorates this modification ever more (ibid.: 5).[4] Lacan's idea, here, is nicely illustrated by a contemporary hard-nosed scientist, who emphasizes that '[r]eal science is a regal application of the full power of human intellect' (Atkins 1995: 100) and that '[f]oremost among these achievements [of science] is the continually renewed reinforcement of the view that the human brain is such a powerful instrument that it can illuminate whatever it selects as its object of study, including itself' (ibid.: 97).

In addition to its vigorous promotion of human rationality and its key function for the precipitation of modern science, the Cartesian *cogito* of course also advances a peculiar relationship between knowledge and truth. In the fourth section of his *Discourse on the Method* Descartes contended: 'I observed that there is nothing at all in the proposition "I am thinking, therefore I exist" to assure me that I am speaking the truth, except that *I see very clearly* that in order to think it is necessary to exist. So I decided that I could take it as a general rule that the things we conceive very clearly and very distinctly are all true; only there is some difficulty in recognizing which are the things that we distinctly conceive' (Descartes 1985 [1637]: 127, emphasis added). In Descartes' philosophy, clear and distinct observations are the prerequisite for the construction of truthful knowledge about the world. What guarantees the essential clarity of our perceptions and what prevents us from dwindling into error is the infinite goodwill of God: 'There is . . . no doubt that God could have given me a nature such that I was never mistaken, again, there is no doubt that he always wills what is best. Is it then better that I should make mistakes than that I should not do so?' (Descartes 1984 [1638–1640]: 38). For Descartes, knowledge is not inherently true, but by virtue of God's benevolence our observations are authenticated and the truth of our knowledge is relatively secure. In the *cogito*, and by extension within Cartesian philosophy in general, knowledge and truth are therefore separate dimensions which are being joined together through God. Of course, the thinking subject can only assume that God is effectively good-natured and non-deceitful. God is the guarantee of truth, but apart from their faith in God individuals have no guarantee that this is a truthful representation of God.

Lacan avers that epistemologists have largely neglected the importance of the modification in our subject position, as inaugurated by

Descartes' *cogito*, for the ascent of modern science. But if epistemologists have minimized the impact of the *cogito*—in favour of Galileo's carefully controlled experiments, for instance—they are also likely to disregard the constitutive axis of psychoanalysis, because according to Lacan this axis is synonymous with the *cogito*, that is, with the subject of science. Bluntly and unequivocally, Lacan states that 'but one subject is accepted as such in psychoanalysis, the one that can make it scientific' (Lacan 1989b [1965]: 8). Presumably aware of the extraordinary tenor of this proposed congruence between the psychoanalytic subject and the *cogito*, he at once concedes: 'To say that the subject upon which we operate in psychoanalysis can only be the subject of science may seem paradoxical' (ibid.: 7). Why paradoxical? For the simple reason, we may assume, that psychoanalysis is traditionally described as a discipline which concentrates on people's irrational motives, on their fantasies, intuitions and emotions, to the detriment of rational beliefs and cognitions. The term 'psychoanalysis' literally refers to a 'liberation of the soul', so that the designation of its central stake as the rational powers of the mind (the subject of science) effectively elicits a sense of paradox.

Lacan steers away from the alignment of psychoanalysis with depth psychology (Lacan 2002f [1960]: 283, 1989b [1965]: 7, 1991 [1969–70]: 61) and also refuses to advocate it as a treatment which derives its power from the illogical, irrational and ineffable aspects of the mind (Lacan 2002f [1960]: 284). Although rooted in the pervasive influence of the unconscious on the human condition, Lacanian psychoanalysis does not define the unconscious as an amalgamation of irrational forces in the depth of the mind which disturbs the conscious order of mental things. In Lacan's theory the distinction between rationality and irrationality does not coincide with that between consciousness and the unconscious. The Lacanian unconscious has the structure of a language, and therefore it can be described and explored as a logical system of combinations between discrete elements (Lacan 1994a [1964]: 203). The Lacanian unconscious is a symbolic chain of elementary linguistic components (signifiers) whose insistence can be compared to that of a memory function in a cybernetic network (Lacan 1988c [1954–55]: 88). Rather than a reservoir of free-floating libido, the Lacanian unconscious emblematizes an inaccessible yet compelling archive of knowledge, a discourse that continues to express itself in the absence of a conscious speaker. Lacan's definition of the unconscious does not differ substantially here from that adduced by Lévi-Strauss in his

1949 paper 'The Effectiveness of Symbols': '[T]he unconscious merely imposes structural laws upon inarticulated elements which originate elsewhere. . . . We might say, therefore, that the pre-conscious is the individual lexicon where each of us accumulates the vocabulary of his personal history, but that this vocabulary becomes significant, for us and for others, only to the extent that the un-conscious structures it according to its laws and thus transforms it into language' (Lévi-Strauss 1968a [1949]: 203).

From this vantage point Lacan underscores that 'every attempt, or even temptation, in which current theory does not stop relapsing, to incarnate the subject earlier, is tantamount to errancy—always fruit-ful in error, and as such mistaken' (Lacan 1989b [1965]: 8, translation modified). Detailing the subject on which psychoanalysis operates as a setback from the subject of science, that is to say, as a being whose thought processes are distorted or whose mind is fixated at an infantile stage of psychosexual development, inevitably gives rise to what Lévi-Strauss called the 'archaic illusion' (Lévi-Strauss 1969 [1949]: 84–97). The subjects psychoanalysts are working with are not people whose mental powers are underdeveloped, primitive, infantile, or pathologically disturbed. Endorsing Lévi-Strauss' argument, and implicitly criticizing Freud's Comtian model in *Totem and Taboo* (Freud 1912–13a) of the phylogenetic evolution of the human mind from magic and animism to science and rationality, Lacan argues that there is no such thing as a non-scientific human mind, whether the latter is situated within a pre-modern or modern society, whether that of a child or an adult, whether suffering from psychic problems or not. Against the prevailing developmental theories of Lévy-Bruhl and Piaget, Lévi-Strauss had indeed suggested that the postulation of a 'primitive mentality' in children and 'savages' neglects the uniqueness of 'a universal substratum the crystallizations of which have not yet occurred, and in which communication is still possible between incompletely solidified forms' (Lévi-Strauss 1969 [1949]: 93). Fully consistent with this outlook, Lacan contends that the devel-opmental approach 'falsifies the whole primary process [the key pro-cess of free-floating libidinal energy animating the Freudian unconscious]' and 'masks the truth about what happens during childhood that is original' (Lacan 1989b [1965]: 8).

Yet beyond the specific realms of depth and developmental psycho-logy, psychoanalysis cannot affiliate itself with the human sciences in general, to the extent that the latter tend to depict human beings as objectifiable, not inherently knowledgeable creatures. Human scientists are inclined to treat the participants in their research projects as less scientifically inclined, diligent and obedient respondents, through which they also fall into the trap of the 'archaic illusion'. A concrete example may clarify this. Assume that a human scientist wants to investigate whether the truthfulness of the stories people tell can be inferred from involuntary non-verbal cues such as blushing, blinking, frowning, etc. Since the discovery of reliable facial indicators for lying would have an enormous impact on police interrogations and court testimonies, a project of this kind requires little justification and is likely to attract substantial funds from social science research councils. If it were proven that there is indeed a correlation between lying and the appearance of certain facial tics, we would have been able to tell whether William Jefferson Clinton was telling the truth when he proclaimed that he did not have sex with 'that woman', so even the wider social relevance of this type of project is easy to justify. In choosing an appropriate design for his research the human scientist might decide to set up a simple experiment in which participants are asked to tell two stories (a true and a false one) in front of a camera recording all their bodily movements. After the data have been collected, the researcher can then try to identify within the series of recorded bogus stories those recurring patterns that are significantly different from observable expressions in the recorded true stories.

What is the catch? Although the experiment seems methodologically sound and likely to generate a good set of results, it can be implemented only on the condition that the participants are willing to subject themselves without resistance to the scientist's instructions. This means that the scientist needs to proceed from the fundamental assumption that, whilst attributing knowledge to him, participants will put themselves into the position of passive, ignorant and reactive subjects who will not try to counter his knowledge with their own. The scientist has to assume that his participants will comply with his instructions, will literally subject themselves to the experimental conditions and will not try to deceive him. In order to implement his project, the scientist thus also has to exclude the possibility of his participants wilfully recounting true stories whenever they are being asked to produce false ones, and vice versa. Yet he also needs to discount the possibility of his participants deceiving themselves in thinking that something actually happened when it did not; that is to say, he cannot take account of the fact that some of the stories produced as true may be true only in terms of his participants' psychic reality, and not in terms of what 'really' happened to them. To the degree that human scientists who engage in empirical research view their participants merely as responsive objects, they reduce the human being to a pre-logical entity, which evidently undermines the validity of their conclusions. But the degree to which they take stock of their participants' potential deceitfulness is equally a measure of their acknowledgement that their epistemological approach is fundamentally flawed and that their methodology cannot yield any reliable and valid results. Lacan does not hesitate to conclude that the human sciences' plan to develop knowledge about the human being is doomed to fail, because 'science's [hu]man does not exist, only its subject does' (Lacan 1989b [1965]: 8).

The temptations of structuralism

If the status of the subject in psychoanalysis precludes its affiliation with the human sciences, are there any disciplines or paradigms which may still have value as models for its praxis? Doesn't the practice of hard science, as the direct outcome of the *cogito* and the most solid precipitation of the human intellect, provide psychoanalysis with a set of stringent methodological parameters? Once again, Lacan's answer is a categorical 'no'. Although the psychoanalytic subject equals the subject of science, this by no means implies that psychoanalysis is or should be a 'hard' modern science. Despite the fact that Freud could not have cleared the path of psychoanalysis without his allegiance to scientism, despite the fact that psychoanalysis bears the essential mark of Freud's scientific ideals (Lacan 1989b [1965]: 6), modern scientific practices do not reflect the ambitions of psychoanalysis.[5] The reason is that modern science, for all its debts to the *cogito*, constantly tries to 'suture' (sew up) the subject of science (ibid.: 10). Whereas the Cartesian subject is fundamentally divided between a certainty of thinking (knowledge) and an uncertainty of truth (the point where knowledge reaches its own limit), which can be lifted only through the introduction of a non-deceitful God, modern science has endeavoured to solve the issue of truth by advancing it as the inherent quality of proper scientific knowledge. Whilst in Descartes' philosophy truth always escapes rationality, in modern science truth has become the hallmark of a properly conducted rational process and its outcomes. As Atkins puts it: '[S]cience is the best procedure yet discovered for exposing fundamental truths about the world . . . Truth invariably prevails in science even though the road to it is not always straight' (Atkins 1995: 97). Unlike those disciplines which implicitly entertain the archaic illusion by operating on a pre-logical, primitive or irrational mentality, modern science eulogizes the powers and achievements of human rationality whilst simultaneously pursuing true products of knowledge, thus suturing the Cartesian rift between knowledge and truth. Lacan concludes that 'science, if one looks at it closely, has no memory. Once constituted, it forgets the circuitous path by which it came into being; otherwise stated, it forgets the dimension of truth that psychoanalysis seriously puts to work' (Lacan 1989b [1965]: 18).

Lacan's definition of truth, here, differs substantially from the traditional ones. Throughout his works, he criticized the time-honoured 'correspondence criterion' of truth, according to which truth is synonymous with a perfect overlap (correspondence) between reason and reality, between the thing and the outside world (*adaequatio rei et intellectus*) (Lacan 2002b [1955]: 136, 1990d [1974]: 20). In this context, Lacan is eager to point out at the beginning of 'Science and Truth' that Freud's reality principle does not entail a disjunction between an objective, 'true' reality that imposes itself onto the subject's senses (the system of perception consciousness) and a less objective 'psychic reality' (Lacan 1989b [1965]: 5). When a child acknowledges that its mother does not have a penis, this perception is not more true owing to its correspondence with a factual reality than the realization that its mother and father are equally endowed, because both observations are part and parcel of a single 'strain of experience sanctioned by the subject of science' (ibid.: 6). Only if we were to adopt an epistemological perspective that defines true knowledge as knowledge which coincides with a factual reality would we be led to consider the first observation as true and the second as false, and would we probably feel inclined to 'correct' the latter in line with the former. Yet the psychoanalyst does not take factual realities into account when judging the truth of an analysand's thoughts, and every attempt at bringing an analysand's experience in line with the facts can be considered an analytic failure, even if the attempt in question actually succeeds.

In Lacan's outlook, truth refers to a human being's incapacity to master all knowledge owing to the absence of a knowing agency at the level of the unconscious. Truth is synonymous with the inexorable insistence of a non-subjectified, unconscious knowledge, which constitutes the very limit of knowledge. When Lacan argues during the mid-1960s and early 1970s that analytic interpretations are correct only if they have an effect of truth (Lacan 1966–67: session of 14 December 1966, 1970–71: session of 13 January 1971), we can therefore read this as a recommendation that analytic interpretations must always be geared towards those points in the analysand's discourse where knowledge shows its inconsistencies, where the nonsensicalities and the stupidities are at work, not in order to reduce these elements and contribute to the enlargement of consciousness, the expansion of self-knowledge or—God forbid—a corrective reorientation of the psyche, but in order to make the analysand experience and acknowledge the ineluctable return of the limits of reason as a *sine qua non* of humanity (Lacan 1968a [1967]: 52–53).

The aforementioned effort to suture the Cartesian subject of science within modern scientific practices can now also be understood as a sustained endeavour to control and evaluate all knowledge, proceeding from the spurious conviction that the rational processes which organize all things worldly will ultimately reveal themselves to the conscious human mind. Analysands engage in a comparable enterprise whenever they fall prey to what Lacan dubbed 'the supposed subject of knowing' (*le sujet supposé savoir*) in the transference, for the function of the supposed subject of knowing signals the analysand's belief in the possibility of achieving complete self-control and full self-realization. Because this supposed subject of knowing also functions as a mental reassurance that the process of gathering knowledge about the world and oneself is not in vain, Lacan identified it in *Seminar XI* with the God of Descartes (Lacan 1994a [1964]: 224–225), and later on with the God of the philosophers in general (Lacan 1968b [1967]: 39, 1968–69: session of 30 April 1969). Both the supposed subject of knowing and Descartes' God are assumptions destined to annihilate the constitutive gap between knowledge and truth, and thus to abolish the unconscious (Lacan 1968c [1967]: 46). The suturing of this gap within modern science is of a similar nature, with the proviso that modern scientists do not have recourse to a belief in a transcendental function or agency in order to reach their goals. They are firmly convinced that knowledge and truth can be matched within the limits of reason alone, because they do not accept the existence of a gulf separating knowledge (rationality) and truth in the first place.

The only frameworks Lacan regards as sufficiently attuned to the subject of science and its inherent division between knowledge and truth, therefore qualifying as suitable partners for psychoanalysis, are those of game theory, linguistics and structural anthropology. Strictly avoiding an evolutionistic, genetic approach to their topic of study, these frameworks are all concerned with the rigorous analysis and systematic classification of the modes of thought people may use to organize their relationship with the environment.

Lacan's espousal of game theory generally follows the works of Williams (1954) and Von Neumann and Morgenstern (1944), whereby the latter work had already been embraced by Lévi-Strauss in 1952 (Lévi-Strauss 1968c [1952]) owing to the strong similarities between the formal models of economic analysis advocated by Von Neumann and Morgenstern, and the structural approach within anthropology. In game theory a person is defined as a distinct set of interests, the description of a conflict situation depends on a calculation of the number of persons involved, and the available strategies can be graphically represented in the form of a matrix. As Lacan put it: 'game theory . . . takes advantage of the thoroughly calculable character of a subject strictly reduced to the formula for a matrix of signifying combinations' (1989b [1965]: 9).[6] As far as linguistics is concerned, Lacan accepts that its case is more subtle, since it must take account of the difference between rational, symbolic systems of language and thought (the subject of science, the produced statements) on the one hand, and the subject who speaks as such (the aspect of enunciation) on the other hand. Nonetheless, he believes that linguistic science was justified in following the anti-psychological directions of the Saussurian paradigm and turning decisively towards the formal study of the language system, rather than the incidence of speech and intonation, for instance. If there was a theoretical divergence amongst contemporary linguists, it was, in Lacan's opinion, not rooted in an incompatibility between their objects of study, but rather in their alternative formalizations of the symbolic system (the battery of signifiers): while syntax was the core organizational principle of language for Chomsky (1957), other aspects were examined by Hjelmslev (1961 [1943]) and Jakobson (1963).

However important the contributions of game theory and linguistics, the discipline of structural anthropology, as inaugurated by Lévi-Strauss during the late 1940s, features first and foremost amongst the frameworks which Lacan identifies as suitable for supporting a psychoanalytic epistemology. In the first chapter of *The Savage Mind* (1966 [1962]: 1–33), Lévi-Strauss gave numerous examples of how allegedly primitive people construct highly sophisticated classifications of fauna and flora, demonstrating how these people rely on thought processes that are not qualitatively different from those activated by so-called scientific minds. Moreover, the so-called primitive classifications 'may anticipate not only science itself but even methods or results which scientific procedure does not incorporate until an advanced stage of its development' (ibid.: 11). Borrowing an example from Deacon (1927), Lévi-Strauss also emphasized, both in his seminal treatise *The Elementary Structures of Kinship* (1969 [1949]: 125–126) and in *The Savage Mind* (1966 [1962]: 251), that informants may be as capable as the scientifically trained anthropologist of drawing the complicated diagrams of the kinship patterns underpinning their communities.

Of course, it is not because the anthropologist's informants are able to reproduce the elementary structures of their community that they are constantly aware of them, nor even that they play an active part in generating them. In Lévi-Straussian anthropology, elementary structures outline a subject's position vis-à-vis the other members in the community, just as much as in game theory a certain symbolic set of strategic principles defines the relationship between the opponents. Subjects act upon a knowledge of these structures without taking them consciously into account all the time, and without contributing wittingly and willingly to their development. Extrapolating these principles to the study of myths in *The Raw and the Cooked*, a book published shortly before Lacan's presentation of 'Science and Truth', Lévi-Strauss explained his approach as follows:

> [S]ince, my ambition being to discover the conditions in which systems of truth become mutually convertible and therefore simultaneously acceptable to several different subjects, the pattern of those conditions takes on the character of an autonomous object, independent of any subject. I believe that mythology, more than anything else, makes it possible to illustrate such objectified thought and to provide empirical proof of its reality. Although the possibility cannot be excluded that the speakers who create and transmit myths may become aware of their structure and mode of operation, this cannot occur as a normal thing, but only partially and intermittently. It is the same with myths as with language: the individual who conscientiously applied phonological and grammatical laws in his speech, supposing he possessed the necessary knowledge and virtuosity to do so, would nevertheless lose the thread of his ideas almost immediately. . . . Mythological analysis has not, and cannot have,

as its aim to show how men think. . . . I therefore claim to show, not how men think in myths, but how myths operate in men's minds without their being aware of the fact. And, as I have already suggested, it would perhaps be better to go still further and, disregarding the thinking subject completely, proceed as if the thinking process were taking place in the myths, in their reflection upon themselves and their interrelation.

(Lévi-Strauss 1983 [1964]: 11–12)

As Lacan points out, Lévi-Strauss 'does not presume to deliver up to us the nature of the myth-maker' (Lacan 1989b [1965]: 11). Although a particular individual may venture a logical analysis of his community's myths akin to that undertaken by Lévi-Strauss himself in *The Raw and the Cooked*, this individual neither creates nor modifies, neither demurs nor assents to the various patterns those myths adopt. If anything, there is 'simultaneous production of myths themselves, by the mind that generates them and, by the myths, of an image of the world which is already inherent in the structure of the mind' (Lévi-Strauss 1983 [1964]: 341). The grammar of kinship and myths constitutes the very fabric of the human mind, without this mind being fully aware of its exact remit and its precise ramifications. It provides the rational building blocks of human experience, pervading the subject's knowledge and actions, and situating him in relation to others. Instead of being located and deployed by the subject, the elementary structures delineate the subject's position and regulate his relationships with themselves and others. Lacan concludes approvingly that the 'object of mythogeny [the study of the genesis of myths] is thus linked to no development whatsoever, nor to an arrest, of the responsible subject. It is not to that subject that this object is related, but to the subject of science' (ibid.: 11, translation modified), that is to say, to a genuine experience of thought which transcends the boundaries of consciousness and whose truth should not be judged by an evaluation of its proximity to an objective reality. Indeed, as can be inferred from the above citation, Lévi-Strauss refers to myths as systems of truth, despite their having no apparent basis in a set of observable facts, and despite the simultaneous presence of ostensibly incommensurable accounts. During the mid-1960s Lacan embraced Lévi-Strauss's structuralist viewpoint wholeheartedly, integrating its main principles into his own psychoanalytic theory of the subject, and believing in the possibility of guaranteeing in this way the scientific status of psychoanalysis. What Althusser was trying to achieve for Marxism, Lacan implemented for psychoanalysis. Structured like a language, the modus operandi of the unconscious in the human mind is held to resemble that of foundational myths and social patterns of kinship. Rather than an object manufactured by a subject, the unconscious structure of language (the chain of signifiers, the Other) manu- factures the subject, and Lacan even went so far as to say that the subject is *caused* by the signifier (Lacan 1995a [1964]: 265). In a text contemporary with 'Science and Truth', he put it as follows: 'The unconscious does not exist because there might be an unconscious desire—obtuse, heavy, Caliban, even animalistic—that is awoken from the depths, that would be primitive and that would have to elevate itself to the superior level of consciousness. On the contrary, there is a desire because there is unconscious, that is to say language which escapes the subject in its structure and effects, and because there is always on the level of language something beyond con- sciousness, which is where the function of desire can be situated' (Lacan 1967 [1966]: 45).

A more radical description of the relationship between the un- conscious structure and the subject appeared in 'Position of the Unconscious': 'The effect of language is to introduce the cause into the subject. Through this effect, he [the subject] is not the cause of himself; he bears within himself the worm of the cause that splits him' (Lacan 1995a [1964]: 265). And farther in the same text: 'The fact that the Other is, for the subject, the locus of his signifying cause merely explains why no subject can be his own cause. This is clear not only from the fact that he is not God, but from the fact that God Himself cannot be His own cause if we think of Him as a subject . . .' (ibid.: 269). Lacan maintains that language is the necessary and suf- ficient precondition for the unconscious, and that the unconscious, which is itself structured like a language, predestines a human being to a state of subjective splitting, inasmuch as the active knowledge residing in the unconscious evades the radius of the conscious subject. Because of Lacan's extension of the sphere of language to the unconscious, rationality is not restricted to conscious processes of thought, and it does not stand in opposition to the splitting of the subject. On the contrary, the symbolic system of the unconscious occasions the distinction between a mental place where 'one' is, and another mental place where 'one' is not, which is tantamount to saying that it gives rise to the experience that 'one' is not one.

Lacan's conviction that the subject is never the cause of itself

(*causa sui*), but is always being caused by the Other, also allows him
to criticize the principal conclusion Descartes drew from his *cogito*,
'I am thinking, therefore I exist' (*cogito, ergo sum*) (Descartes 1985
[1637]: 127), as well as Freud's clinical imperative, 'Where Id was,
there Ego shall be' (*Wo Es was, soll Ich werden*). As far as Descartes'
formula is concerned, Lacan argues that it erroneously proposes a
causal relationship between subjective reasoning (*cogito*) and a subjective existence (*sum*) that transcends the thought process, whilst
Descartes' *ergo sum* is as much tributary to speech and language as
his *cogito*. In *Seminar XI* he had already explained this point in
relation to the first part of Descartes' formula: 'Descartes tells us—
By virtue of the fact that I doubt, I am sure of thinking [de penser],
and—I would say, to stick to a formula that is no more prudent than
his, but which will save us from getting caught up in the *cogito*, the
I think—*by virtue of thinking, I am*. Note in passing that in avoiding
the *I think*, I avoid the discussion that results from the fact that this
I think, for us, certainly cannot be detached from the fact that he can
formulate it only by *saying* it to us, implicitly—a fact that he forgets'
(Lacan 1994a [1964]: 35–36, translation modified).[7]

Likewise, Descartes can conclude his own existence only 'by saying
it to us', and without even realizing that this is what he actually does.
Therefore, Lacan rewrites Descartes' adage as 'I am thinking: "therefore I exist" '(Lacan 1989b [1965]: 13), through which the *sum* in the
statement accedes to the level of thought, the *ergo* loses its function
as a logical implication, and the issue of existence is relegated to a
dimension beyond the statement. This alternative formula also indicates that Descartes' own conscious reasoning (the reflection upon
his own thought) does not elicit his meta-rational existence, but that
the entire linguistic operation, of whose impact the philosopher
himself was not fully aware, induced his split subjectivity.

Lacan detects a similar 'paradox . . . that presses me to assume my
own causality' (ibid.: 13) in Freud's well-known motto, *Wo Es war,
soll Ich werden*, which Lacan translates as '*là où c'était, là comme
sujet dois-je advenir*, 'there where it was, there must I, as subject,
come to happen' (ibid.: 12, translation modified).[8] Urging his audience to read Freud's formula backwards (*à revers*), that is to say, to
'invert its direction' (*d'en renverser le sens*) (ibid.: 13, translation
modified), Lacan contends that the ensuing *Ich soll werden wo Es war*
indicates sufficiently how the subject's mandatory happening does
not tap from any other force than that which inhabits the subject
itself. Here too the subject appears as *causa sui*.[9]

The material cause

Lacan's overarching aim in 'Science and Truth' is to reduce the multifarious formations of the unconscious to their structural invariants in order to lay the foundations for an epistemology of psychoanalysis that is in keeping with the nature of its clinical praxis. The first half of Lacan's text yields at least three such elementary components:

1   The subject on which psychoanalysis operates is invariably the subject of science (an experience of thought).
2   The subject of science is divided between knowledge and truth.
3   The unconscious, as conditioned by and structured like a language, encapsulates an independent thinking process devoid of a thinking agency, which permeates conscious reasoning.

However necessary these three invariants may seem as cornerstones for a solidly constructed psychoanalytic praxis, in Lacan's mind they insufficiently convey the specificity of psychoanalysis. Insofar as psychoanalysis operates on the subject of science, 'I do not believe,' he concedes, 'that, in this respect, psychoanalysis lays claim to any special privileges' (Lacan 1989b [1965]: 8). Cartesian philosophy also operates on the subject of science, as do the disciplines of structural anthropology, linguistics and game theory. The constitutive division between knowledge and truth emanates from Descartes' struggle to find a reliable criterion for the clarity of his perceptions, and it is also entertained within structural anthropology. The linguistic structure of the unconscious and its pervasive influence on the human condition had already been accounted for by Lévi-Strauss.

As a result, Lacan starts looking for another, more distinguishing invariant, which he identifies in the function psychoanalysis accords to the truth as cause. This specific function of the truth as cause in psychoanalysis also emboldens him to widen the gap between psychoanalysis and modern science, and to take issue with reigning conceptions of psychoanalytic practice as a Western version of shamanism or an alternative religion. The former analogy had, of course, been adduced by Lévi-Strauss in 'The Effectiveness of Symbols' (Lévi-Strauss 1968a [1949]: 198–204), and it had prompted Lacan to admit in his 'Rome Discourse' that the psychoanalyst 'is not far from regarding [the status of his action] as magical' (Lacan

2002a [1953]: 34). The second parallel has less noble origins and more widespread ramifications amongst the numerous detractors of psychoanalysis. Indeed, the idea that psychoanalysis is but a secular belief and that its 'rites' of initiation' are not dissimilar to those preserved by religious cults continues to underpin many a Freud basher's exposure of the psychoanalytic fallacies.

In order to define the additional invariant of psychoanalytic praxis, simultaneously separating psychoanalysis from modern science, magic and religion, Lacan takes his inspiration from Aristotle's classic tabulation of the four causes in the second book of his *Physics* (Aristotle 1996: 38–42): the efficient cause, the final cause, the formal cause and the material cause. The difference between these four causes is traditionally explained with the example of the construction of a house. The efficient cause refers to the time and effort invested in the construction process; it is synonymous with the general expenditure of energy required to build the house. The final cause concerns the aims and objectives of all those people involved in the construction; if nobody had the intention to build, the first stone of the house would not even be laid. The formal cause is related to the construction plan, the outline of work procedures, and the general application of certain mathematical laws. Every act of construction corresponds to a systematic arrangement within a pre-conceived plan, without which the house would never subsist as a solid piece of work. The material cause reflects all the equipment and natural resources necessary for giving shape to our intentions, efforts and plans. No matter how great one's enthusiasm, detailed one's plans, and clear one's intentions, the house cannot exist without stones or wood.

Lacan argues that the function of truth as cause within magic, religion, modern science and psychoanalysis always follows one of the four causes within Aristotle's theory of causality. 'Magic involves the truth as cause in its guise as efficient cause' (Lacan 1989b [1965]: 19). In religion, 'truth appears only as a final cause' (ibid.: 20). And whereas 'the truth as cause in science must ... be recognized in its guise as formal cause', psychoanalysis envisages the truth as a material cause (ibid.: 22). How are we to read each of these connections? What does it mean for the truth to function as an efficient cause in magic, for instance? From the vantage point of our common-sense understanding of causality, whereby a cause is simply everything responsible for the production of an effect, it is difficult to see what Lacan is trying to convey. Yet he mentions explicitly that his programme does not entail 'the cause as logical category, but as causing the whole effect' (ibid.: 17), and we also ought to bear in mind that some of Aristotle's causes are completely alien to our contemporary definition of a causal factor.[10] Nowadays few if any people would presumably agree that a pile of bricks is the cause of a house. The causes in Lacan's schema should therefore not be understood in logico-mathematical terms, and not be diverted from their meaning in Aristotle's physics.

The function of truth as an efficient cause in magic indicates that the truth of a magical phenomenon, whether a shamanistic healing practice or the cursing of natural forces, is always attributed to power, energy or (super)natural abilities. Even when a shaman knows that he is merely practising the art of deception, as in the famous case of Quesalid reported by Boas and immortalized by Lévi-Strauss (1968b [1949]: 175–178), his confrontation with the fact that his own deceptive practice seems to be more effective than that of others may instil the seeds of doubt into his mind, and trigger explanations of the truth of the patient's cure in terms of his own divine powers. By contrast, in religion the truth of a phenomenon does not lie within the efforts required to produce it, but mirrors the unfathomable intention of God. Here, the final cause is being invoked as *primus inter pares* amongst the causes: the will of the Creator controls the expenditure of energy and the planning, as well as the available materials. In 'Science and Truth' Lacan formulates this dynamics as follows: 'Let us say that a religious person leaves responsibility for the cause to God, but thereby bars his own access to truth. Thus, he is led to place the cause of his desire in God's hands, and that is the true object of the sacrifice' (Lacan 1989b [1965]: 20). The truth of the endless spiral of nature, including the individual's private psychic dwellings, is firmly in the hands of God, who pursues a superior goal. In modern science, then, truth appears as a formal cause, which means that modern scientists are willing to admit that they have discovered the true nature of a phenomenon only if they have succeeded in formulating the laws governing its manifestations. Whereas a religious person is likely to explain biological diversity with God's plan of creation, the scientist will engage in a series of carefully controlled studies and, armed with Darwin's theory of evolution, contribute to the development of natural laws emblematizing truthful scientific knowledge. Furthermore, the truth value of a scientific formula will be judged on the basis of the number of phenomena it is capable of explaining. Rules to which there are many exceptions are less true than rules applicable to anything in each and every context. The central message of Lacan's distribution of the Aristotelian causes over magic, religion and modern science entails that in their reliance on the efficient, final and formal causes, respectively, none of these three realms of action really acknowledge the truth as cause. This is why he contends that in magic, religion and modern science the truth as cause 'appears as', or must be recognized 'in its guise' as an efficient, final and formal cause. To Lacan, the key feature of the truth as cause is taken into account only in psychoanalysis, for only psychoanalysis accepts that truth functions as a material cause. For a psychoanalyst, the truth of a phenomenon, action or process lies neither in the effort invested in it, nor in its goals or its logical plan, but only in its building blocks, which are made up of speech and language. Putting the truth to work as a material cause thus implies that the symbolic make-up (the signifying dimension) of an event is being taken seriously. Lacan further complicates his account by arguing that magic, religion and modern science do not disregard the truth as cause in the same way (Lacan 1989b [1965]: 22). In its promotion of the efficient cause, magic displays a repression (*Verdrängung*) of the truth as cause: it is as if the magician says, 'My words and actions are part of the ritual, yet they have nothing to do with the effect, since my power is the only thing that counts.' Religion, by contrast, maintains a negation (*Verneinung*) of the truth as cause: 'You may think that these words and actions are mine, but they belong only to God.' Finally, foreclosure (*Verwerfung*) of the truth as cause is the province of modern science: 'My words and actions do not exist at all within the equation; the truth transcends my existence, yet my knowledge can capture it in such a way that it is unaffected by my words and actions.' The fact that Lacan uses the term 'foreclosure' (*Verwerfung*) here is telling, for it implies that a psychotic mechanism resides at the heart of modern science. Lacan intimates that if the modern scientist is absolutely convinced that she is able to realize her scientific aims and objectives, she joins the psychotic in the conviction that she has privileged access to the knowledge of a truth that is independent of her own existence.

More concretely, Lacan's gloss on the truth as material cause in psychoanalysis emphasizes that all formations of the unconscious derive their existence from the material of language, and that a psychoanalytic praxis cannot be deployed without these symbolic elements (signifiers). In light of the above considerations on the unconscious as a symbolic system without a knowing agency, it should be noted that the formations of the unconscious stem from the synergetic, albeit thoroughly conflictual action of the subject's conscious speech and his or her unconscious 'being spoken'. Although the truth of a symptom, its emergence and disappearance, lies in the signifier, this truth has to be situated on the level of the unconscious, within a discourse from which the subject is barred. Of course, this does not imply that the unconscious is prevented from expressing itself. On the contrary, as Lacan had daringly demonstrated with a lengthy rhetorical figure, the truth (the fact that there is no subject in the unconscious and that knowledge reaches its limits in the emergence of unconscious formations) speaks vigorously and eloquently.[11]

Beyond structuralism

Lacan's arguments in 'Science and Truth' inspire some bewilderment as to his exact position concerning the scientific status of psychoanalysis. Whereas in *Seminar XI* he had drawn attention to the 'ambiguity that persists in the question as to what in psychoanalysis is or is not reducible to science' (Lacan 1994a [1964]: 265), in 'Science and Truth' some ambiguity persists as to whether Lacan is keen to reduce psychoanalysis to a science or not. On the one hand, he is adamant that psychoanalysis operates on the subject of science, that this is the only subject that should be tolerated within psychoanalysis, and that this is the subject which can make a psychoanalytic praxis scientific. On the other hand, he criticizes contemporary scientific practice for its inherent closure of the gap between knowledge and truth, and its spurious reliance on the truth as a formal cause. On the one hand, he is extremely dismissive of the way in which modern science seems to have forgotten how to recognize the subjective *Spaltung* that presided over its birth, and he goes so far as to suggest that scientific practice becomes synonymous with a psychotic delusion in its total rejection (foreclosure) of the material cause of truth. On the other hand, he remains extraordinarily keen to establish the scientificity of psychoanalysis in defiance of modern scientific practice and against its epistemological assumptions.

On the basis of 'Science and Truth', Milner (1991, 1995) has argued that Lacan finally relieved psychoanalysis from the burden of the ideal of science, adding provocatively that scientists could definitely benefit from the ideal of psychoanalysis. Whilst we remain unsure about the ideal character of (Lacanian) psychoanalysis, we tend to agree with Milner's first proposition, if only the term 'science' is restricted to those modern disciplines which favour the quantitative experimental method and the hypothetico-deductive approach. For nowhere in 'Science and Truth' does Lacan intimate that a psychoanalytic praxis does not deserve to be qualified as scientific, if only the term 'scientific' is expanded in a Lévi-Straussian way, so that it encompasses all activities involving the systematic classification, detailed description and rational explanation of empirical data, regardless of whether this knowledge is absolutely true, and taking account of the symbolic universe in which the subject is situated. Lacan is happy for psychoanalysis to flourish amongst linguistics, game theory and structural anthropology—disciplines whose main representatives have championed the scientific value of their observations. Hence, it would be unfair to say that during the 1960s Lacan refused to adorn psychoanalysis with the label of science. His entire trajectory in 'Science and Truth' reflects an ardent desire to situate psychoanalysis within the Cartesian tradition of rationality which had given birth to modern science, a tradition which modern science itself paradoxically exchanged for the seductions of objectivity and true knowledge. Our alternative to Milner's aforementioned statement therefore reads that Lacan refused to expose psychoanalysis to the ideal of modern science, not because modern science is too empiricist, rational and detached, but because modern science is no longer scientific, or is not scientific enough.

And yet, as Lacan realized during the early 1970s, the epistemology of psychoanalysis also sits uneasily with the tenets of structuralist science. Lacan's progressive detachment from structuralist linguistics and structuralist anthropology may first of all be explained through the fact that, as a psychoanalyst, he was not particularly interested in the study of language as an abstract formal system nor, for that matter, in the classification of the transformative rules that govern patterns of kinship and myths. Psychoanalysts deal with the signifier as it is articulated by a particular subject within a singular social setting, and the process of articulation matters at least as much as, if not more than, the articulated product. Confronting Roman Jakobson in a memorable session of his *Seminar XX*, Lacan proclaimed that psychoanalysis does not require linguistics (*linguistique*), but is in need of a science of 'linguistricks', 'linguistrickery', 'linguisteria' (*linguisterie*)—a science that takes account of the tricks language plays upon us, a science that renders the linguistic trickeries with which an analysand presents himself, a science that takes seriously the linguistic twists and turns underpinning the symptoms of hysteria and the intricacies of the hysterical discourse (Lacan 1998b [1972–73]: 15).

At a more fundamental level, Lacan gradually came to realize that structuralist science, in its relentless emphasis on the operative mechanisms of reason, including in those places where reason has been annihilated and rejected as irrationality, madness and stupidity by the authoritative voices of scientific ideology, had failed to recognize the very limits of reason. By reducing everything to the formal operations of language, structuralist science becomes a tyrannical superpower in its own right, which crushes the significance of any resistant core of non-knowledge within operative systems of thought, be it those animating the unconscious. In response to structuralist science, and as an alternative to the all-encompassing terror of its linguistic premises, Lacan subsequently developed a discourse theory (Lacan 1991 [1969–70]) in which a crucial place is reserved for the 'object *a*', the object which defies reason and which links truth (the intrinsic boundary of knowledge, the perpetual evaporation of meaning) to the dimension of jouissance. This relationship between knowledge, truth, meaning and jouissance will be explored in the next chapter.

Chapter 3

The punning of reason: meaning, nonsense and the limits of psychoanalytic language

> When the space of a lapsus no longer carries any meaning (or interpretation), then only is one sure that one is in the unconscious. *One knows.*
>
> Jacques Lacan, Preface to the English-language edition of
> *Seminar XI*, xxxix

> Ut translatio Natura.
> Motto of the Museum of Jurassic Technology

On learning to speak Lacanese

There is a colloquial expression in French which one can sometimes hear in the company of psychoanalysts, but with increasing frequency also amongst 'educated lay people', and which serves to emphasize the excruciatingly awkward formulation of a spoken sentence or written statement. Faced with his complete failure to fathom the significance of a text, confronted with her radical inability even to begin to understand the meaning of a phrase, a person may be heard to say: '*Eh bien, c'est vraiment du Lacan, ça!*' Translated back into English, the exclamation would probably sound something like: 'Wow, this is genuine Lacan!' Perhaps the *éminences grises* of the Académie française will one day discuss whether to admit a new word into the language and thus into the pages of the great French dictionaries: '*lacan [lakã] <m.> 0.1 mot/passage difficile, impossible à comprendre; 0.2 personne qui parle ou écrit de façon difficile.*' Perhaps they will one day even debate whether to give their blessing to the language system that gives birth to these difficult words and passages: '*lacanien [lakanjɛ] <m.> 0.1 adhérent/praticien de la psychanalyse lacanienne, tradition développée par le psychiatre* *français Jacques Lacan (1901–1981); 0.2. langage parlé par les lacaniens; 0.3 langage difficile/incompréhensible; <> 3.2 parler lacanien ~ fig. parler de façon difficile/incompréhensible; cf. parler chinois'.* Now that 'Lacan' is no longer simply recognized as a proper name, but has acquired the status of an appellation in popular parlance, perhaps we will one day indeed be entitled to use 'Lacanian' as a synonym for 'unfathomable, convoluted, twisted, inaccessible, gobbledegook'. Students whose written work falls far below common academic standards of readability might then be told that their essays are too 'Lacanian', contain too many 'Lacanisms', and consequently be asked to put them into 'proper' language.

One category of students, however, would never run the risk of their papers being criticized for 'intermittent Lacanianisms', 'Lacanian turns of phrase', 'high Lacan-quality', etc. In this bracket we find, of course, the boys and girls who aspire to become 'adherents/practitioners of Lacanian psychoanalysis, the tradition developed by the French psychiatrist Jacques Lacan (1901–1981)'. Since the process of initiation and ordination into this tradition involves acquiring its language, a totally unique idiom with a specific grammar and vocabulary, the aforementioned criticisms would no doubt become coveted accolades and well-received tokens of intellectual achievement. Lacanian (or Lacanese, as it is sometimes called) is, after all, the language of professional exchange within the Lacanian community, and the extent to which someone is able to utilize it fluently and flexibly counts as an established criterion for assessing the degree of his or her social integration in the field. Nothing worse for enthusiastic travellers in the realm of 'Translacania'— as François Perrier (1985) once called it—who want to befriend the natives, adopt their customs and contemplate settling down with a view to becoming permanent residents, than to hear that they have insufficiently mastered the idiom, their language containing too many barbarisms, too many incompatible residues of previously acquired discourses, or too many syntactic and semantic errors.

As a prerequisite for gaining acceptance within the Lacanophone territories, learning to speak and read Lacanese constitutes an enormous task, and many an apprentice's patience has been tested to such a degree that dropping out of the training process offered itself as the only viable protection against joining the ranks of other apprentices' patients. For being fluent in Lacanese does not so much require learning the meaning of words (or 'signifiers' as they are called there), and how to use them in the right context, as learning that meaning is fleeting and that signifiers should never be used in predetermined semantic configurations. Or, as Lacan himself put it in a famous statement from the early 1970s: 'The meaning of meaning in *my* practice is conceivable (*Begriff*) because it escapes: to be understood as leaking from a barrel, not as scampering off. It is because it escapes (in the barrel sense) that a discourse finds its meaning: in that its effects are impossible to calculate' (2001g [1973]: 553).[1]

Fortunately, the novice can now have recourse to excellent 'dictionaries', 'glossaries' and 'thesauri', in which key Lacanian notions are being explained and translated in not-too-meaningful and not-too-calculated terms. A recent 'travel guide' by Corinne Maier cannot be recommended too highly, if only because it also provides concrete examples of how to render everyday expressions in perfect Lacanese, thus ensuring the subject (a good word, if there ever was one) full-blown recognition (the desire of the Other willing, of course) as a member of the Lacanophone community. A couple of excerpts may illustrate the meaning of the principle (in the barrel sense, of course). The proper way of saying 'I am ill' in Lacanese is: 'My symptom does no longer succeed in quilting my lack of being' (Maier 2003: 52). In Lacania, a woman who wants to speak to her friend because her husband has just left her says: 'For the subject who is now confronted with its lack of being, the hole of the loss in the real mobilizes the signifier' (ibid.: 62). Needless to say, it is much more difficult to translate from Lacanese into English than vice versa, which is exactly what the existing 'dictionaries', 'glossaries' and 'thesauri' prove. When a Lacanian points out that 'his scopic drive is searching to satisfy itself with a new object *a*', the addressee will no doubt wonder whether he is expressing a certain sexual interest here, yet he may simply feel like going to the cinema. And the addressee should definitely avoid asking the Lacanian in question whether he means one or the other, because it is likely to be neither, which will leave him, the addressee, in the potentially embarrassing position of having given meaning to the discourse of the Other, that is to say, having revealed the symbolic structure of his own unconscious. The best Lacanian answer to enigmatic Lacanian expressions such as these—but is there really such a thing as a non-enigmatic Lacanian phrase?—is always 'What do you want?', preferably put in Italian, as '*Che vuoi?*' (Lacan 2002f [1960]: 300), because it will give the subject an opportunity to mobilize the signifier and, on a good day, to commence the long road towards the traversal of the fantasy (Lacan 1994a [1964]: 273).[2]

This difficulty of knowing what a Lacanian phrase means, of understanding its signification, is not only inherent to the semantic pluralism of the Lacanian signifiers but actually defines the very 'essence' of Lacanese, as a potentially untranslatable discourse whose significance can apparently be gauged only through careful deciphering, lengthy exegesis and prolonged interpretive probing into the metonymical ramifications of its textual desire. Indeed, if '*le docteur Lacan*' was right (and Lacanians have the annoying habit of believing that, even on a bad day, he always was) and 'the meaning of meaning' is that it escapes, and this applies par excellence to the meaning of his own discourse, then the implication can only be that Lacanese is untranslatable. This point could be justified by conjuring the authoritative voice of Lacan's 'friend' Claude Lévi-Strauss, who argued 'that "to mean" means the ability of any kind of data to be translated in a different language . . . not . . . a different language like French or German, but different words on a different level' (Lévi-Strauss 1978: 9), yet the French colloquialism mentioned at the start of this chapter suffices to understand the principle. Stubborn untranslatability, after all, is the main reason why an ostensibly meaningless, undecipherable phrase is called '*du Lacan*'. The devoted English translators of Lacan's works have given further evidence of the difficulty to translate the 'Lacanian language' into a 'natural language' by deciding to leave crucial Lacanian concepts such as '*méconnaissance*', '*jouissance*', 'objet *a*', etc., untranslated. In the latter case they have thereby granted Lacan's own explicit request to treat his invention as an algebraic formula: not to be translated for untranslatable.

[margin note: Lacanese is untranslatable]

Doing the impossible

In light of the untranslatability of the Lacanian discourse, it does not come as a surprise, then, that Lacanians often measure Lacanian excellence by someone's ability to unlock the hermetic closure of the idiom or, to put it in Lacanese again, by the subject's 'success at symbolizing the traumatic impact of the real'. Acceptance within the Lacanophone community may thus very well be achieved through learning the skills and the knowledge that facilitate understanding of the intricate twists and turns of the language, yet true mastery will be gained (and granted) only from cracking the real, from doing the impossible, from knowing how to interpret, that is to say, translate, the master's knowledge into a diversified set of meaningful principles.

Some how significant

Would it be sacrilege to say that the attribution of mastery, here, simply follows the same rules as those informing a sovereign's decision to award heroic soldiers the insignia of courage? For translating the untranslatable, making the impossible possible, surely not only constitutes a self-confident act of bravery, but also betrays a defiant and persistent will to break strategic pockets of resistance, in this case the hermetic closure of the text.

It was probably not a coincidence, then, that this act had to be incumbent upon a young stranger called Jacques-Alain Miller, who was quite unaware of the devastating intrigues tearing apart Lacan's entourage of warring psychoanalysts, and quite unconcerned by the risk of being exiled from the Lacanian city, since he was but an innocent, if not naïve participant in the wider intellectual landscape of Paris during the early 1960s. As Derrida (2000 [1997]) has reminded us, from Plato's dialogues it can already be seen that it is often the stranger who formulates 'the intolerable question', who unwittingly challenges the authority of the master, who is not scared to jeopardize the hospitality he has received. The stranger need not *the stranger the one who is unfamiliar* worry that his questions will be regarded as anathema, for he can claim unfamiliarity with the doctrinal tenets that have been passed on from master to disciple, from elder to novice, from father to son. The stranger need not worry that the questioning nature of his statements will stir the community, for he has no knowledge about the truth of the existing agreement regarding the ban on any type of question. The stranger speaks from ignorance and thus forces his interlocutors to break the silence that governs mutual understanding and to explain at length what they think they know. Combining within his presence, as Simmel (1971 [1908]) put it, physical proximity and social remoteness, geographical nearness and mental distance, the person of alien origin occupies a privileged position, which gives him the opportunity to cross boundaries and somehow be exonerated by reason of ignorance, and which can make him privy to secrets that will never be revealed to any 'regular' inhabitant of the community.[3]

Hence, the moment of the arrival of the nineteen-year-old Miller at Lacan's seminar in 1964 was perhaps already pregnant with the historical meaning of the stranger's privilege of being allowed to read, question, interpret, translate and transcribe the unreadable, uninterpretable, untranslatable and untranscribable discourse of the master—to the point of being eventually recognized as a master in his own right by virtue of having undertaken (and continuing to do so) the impossible. Lacan saluted the questioning stranger, who had by then—supreme testimony to the master's unquestionable hospitality?—already been adopted into the psychoanalytic cenacle of the École freudienne de Paris (despite not being a psychoanalyst) and had become a full member of the master's Roman Catholic household (despite being Jewish), with the not-too-meaningful apodictic formula: 'He who interrogates me also knows how to read me' (Lacan 1990d [1974]: 1). apodictic (adj) of a proposition

During the 1950s, Lacan himself approached Freud's discourse as an enigmatic code at a time when it had become so understandable and so understood that even psychoanalysts no longer seemed to bother reading the original texts. His Freud was therefore above all a 'Lacanized' Freud, inasmuch as he treated the Freudian corpus as a mysterious, untranslatable body of knowledge that could only be conquered through a meticulous and painstaking labour of interpretation on its linguistic singularities. Lacan spent the first years of his public seminars at Sainte-Anne Hospital criticizing the existing French renditions of Freud's work, trying to find more accurate translations for the essentially untranslatable idiom pervading the Freudian text. Without claiming that he could understand what Freud had written, he made it clear to his audience that he had at least understood the necessity to reduce the understandability of the Freudian text. Lacan demanded that Freud be demanding, that the Freudian text pose constant challenges to common intelligibility, be unforgiving in its relentless recourse to discursive simulacra, block easy access to its intellectual riches, defy any attempt at discovering its message with the cursory glance of the casual reader.

Much later even, when his references to Freud had all but collapsed under the weight of an increasingly self-referential system of thought, Lacan continued to emphasize the fundamental untranslatability of key Freudian notions. Talking about Freud's terminology in a 1967 interview with François Wahl, shortly after the publication of Écrits, he posited (and the reader will forgive us for not translating here): 'Freud n'a jamais parlé d'instinct mais de quelque chose dont le terme est en somme parfaitement intraduisible, il s'agit du Trieb, qu'on traduit par "pulsion" mais, à la vérité, on le traduit surtout mentalement par instinct avec pour résultat la confusion la plus parfaite' (Lacan 1983 [1967]: 6). Freud's notion of Trieb is considered 'perfectly untranslatable', which of course did not prevent Lacan from translating it himself as 'dérive' (Lacan 2001f [1972]: 485, 1981 [1972]: 13, 1978b [1973]: 70).[4] On numerous occasions,

Lacan scorned the authorized French translation of Freud's famous maxim, '*Wo Es war, soll Ich werden*' (Freud 1933a [1932]: 80), hinting at the radical untranslatability of the phrase, yet nonetheless suggesting various alternative and improved renditions (Lacan 2002c [1957]: 162, 2001a [1958]: 172).

The problem Lacan highlighted, here, once again concerns the meaning of meaning, yet we must guard against the conclusion that the relative untranslatability of a text is a reliable measure of its meaninglessness. If there is a relationship between meaning and translatability, then the two variables are not directly, but inversely proportional: the more translatable, the less meaningful and vice versa. In other words, Lacan's insistence on the difficulty of finding a proper translation for Freud's idiom, to the point of regarding it as totally untranslatable, is a way of doing justice to its semantic saturation, its perennial polysemy, its superabundance of fluctuating significations. What he despised in the existing translations of Freud was therefore less their linguistic inaccuracy than their total disregard for the multilayered dynamics of meaning operating underneath the superficial accessibility of the signifiers, especially in those cases where Freud was not having recourse to technical terms but to everyday German words such as *Ich* and *Es*. For all the technical meaning these notions may have acquired, they are omnipresent in everyday German language with a wide range of significations, and these resonances are threatened if the notions are not approached with caution.

It is interesting to note that when questioning the available translations of the Freudian text Lacan, too, already occupied an eccentric position. Although he had gained a certain reputation with seminars on Freud's major case studies during the early 1950s, his critical attack on the established versions of purportedly Freudian psychoanalysis did not gain momentum until after his provisional exclusion from the International Psychoanalytic Association (IPA) in 1953 (Miller 1976). It would be quite untrue to claim that Lacan was a total stranger in the psychoanalytic arena, yet, as a subject exiled from the bosom of the official establishment, he was able to observe its workings from a viewpoint which few, if any other contemporary psychoanalysts would have had, intermittently returning to the scene of the action as an intellectual tourist cum vagabond whenever he believed it possible to benefit from its proceedings.

Unlike the Freudian text, Lacan's own discourse has not required the intervention of an outsider to make it less intelligible. By virtue of the fact that Lacan's discourse was quite unintelligible in itself, it did not need the eccentric appearance of a courageous figure to emphasize its radical Otherness. Whereas Lacan first needed to demonstrate the untranslatability of Freud's text before he could proceed to do the impossible and translate it anyway, Miller had in some way the advantage of being directly confronted with an idiom that already defied intelligibility. For many a speaker of Lacanese, this unintelligibility is of course a virtue which should not only be preserved at all costs, but also aggrandized, embellished and disseminated far beyond the boundaries of the Lacanian community. For if understanding is but a semblance of communication, and a discourse that might not be made out of semblance is impossible to conceive (Lacan 1970–71), we might as well all try to speak a language that nobody, including ourselves, can understand. Yet if the challenge of learning Lacanese is about familiarizing oneself with the idea that meaning escapes, this does not preclude the fact that meaning exists and that its flow can be delineated. The power to delineate the flow of meaning is precisely what the inhabitants of the Lacanian city appreciate in their rulers.

In addition, the forbidding character of the Lacanian idiom has never deterred students from trying to acquire its terms and practices. On the contrary, the exceedingly convoluted syntax, the highly peculiar vocabulary and the unusually complex pragmatics of the language exercise an extremely seductive power over the minds of young adults. Involuntarily drawn to the incomprehensible yet euphonic sounds of the Lacanian signifiers, surreptitiously enticed by the unfathomable yet peculiar composition of the Lacanian text, many an unsuspecting subject finds himself suddenly fascinated, devoted and enthralled. The house of Lacan is everything but hospitable to strangers, its threshold is so high and difficult to cross that only the most determined people will eventually gain access to its premises, it does not particularly welcome visitors and is especially unfriendly towards miscellaneous day trippers and minibreakers— and yet all of these features have made it not into a spectral dwelling, but into a highly coveted residence for the pursuit of profound analytic reflection. And for those whose calling has been answered by the masters of the house, when the entry request has been recognized as harbouring a truthful desire, their new-found territory is likely to become their home, the more so as they are feeling finally rewarded for their protracted efforts.

A ludic dream world of language

At this point, we need to take away any doubts on the part of the reader concerning the seriousness of this chapter and the importance of learning Lacanese. Although much of what we have said in the previous sections may deservedly be regarded as ironic, it is not our intention to follow Erasmus in his *Praise of Folly* (Erasmus 1993 [1509]). The impenetrability of the Lacanian wall of language and its extraordinary resistance to destructive external forces have made it into one of the most seriously solid (and solidly serious) intellectual buildings of the twentieth century. This is not to say that its conceptual brickwork has never faltered, yet, as we shall see in the next chapter, with few exceptions all the serious cracks in the construction have been caused by internal struggles, Lacanians arguing over the interpretation of the master's words, the ownership of his intellectual legacy and the principles governing the maintenance of his school. Lacan's discourse is serious precisely because it defies common intelligibility. And it became progressively more serious during the 1960s and 1970s, when he gradually moved away from Freud's terminology in favour of the development of a much more idiosyncratic language, sustaining the acquired taste for syntactic oddities yet adding a supplementary degree of linguistic playfulness. It is as if Lacan eventually managed to overcome the force of gravity which had kept him firmly on Freudian ground during the first ten years of his seminar, and, once airborne, celebrated his freedom of movement with the creation of a new idiom, bristling with infinite semantic pluralism and reflecting virtuoso stunt work on the connotations of his own conceptual inventions.

Both within and outside the psychoanalytic community, Lacan had of course always surrounded himself with an aura of ludicity, amusing friends and colleagues with long improvised speeches on serious and not-so-serious topics, brightening up austere professional gatherings with his bohemian dress and confusing his audience by speaking not only in tongues but in different names and with different voices. Madeleine Chapsal recalled that the first time she met Jacques Lacan he was wearing a large and hairy, red wig and invited her to dance (Chapsal 1984: 31). It is no coincidence that the larger-than-life 'Docteur' became the hilarious protagonist, under the name of *le grand vizir*, of François Weyergans's ode to the jester (Weyergans 1974).[5] How many psychoanalysts will ever be remembered with a collection of trivia such as that compiled by Allouch

(1998), crammed with real-life jokes and nonsense exchanged by gossipy analysands killing time in the waiting-room? In 1972, Lacan arrived in a packed lecture theatre at the Catholic University of Louvain sporting a huge fur coat, the trademark 'twisted cigar' directly imported from Cuba and a groovy, psychedelic shirt, whose attached 'cravate' proved to be an obstacle to the microphone. The drollery of Lacan's presence contrasted sharply with the sobriety of his message—on the (totally un-Catholic) idea of death being driven by faith—yet the latter's painful impact did not seem to be made any more bearable by the buffoonery of the performance (Lacan 1981 [1972]).

At the level of Lacan's language, however, a remarkable change took place towards the end of the 1960s, more specifically during the time of his seminars on *The Logic of Fantasy* (1966–67) and *The Psychoanalytic Act* (1967–68). For the first time Lacan continually peppered his language with wordplay, launching a barrage of homonymic and polysemic puns, creating neologism after neologism, and cleverly justifying the semantic instability of existing terms with reference to their etymology. This process reached its high point between 1972 and 1975, when Lacan not only committed himself to exploring the knotty problems in the work of James Joyce, but also increasingly started to speak like Joyce, that is to say, his spoken discourse came to resemble Joyce's style of writing in *Ulysses* (Joyce 1961 [1922]) and, more radically, in *Finnegans Wake* (Joyce 1992 [1939]).

At the occasion of the publication of an exhaustive glossary of Lacan's wordplay (Bénabou *et al.* 2002), Jacques-Alain Miller argued that, at least according to classic definitions of what constitutes a neologism, Lacan should not be regarded as a 'neologist' (Miller 2002b). If a neologism is a newly invented word, manufactured in order to capture the 'exactly that' of a new experience or event, the 'thing' which no other existing word can render with sufficient accuracy, then Lacan's 'Lacanisms' are not neologistic because, according to Miller, Lacan was never really driven to find the right word, to invent a term which would convey exactly the right meaning, given the nature of the event. The art of naming, insofar as it operates with the expectation of reducing ambiguity and (re-)creating unequivocal labels, was not Lacan's concern. On the contrary—and this chimes with our observations on the relationship between meaning and translatability above—Lacan seemed much more attuned to doing exactly the opposite: questioning the correctness of existing words, extending their semantic realm, opening up sclerotized centres of meaning and making it escape again (in the barrel sense . . .). Miller subsequently posited that what is often designated as a neologism in Lacan's discourse is actually a linguistic joke, a clever pun of the sort analysed by Freud in his third volume on the formations of the unconscious (Freud 1905c). There is definitely something to be said in favour of Miller's argument here. Lacan's 'new language', which came to full fruition between the late 1960s and the mid-1970s, was not a sophisticated designer idiom for the improved description and communication of a new set of meanings, but a joyful and often dazzling series of exercises on sound similarity and semantic richness, mostly within one and the same natural language (French), but from time to time also across languages (French, German, Latin, etc.). In Lacan's hands the natural language acquired a new form of elasticity; it became a stretchable and squeezable object whose matter allows for endless twisting and turning, much like the topological figures and knots with which he was obsessed during the last years of his life. The comparison between Lacan's 'mature discourse' and his *savoir-faire* with topology is everything but gratuitous here, for it was precisely within the context of his exploration of Joyce's text, and his concurrent espousal of the writer's 'decomposition' of language, that he found the best opportunities for testing the limits of the Borromean knot (Lacan 1976–77 [1975–76]). Yet Lacan's ostensibly 'senseless' manipulation of bizarre topological shapes, such as the Moebius strip, the torus and the cross-cap, should also be situated on the same level as his apparently nonsensical cornucopia of puns: the flexible 'structure' of topology equals the structuring 'flexibility' of language and, by extension, the squeezable and stretchable fabric of knowledge.

Just like 'Lacan the topologist', 'Lacan the punster' could pride himself on an amazing ability to practise every possible trick of the genre. Intralinguistic homophones occupy all of the titles he allocated to his seminars from 1972 to 1976. The best known of these is no doubt *Seminar XX*, which was actually retitled *On Feminine Sexuality, the Limits of Love and Knowledge* for the official English edition, with the homophonic French title of *Encore* ('en corps') added in brackets (Lacan 1998b [1972–73]). The first sessions of his *Seminar XXIV* revolved entirely around the exploration of the cross-linguistic homophone *une-bévue* ('one-blunder'), which he suggested as a possible 'translation' for Freud's term *Unbewußte* (unconscious), yet the entire title of the seminar was one sustained pun: *L'Insu-que-sait de l'une-bévue s'aile à mourre, L'Insucces de l'Unbewußte c'est l'amour, L'un succède l'Unbewußte et scelle l'amour*, etc. (Lacan 1977–79 [1976–77]).[6] In *Television* (Lacan 1990d [1974]), Lacan illustrated the identification of the Other with the One through the anagrammatic pun of *ennui* (annoyance, boredom) and *unien* ('oneyance'), before launching into an unstoppable stream of portmanteau words—*tu-émoigne, humanitairerie, di-eu-re de l'amour, l'en-gage*—and finishing off his bravura performance with a stunning paranomasia: '*De ce qui perdure de perte pure à ce qui ne parie que du père au pire*'. '*Eh bien, c'est vraiment du Lacan, ça!*' Dr William Archibald Spooner was not a stranger to him either, for Lacan freely admitted that he had arrived at the word '*lituraterre*' 'through this wordplay with which one happens to make a witticism: the spoonerism appearing on the lips, the reversal at the ear' (Lacan 2001e [1971]: 11), although the 'tip of the slung' subsequently received the most elaborate theoretical justification imaginable. In Lacan's book, 'literature' could never be as semantically revealing, conceptually challenging and psychoanalytically relevant as its playful macaronic counterpart, which again indicates how the ostensible absurdity of the linguistic 'accident', and the gist of the Lacanian discourse in general, ended up being transformed into a deadly serious matter for theoretical research and development.

'Pata-psychoanalysis?

Few people have unravelled the intricate fabric of Lacan's constant wordplay, despite the fact that it probably does not have its equal in the whole history of psychoanalysis. Of course, if already within literary studies puns are often looked down upon as the lowest form of wit—following John Dennis's claim that 'he that would pun would pick a pocket' (Culler 1988: 4)—there is probably no reason to assume that Lacan's puns would fare any better. On the contrary, 'serious' psychoanalysts and scholars may be 'seriously' irritated by the 'non-seriousness' of Lacan's linguistic tricks. And the realization that we are dealing with a discourse that aspires to be, if not scientific, at least professional and instructive makes its 'punning quality' all the more difficult to digest, not to mention the fact that the discourse in question, and the knowledge it carries along, is supposed to help psychoanalysts conduct their clinical practice. How dare he enjoy himself with stupid jokes when the misery of human beings is at stake!

Yet 'Lacan the punster' has not gone totally unnoticed and a handful of writers have even tried to clarify the reasons for his insistence. Cathérine Clément has suggested that Lacan started punning in order to make the theoretical heaviness of his discursive production more bearable for his audience, like a lecturer who has recourse to the technique of intermittent joking as a means of maintaining his students' attention when the knowledge he needs to transmit is dead boring. Yet Clément claims that Lacan eventually became a victim of his own success, and progressively started employing punning as a *captatio benevolentiae*, because he knew that this was what people in the room wanted to hear and what kept them coming to the lecture theatre (1983 [1981]: 32–34). A much more incisive reading has been advanced by François Roustang, who posited in *The Lacanian Delusion* (Roustang 1990 [1986]) that through constant punning Lacan merely endeavoured to fool his audience into believing that he had something profound to say, whereas behind the wordplay there was but the gaping failure of his attempt to found a new, psychoanalytic science of the real. Whereas Clément's Lacan appears as a slightly pitiful figure, who cannot resist the temptations of public recognition, fails to withstand the narcissistic gratifications of being applauded, and succumbs to his fan base's insatiable demand for more (of the same), Roustang's Lacan is a much more deliberately disingenuous and deceiving character, who is actively seducing his audience with false sophistication and empty rhetoric.

Regardless of these assertions, whose value should not be overlooked yet which are probably situated as much within the context of their authors' personal experiences as within Lacan's intellectual ambitions, the development of Lacanese from a difficult professional jargon to a full-blown idiom infested with puns could be looked at in yet another way. From the moment Lacan arrived on the psychoanalytic scene, he modelled his own discourse on the very rhetoric of the unconscious, which he believed to have discerned in Freud's foundational accounts of dreams, slips of the tongue and jokes (Freud 1900a, 1901b, 1905c).

Here is what Lacan had to say about dreams in the 1953 text that signalled the start of the Lacanian movement: 'What is important is the version of the text, and that, Freud tells us, is given in the telling of the dream—that is, in its rhetoric. Ellipsis and pleonasm, hyperbaton or syllepsis, regression, repetition, apposition—these are the syntactical displacements; metaphor, catachresis, antonomasia, allegory, metonymy, and synecdoche—these are the semantic condensations; Freud teaches us to read in them the intentions—whether ostentatious or demonstrative, dissimulating or persuasive, retaliatory or seductive—with which the subject modulates his oneiric discourse' (Lacan 2002a [1953]: 57). A basic knowledge of rhetoric probably suffices to ascertain that each of the figures distinguished by Lacan in this passage, and attributed to the language of dreams, also constituted a regular feature of his own discourse during the 1950s. One could even venture the claim that compared to the stylistic intricacies of Lacan's own discourse, the rhetorical power of dreams is still rather limited, for the former also included extensive use of irony and sarcasm, not to mention the notorious figure of the prosopopoeia in 'I, the truth, am speaking' (Lacan 2002b [1955]). Apart from the syntactic difficulty, it is precisely this recurrent and often surreptitious presence of sophisticated rhetoric which makes Lacan's discourse extremely challenging for the reader. One is often left wondering with whose voice, in whose name and with what intention he is speaking and writing. Indeed, one is often left wondering which meaning lies buried beneath the excess of rhetorical force. Or, rehearsing Lacan commenting on Freud, one might say that in confrontation with Lacan's text the reader is challenged to read in it 'the intentions—whether ostentatious or demonstrative, dissimulating or persuasive, retaliatory or seductive'—with which the author modulates his discourse. Much like the psychoanalyst dealing with the obscure text of an analysand's dream, the reader is faced here with a task of translation and deciphering, although this might not necessarily imply that a good interpreter of Lacan's texts is therefore also a good psychoanalyst, and vice versa.

The strict compatibility between Lacan's account of the rhetoric of the unconscious and his own rhetorical strategies in his texts from the 1950s does not, as such, explain the emergence and proliferation of punning in his later discourse. If 'the pun in Lacan is intimately related to his notion of metonymy and metaphor . . . [and] partakes of the rhetorical structures of the Lacanian unconscious', as Françoise Meltzer has claimed (Meltzer 1988: 156–157)—and indeed jokes are one of the key formations of the unconscious—then this association does not do full justice to the extraordinary playfulness of Lacan's punning, as opposed to the stern rigour of his rhetorical pursuits. As Jacques-Alain Miller has pointed out in his seminar of 1995–96 on *La Fuite du sens* (encore, the flight of meaning), Lacan's conception of language and the unconscious changed dramatically during the late 1960s (Miller 1996). Up until then, Lacan had observed the unconscious through the Saussurean/Jakobsonian lens of structuralist linguistics, conceiving it as a mental machine for processing repressed symbolic knowledge. This also entailed the radical separation of language and enjoyment (jouissance), on a theoretical as well as a clinical level, with the analyst being asked to interpret in such a way that the analysand's shifting (metonymical) desire takes control over the repetitive factor of enjoyment. As we mentioned at the end of the last chapter, Lacan at one point gave up on his unconditional belief in the structuring power of a pure language system. Although he remained convinced that the unconscious is structured like a language, he no longer believed that the language system conditioning the unconscious is made up of an exclusively symbolic series of relationships between signifiers, that is to say, of an exclusively epistemic network of materials. What testifies to this shift of perspective, according to Miller, is Lacan's promulgation of the term *lalangue*, in which the noun *langue* (language system) is joined together with its pronoun *la* (Lacan 1971–72: session of 4 November 1971).[7] Lacan's *lalangue* latches onto 'lallation', which refers to the babbling of a baby, the first indications of an infant's being affected by language. *Lalangue* is a language, for sure, yet it is not one of 'the' known languages, inasmuch as it is replete with strange amalgamations of sounds and seemingly punctuated by bizarre, barely distinguishable changes in intonation. As Jean-Claude Milner has put it (in a sample of excellent Lacanian phraseology): 'Lalangue is a crowd of swarming ramifications to which the subject attaches its desire. . . . The point of subjectivation is always one amongst others and the chain where it is distinguished is hardly situated for a thousand analogous chains to emerge' (Milner 1978: 104). What Lacan designated as *lalangue* refers to the enjoyment of speaking, the satisfaction derived from engaging in verbalization, the urge to say something for the sake of saying rather than for the communication of a message. Or, in Miller's words: 'The essential phenomenon of what Lacan has called "lalangue" is not meaning . . . but jouissance' (Miller 1996: 12).

By promoting, against Saussurean linguistics, the impact of a language system tainted with enjoyment, Lacan inevitably had to change his view on the structure of the unconscious. Instead of a rational, memory-like network of purely symbolic signifying connections, the unconscious thus came to be regarded as an enjoyment-driven, pulsating voice whose messages are more conditioned by the satisfactory release of their animating force than by the syntactic and semantic features of their manifest/latent contents. In light of this contamination of unconscious reason, we can now begin to delineate, over and above the personal reasons mentioned by Clément and Roustang, another motive for Lacan's consistent recourse to punning. Overall, Lacan's strategy during the late 1960s and early 1970s did not differ significantly from that which he had adopted earlier: detailing the linguistic complexity of the unconscious structure through the intentional mimicking of its characteristics; rendering the nature of the discourse of the unconscious through a direct representation of its discursive oddities; producing knowledge of a type that is strictly in accordance with the truth of the unconscious. Yet with the modification of the linguistic system presiding over the unconscious—from an exclusively symbolic rhetorical machinery to a 'checked', 'free-floating', 'babbling' language force—Lacan's own discourse transformed into an exceedingly playful, more seemingly nonsensical and less immediately meaningful concatenation of polyphonic sounds. Here, his original 'return to the reason of Freud' and that of the unconscious (Lacan 2002b [1955]) gave way to a second return, a 'return to the return', involving the 'enjoyification' of language, the 'checking' of the unconscious, the 'punning' of reason, an idiosyncratic mixture of science and poetry along the lines of Jarry's 'pataphysics or, more performatively, the installations in Los Angeles' Museum of Jurassic Technology. It would therefore be a mistake to dismiss the proliferation of wordplay in high Lacanese with Derrida's scathing critique on the pun as clear evidence of Lacan's 'complacent and slightly narcissistic relation to language, the exercise of virtuosity to no profit, without economy of sense or knowledge, without any necessity but that of enjoying one's mastery over one's language and the others' (Derrida 1986: 18). Instead of a self-indulgent act of narcissistic complacency, the punning betrays a radically reflexive attack on the presupposed virtues and scientific assumptions of structuralist reason, which is actually already more Derridean in its assumptions than is generally accepted (Nobus 2001). It is no coincidence, then, that at the pinnacle of his punning period Lacan expressed a vote of no confidence in the value of structuralist linguistics for psychoanalysis, proclaiming, as we noted at the end of the last chapter, that what he needed was not linguistics but *linguisterie* (Lacan 1998b [1972–73]: 15).

Poetic wisdom in practice

The 'punning of reason' which characterizes Lacan's mature discourse has many other sides to it. First of all, whereas the rhetorical complexities of Lacan's project during the 1950s were primarily noticeable at the level of the text, that is, in the product of writing rather than the production of speech, the wordplay of the late 1960s and early 1970s was predominantly situated in the area of spoken language; or, to be more precise, it explored the boundaries between speaking, hearing and writing. On more than a few occasions Lacan had to draw his audience's attention to the homophonic and polysemic aspects of his speech by literally spelling out or physically writing down the sound images in letters on the blackboard. The pun presiding over his *Seminar XXI* (Lacan 1973–74) would probably never have been clear to his audience if he had not written it down as *les non-dupes errent.*[8]

The moving threshold between speaking and writing preoccupied Lacan more than ever before during these 'punning years', and it is not always clear whether it bothered, fascinated or annoyed him. Witness the following passage from his contribution to the Fifth International Joyce Symposium which, for reasons that will become clear immediately, we shall once again not translate:

> *LOM: en français ça dit bien ce que ça veut dire. Il suffit de l'écrire phonétiquement: ça le faunetique (faun . . .), à sa mesure: l'eaubscène. Écrivez ça eaub . . . pour rappeler que le beau n'est pas autre chose. Hissecroibeau à écrire comme l'hessecabeau sans lequel hihanappat qui soit ding! d'nom dhom. LOM se lomelise à qui mieux mieux. Mouille, lui dit-on, faut le faire: car sans mouiller pas d'hessecabeau. LOM, LOM de base, LOM cahun corps et nan-na Kun. Faut le dire comme ça: il ahun . . . et non: il estun . . . (cor/niché).*

(Lacan 2001h [1975]: 565)

If the rhetoric of the unconscious poses particular challenges to the reader's interpretive abilities, then the punning of reason seems to defy any attempt at translation here. Before we could begin to translate '*Hissecroibeau à écrire comme l'hessecabeau sans lequel hihanappat qui soit ding! d'nom dhom*' into English, we would need to start translating the sentence into French first, yet even if we were to arrive at '*Il se croit beau à écrire comme l'escabeau sans lequel il n'y en a pas qui soit digne de nom d'homme'*, this translation may generate a certain meaning (but does it really?) without thereby offering much space for a truthful retranslation into English. The issue of translating puns has been addressed by specialist linguists (Delabastita 1997), yet they might not be ready for the cunning pun stunts of Lacanese. In other words, with his punning of reason Lacan takes the untranslatability of his idiom and, lest we forget, of the discourse of the unconscious, to its uttermost limit. And if we are to accept *lalangue* as the structure ruling the unconscious, then the question of its untranslatability must inevitably affect the psychoanalyst's technique of interpretation during the course of a psychoanalytic treatment. Freud may have been able to teach us how to 'see through' the rhetorical cobweb of the unconscious, but would anyone, including Lacan, be able to teach us how to operate with its mixture of language and jouissance, unless the analysand's 'accidental' production of an 'unintended' pun, which does constitute an important difference with Lacan's 'intentional' wordplay, makes the task somewhat easier? Apart from the problem of translation, the homophonic nature of spoken high Lacanese puts the listener at the constant risk of producing 'mondegreens', that is to say, accidental mishearings, unless the speaker were indeed to reduce the homophony of his speech by spelling out and/or writing down the signifier.[9] By definition, mondegreens can occur only at the level of speech (hearing, sound image, signifier) and technically involve the attribution of a different signified to the one intended, via the accidental misinterpretation of a sound image. Mondegreens do not occur at the level of writing—when reading a text—but take hold of every possible similarity in sounds to let themselves be known.[10]

However, if Lacan's insistence on the 'fleeting nature of meaning' and his radical 'punning of reason' serve to represent the mixture of knowledge and jouissance that makes up the discourse of the unconscious, we may draw some consequences from this for the analyst's direction of the treatment. If, as we have demonstrated in Chapter 1, the analyst focuses on the ostensibly marginal, insignificant trifles of the analysand's discourse with a view to pinpointing the formations of the unconscious as the inherent limits of conscious knowledge, then there is no reason why the analyst should not intentionally employ 'mondegreens' as a technique of interpretation. For by actively 'misdirecting' interpretation towards the meaning the analysand does not intend to convey, meaning may become less fixated to its signifiers and may start to 'leak from the barrel of language'. In his *Seminar XVII*, Lacan suggested the enigma and the citation (the analyst 'quoting' the analysand) as techniques of interpretation with which the analyst conveys neither meaning nor non-meaning, but engages in an apophantic 'half-saying', in conformity with the aim of the analytic discourse (Lacan 1991 [1969–70]: 40)[11]. But exactly the same could be said about an 'intentional mishearing': in exchanging the intended meaning of a message for another, unintended one, neither meaning nor non-meaning is being added to the discourse, but a known existing meaning is destabilized in the direction of non-knowledge, that is to say, in the direction of the certainty that meaning is fundamentally unstable owing to the inadequacy of the knowledge used to convey it. The 'mondegreen' might indeed be the most radical form of what Lacan, following Reik (1949: 503–514), intermittently referred to as the analyst's courage *not* to understand (Lacan 1988c [1954–55]: 87, 1993 [1955–56]: 6–7).[12]

In any case, it is clear that *du Lacan* (as an appellative phrase) encompasses too narrow a set of meanings when merely used with reference to an incomprehensible phrase or an exceedingly awkward formulation. Much like the unconscious, *du Lacan* is difficult, for sure, and the revelation of its secret does not respond well to magical incantations. Much like the unconscious, *du Lacan* is not hospitable, 'as it is an entrance one can only reach just as it closes (the place will never be overrun by tourists), and the only way for it to open up a bit is by calling from the inside' (Lacan 1995a [1964]: 267). Yet beyond these qualities, *du Lacan* epitomizes a body of knowledge that is strictly in accordance with the nature of the knowledge it intends to describe. In order to render the 'headless' state of unconscious knowledge, and the interpenetration of language and jouissance that constitutes its fabric, Lacan endeavoured to construct his own knowledge in accordance with the object knowledge he was investigating. Rather than producing a discourse on truth, or trying to be truthful about the truth, he let the truth speak with its own voice.

The upshot is that Lacan's own discourse appears as 'headless', 'stupid' and 'nonsensical', that his interventions inevitably upset established hegemonies of knowledge, both within and outside the psychoanalytic community, and that his own knowledge is itself in a constant state of crisis. In the next chapter we will concentrate on the way in which the (Lacanian) psychoanalytic community has struggled (and continues to battle) in order to protect the autonomous knowledge of the unconscious and its intrinsic defiance of legitimacy against the transformation of its discourse into a formalistic, regulated set of principles that is acceptable within the market economy of goods.

Chapter 4

Knowledge in failure: crises of legitimacy and the emergence of institutionalized doctrine

All the limitative Theorems of metamathematics and the theory of computation suggest that once the ability to represent your own structure has reached a certain critical point, that is the kiss of death: it guarantees that you can never represent yourself totally. Gödel's Incompleteness Theorem, Church's Undecidability Theorem, Turing's Halting Theorem, Tarski's Truth Theorem—all have the flavor of some ancient fairy tale which warns you that 'To seek self-knowledge is to embark on a journey which . . . will always be incomplete, cannot be charted on any map, will never halt, cannot be described.'

Douglas R. Hofstadter, *Gödel, Escher, Bach*, 697

Disputed legacies

Of all the different strands of psychoanalysis that developed after Freud, the Lacanian tradition has been most animated, permeated and devastated by debates concerning theoretical credibility, clinical legitimacy and epistemological veracity. This is not to say that prior to Lacan's arrival on the psychoanalytic scene and prior to his creation of his own school, the psychoanalytic movement was entirely homogeneous, perfectly harmonious and completely free of professional conflict. From the moment Freud planned to give psychoanalytic knowledge a formal, institutionalized base in the International Psychoanalytic Association (IPA), dissent followed upon secession, and newly found allegiances replaced former alliances turned sour. Yet more than was ever the case within the Freudian movement, the Lacanian tradition within psychoanalysis has been incessantly ravaged by vehement discussions over the correct application of its knowledge base. Epistemological issues presided over the birth of Lacanian psychoanalysis as such, yet they continued to affect its institutions until the very end of Lacan's life, and they may very well be responsible one day for the downfall of its entire edifice. Also, much more than within any other psychoanalytic community, the debates pervading Lacanian psychoanalysis have been sustained by three different adversaries, none of them very willing to compromise: anti-Lacanian psychoanalysts wanting to protect psychoanalytic orthodoxy against the infiltration of purportedly metaphysical forces, external (non-psychoanalytic) agencies perceiving the Lacanian 'ideology' as the pinnacle of an inherently abusive scheme, and Lacanian psychoanalysts themselves, pitting one interpretation of the master's narrative against the other, in an attempt to preserve the purity of his doctrine, be it as a non-doctrinal type of enquiry. Amongst these detractors, the last have not so much acted as latter-day Jung- or Adler-style intellectual dissidents, because they have generally disputed the legitimacy of the Lacanian party line for its unfaithfulness to Lacan's own discourse, not disagreeing with one or the other of Lacan's radical principles but exposing the low Lacan content of a certain type of Lacanianism.

Within this quagmire of stakes, interests, parties and stakeholders, the Anglo-American reader is probably most familiar with the acrimonious argument that prompted Lacan to present himself, during the early 1950s, as the figurehead of a maverick group of French psychoanalysts. This conflict, which has been documented in many a primer of Lacanian psychoanalysis, ignited the first schism within the French psychoanalytic world, signalled Lacan's historical departure from the psychoanalytic mainstream, and features most conspicuously in Lacan's own writings. Subsequently, Lacan proposed his famous 'return to Freud' as an alternative to the reigning doctrinal tendencies of ego psychology and, to a lesser extent, object relations within the IPA. Yet while this antagonism generated a new set of loyalties, it did not suffice to maintain the unity of the Lacanian group. As Lacan gained more recognition and admiration as a maître-à-penser, his authority as the self-proclaimed recipient of Freud's legacy came more and more under attack from people who had initially supported him. As ego psychology disappeared from the Lacanian cenacle as the psychoanalytic bugbear par excellence and Lacan progressively moved from fairly intimate seminars on Freud's texts to large-scale public events promoting his own theory, he himself started to occupy a place of contention for his followers. This eventually led to a series of institutional implosions, crowned by

Lacan's unilateral 'dissolution', in January 1980 (Lacan 1990e
[1980]), of the École freudienne de Paris, the school he had single-
handedly created some fifteen years earlier (Lacan 1990a [1964]).[1]
    Since Lacan's demise, in September 1981, the newly established
'Freudian Field' (Le Champ freudien) has been in constant turmoil,
on the one hand losing valuable strategic parts of its intellectual
territory in France, whilst on the other continually expanding its
sphere of influence beyond the geographical and linguistic boundaries of its homeland. At an institutional level this has coincided
with the eruption, in increasingly rapid succession, of new formal
and informal groups devoted to Lacanian psychoanalysis, some of
which are strictly controlled in their function as satellite units by a
central governing body, whereas others are more 'devolved' and
therefore designed to run a more independent and self-governing
course.[2] At an intellectual level, the tumultuous existence of the
'Freudian Field' has coincided with the emergence of new rivalries
over the moral ownership of Lacan's intellectual heritage and ardent
discussions over the preservation of Lacanian theory as an anti-
dogmatic corpus. These conflicts have no doubt been exacerbated by
the fact that both the institutional and the intellectual centres of the
'Freudian Field' are, if not directed, at least closely monitored by
Jacques-Alain Miller, Lacan's son-in-law, who has come to represent
for many an adversary the conflation of doctrinal concerns and
genealogical authority at the highest level of Lacanian officialdom.
    Teasing out the intricacies of this complex configuration consti-
tutes a massive task, which far exceeds the scope of our book.[3] For
the purposes of our argument in this chapter, we shall restrict ourselves to a discussion of how epistemological issues have affected
Lacan's own trajectory in its theoretical, technico-clinical and institutional ramifications, how these issues have divided the Lacanian
community until the present day, and how the process of institutionalization has modified the transmission and exchange of psychoanalytic knowledge. In the first section of the chapter, we shall outline
how Lacan himself endeavoured to 're-own' Freud's knowledge, and
how his intellectual parentage influenced the conception and development of the 'French Freud' (Mehlman 1972; Dufresne 1997).
Following on from this, we shall concentrate on Lacan's most controversial contributions to psychoanalytic theory and practice, and
how some of these ideas have managed to antagonize generations of
psychoanalysts, including those trained by Lacan himself. In the
final section, we shall then attempt to present the gist of ongoing

discussions over the intellectual ownership of Lacan's assets, including the vexed question of the transcription of his seminars, the publication and translation of his writings, the correct implementation of his training principles, and the general dissemination of his ideas. Here, we shall also try to open a critical perspective on what a Lacanian interpretation of epistemological 'ownership' might entail, and how this conditions the outlook of a psychoanalytic epistemology.

Reappropriating Freud

In a famous quotation from his 1953 'Rome discourse', a text which may be regarded simultaneously as the intellectual bedrock, the organizational mission statement and the political manifesto of Lacanianism, Lacan justified his polemical intervention in the field of psychoanalysis as follows:

> In any case, I consider it to be an urgent task to isolate, in concepts that are being deadened by routine use, the meaning they recover when we reexamine their history and reflect on their subjective foundations. That, no doubt, is the teacher's function—the function on which all the others depend—and the one in which the value of experience figures best. If this function is neglected, the meaning of an action whose effects derive solely from meaning is obliterated, and the rules of analytic technique, being reduced to mere recipes, rob analytic experience of any status as knowledge [*connaissance*] and even of any criterion of reality.
>
> (Lacan 2002a [1953]: 34)

Like so many of Lacan's statements, this proposition probably requires some clarification, if only because of the characteristically elliptic and allusive style in which it is couched.[4] The 'concepts' Lacan is referring to here are of course those employed by Freud when he explained the mechanisms of the human mind and the clinical process of psychoanalysis. According to Lacan, these concepts and, by extension, Freud's entire theory had completely lost their cutting edge—the French refers to *notions qui s'amortissent*, which literally means a 'softening' or 'blunting' of notions—through the uprooted fashion in which they were being applied and transmitted within the psychoanalytic training institutions. Lacan went even so far as to accuse his colleagues of no longer being interested in Freud's works and preferring, for instance, Marie Bonaparte's watered-down 'manual' on the theory of the drives (1934) over the founder's original contributions to sexuality—just as undergraduate students would in these days acquire knowledge of their discipline via a series of textbooks rather than via the study of primary source materials (Lacan 2002a [1953]: 40). The inevitable upshot, Lacan argued, was a symptomatic de-Freudianization of psychoanalysis, somehow in need of analysis itself (Lacan 2002a [1953]: 36, 1988b [1953–54]: 24). Lacan's proposed solution to the conceptual deadlock thus entailed the implementation of the very principles Freud had adduced as the defining characteristics of the psychoanalytic treatment: an in-depth investigation of the historical origins of the materials at hand and a profound reflection upon their subjective significance.

The main difference between this 'analysis of analysis' and the traditional, clinical application of analytic principles lay in the position Lacan reserved for its initiator; in this case, Lacan himself. Only by adopting the position of a teacher, and therefore seemingly not as an analyst, would the analyst be capable of overcoming the stalemate of the analytic discourse. Yet when Lacan subsequently commenced his public seminars at Sainte-Anne Hospital in Paris, he remained quite careful not to identify with the omniscient professors and intellectual guides whose unassailable knowledge had contributed to the disappearance of the spirit of discovery within contemporary psychoanalysis. As a teacher, Lacan preferred the auspices of the Zen master, who 'conducts his search for meaning' without teaching 'ex cathedra a ready-made science', and who 'supplies an answer when the students are on the verge of finding it', thus exemplifying the 'refusal of any system' and favouring the revelation of 'a thought in motion' (Lacan 1988b [1953–54]: 1).[5] And indeed, Lacan's 'early seminars' were perfect illustrations of interactive, learner-oriented instruction, geared towards uncovering the elusive meaning of Freud's texts through a critical dialogue with the audience. In the presence of a small group of enthusiastic seekers, Lacan would often formulate more questions than answers, constantly prompting his audience to read, work and present their way through the conceptual maze of Freud's papers, and testing the results of this procedure against the hallowed interpretations of the same ideas. True to his own motto, Lacan also regularly referred to the original, German version of Freud's texts, sometimes inviting selected participants of the seminar to flesh out the nitty-gritty details of one entire

document, as in the case of the renowned Hegel scholar and transla-
tor Jean Hyppolite, who was charged with the task of preparing an
intervention on Freud's notoriously difficult paper 'Negation' (Freud
1925h; Lacan 1966a [1954], 1966b [1954], 1988b [1953–54]: 289–297).
With hindsight, Lacan's strategy was unique, exciting and clever.
It was unique because the format of weekly, small-scale interactive
lectures on a sharply delineated set of texts was virtually unheard of
within the existing psychoanalytic training institutions. When reading the transcriptions of these seminars, one is involuntarily reminded
of the atmosphere surrounding a group of conscientious students
discussing a 'great book' in a far-away corner of an academic library.
There is no doubt that Lacan stood out as the focal point of intellectual convergence, yet it is equally indubitable that the participants
felt capable and confident enough to push forward, to extrapolate
and sometimes to challenge his ideas. One could compare Lacan's
early seminars to a jazz workshop in which the leader brings together
a group of trusted sidemen, known for their technical skills, their
ability to empathize and their improvisational talents, in order to
extract a new, creative piece of music from a long-established mel-
ody. Lacan may have based this format on what he himself had
experienced during the 1930s at Kojève's seminar on Hegel (Kojève
1969 [1933–39]), and this would also explain why he decided to give
absolute priority to the *reading* of Freud. The seminars at Sainte-
Anne Hospital bore more resemblance to a scientific laboratory in
which young researchers are on the track of a new formula than to
an academic lecture theatre in which students quietly assimilate
grand narratives of solid knowledge. In trying to rescue Freud's
spirit of discovery from the clutches of his contemporaries, Lacan
endeavoured to create surroundings in which people could also
breathe this same spirit.
    For precisely these reasons, Lacan's early seminars were also in-
credibly exciting, although one should not discount the importance
of the transference towards Lacan, especially amongst the younger
generation. In a barely concealed moment of nostalgia, Wladimir
Granoff, one of the most active figures during the first ten years of
Lacan's teaching, captured the events:

> One day the historian will be faced with the task of explaining
> why Lacan's teaching, notably during this introductory phase,
> was received with so much enthusiasm. No doubt it is partly to
> do with fortunate circumstances concerning the quality of the

first epigones ... I nonetheless believe that the essence was elsewhere. On the side of the joy of revenge. It is a common observation that school results and the taste for study improve amongst students who were previously described as bad when a person who is heavily invested with transference condemns the masters, the manuals and the taught materials. From the start of the game, Lacan told us that we were being taught stupid things and that those who taught us were fools. I still believe he had a point.

(Granoff 1986: 38)

For the record, it should be added that Granoff's enthusiastic commitment may also have been sustained by the way in which Lacan was able to handle the transference within the classroom, refusing to employ it as a lever for driving home distinct units of knowledge, but letting it run as the silent engine of a mutual influencing process. In other words, apart from their being taught 'less stupid' things, the students' interest may also have been stimulated by the fact that Lacan modified the process of teaching itself, so that participants felt less objectified and infantilized.   *Lacan's teaching style*

Above all, Lacan's early seminars were exceedingly clever, not so much in terms of the quality of the knowledge transmitted but with regard to the general instructional method employed. Here was a charismatic and allegedly knowledgeable analyst who did not define his position *per via di porre*, by adding lots of new things to the established canon of ideas, but *per via di levare*, by taking away the dirt that had settled over the Freudian constructions in the unfriendly climate of the psychoanalytic institutions, in order to let it shine again in all its naked glory.[6] Thus, paradoxically, Lacan became an innovator less by presenting something entirely new, than by recovering the old and forgotten, that is to say, by resuscitating discarded fragments of the past, in this case the cutting-edge significance of Freud's original insights. This was the overarching objective of what came to be designated as 'the return to Freud' or, as Lacan himself put it in a famous line from the mid-1950s, 'The meaning of a return to Freud is a return to Freud's meaning' (Lacan 2002b [1955]: 110).

To justify the necessity of such a project, Lacan first of all needed to show that the psychoanalytic establishment had completely misappropriated Freud's body of knowledge. He had to prove that the existing versions of Freud were erroneous, misguided and potentially destructive of the future of psychoanalysis. During the early 1950s, Lacan carried out this critique of psychoanalysis—in the name and for the sake of Freud—on at least four different levels. Textually, he pointed out that Freud's works had filtered through the French psychoanalytic community in appalling translations, which sometimes failed to convey important nuances in Freud's writing, but quite often also rendered his words into phrases carrying completely different meanings (Lacan 1988b [1953–54]: 38–51). At a theoretical level, Lacan argued that established psychoanalytic doctrine tended to look at Freud's entire oeuvre through the lens of his 'structural' distinction between the Ego, the Id and the Superego (Freud 1923b), thus promoting one particular 'dissection of the psychical personality' (Freud 1933a [1932]: 57–80) to the highest ranks of conceptual achievement, at the expense of numerous other distinctions (Lacan 1988c [1954–55]: 11–12). In terms of clinical practice, Lacan scorned contemporary psychoanalysts for turning Freud's flexible 'recommendations' on how to conduct the treatment into a formalistic set of simplistic and rigid algorithms that not only discourage the analyst from taking the initiative (Lacan 2002a [1953]: 33) but also potentially turn the entire analytic experience into a professionally conducted obsessional neurosis (ibid.: 37–38). Beyond these technical issues, Lacan also exposed the accepted goals of analysis within the various post-Freudian schools as non-psychoanalytic deviations: the ego-psychological aim to readapt the patient to external reality reduces psychoanalysis to behavioural engineering; modelling for the patient an image of a strong, mature personality in view of her becoming an active, competent citizen drives psychoanalysis into the realm of social re-education; restoring the patient's genital object relations in order to induce the degree of sexual normalization necessary for the appearance of a solid character structure infects psychoanalysis with spurious moralistic ideals (ibid.: 35–40). Finally, at the institutional level, Lacan reacted against the authoritarian principles presiding over the existing psychoanalytic training institutes, as epitomized in their allegiance to strict hierarchical divisions between training analysts, 'simple' analysts and analytic trainees, as well as in their policies for dispensing and controlling clinical experience. In a bitterly sarcastic comment he posited that the predominant conception of analytic training was 'like that of a driving school which, not content to claim the unique privilege of issuing drivers' licenses, also imagines that it is in a position to supervise car construction' (ibid.: 34).

During the 1950s, all of this contributed to the conception and development of the 'French Freud', as distinct from the 'Anglo-American Freud', although the 'French' incarnation remained less confined to its geographical boundaries than its 'Anglo-American' adversary. Lacan was not so much struggling with enemies on the other side of the Atlantic as with 'Americanized' psychoanalysts at home and around Europe. Insofar as the 'French Freud' steered away from ready-made, 'instant' varieties of psychoanalytic experience and advocated a much more conflict-ridden, restless and dialectical type of knowledge than its counterpart, it was by no means typically French, since the majority of French psychoanalysts, at least during the 1950s, 'owned' the 'Anglo-American Freud'. It was only after Lacan's progressive 'disowning' of the psychoanalytic establishment, and his concurrent reappropriation of the 'original Freud' that the 'French Freud' started to spread across Europe. For many of Lacan's followers, this 'French Freud' would have been 'Lacan's Freud', as they would have been eager to emphasize the idiographic factor over national identity. Yet, for Lacan himself, the Freud he set out to disseminate would have been neither French nor Lacanian, but simply 'Freudian'.

Lacan's assets

This complex dynamics of reappropriation, which eventually gave rise to a genuine cult of Lacanianism, did not trigger the institutional schism within the French psychoanalytic community. It was not Lacan's vituperative dismissal of his contemporaries' ideas, their shared conception of psychoanalytic theory and practice, and their proposed organization of psychoanalytic training, that elicited the earthquakes which divided the French psychoanalytic landscape, either the first time (in 1953) or the second time (in 1963). Indeed, it was exactly the other way round, Lacan's 'return to Freud' emanating from and consolidating itself through an institutional split. Lacan's reinvention of Freud thus occurred on the ruins of an institutional collapse, instead of the institution collapsing in the aftermath of Lacan's project. It is as if the first schism within the French psychoanalytic community released psychoanalytic knowledge from its doctrinal shackles and cleared the path for the 'return to Freud' that would establish Lacan's reputation.

At the same time, Lacan did play a major part in the institutional conflict, not least because the crisis revolved mainly around the clinical legitimacy of one of his technical assets, namely, the infamous principle of the variable-length session (Eissler 1954). This contentious principle, which allows the psychoanalyst to interrupt the session at will and therefore also, for instance, after five or ten minutes, contravened the rule of the fifty-minute hour within the IPA and was regarded by its representatives as a dangerous deviation from the norm—abusive when applied in the treatment of regular patients and unethical when utilized within the context of a training analysis. Whatever else they may have (dis)liked about Lacan's uncompromising character, the leading figures within the French psychoanalytic society were consequently concerned about the clinical authority which he granted himself by manipulating the temporal structure of the treatment, and even more seriously concerned about the possible ineffectiveness of the training analyses he was conducting. The latter issue was considered more pressing because training analyses had always been more strictly regulated than 'regular' analyses, and any failure to comply with these regulations on the side of the training analyst could have resulted in trainees being badly trained and subsequently practising as insufficiently trained ('wild') psychoanalysts.[7] The possibility of patients being mistreated by these psychoanalysts could have posed a problem, then, not only for the legitimacy (and the survival) of the psychoanalytic training institution, but also for the assurance of public health. Furthermore, if the IPA refused to ratify Lacan's practice of variable-length sessions, those trainees who had been allocated to him for their training analysis would never have been able to become members of the association unless they started all over again with a different training analyst.

Aggravated by personal rivalries and exacerbated by Lacan's ostensible intransigence, discussions over the principle (and associated institutional matters) reached a breaking point in June 1953, when Lacan was forced to resign as president of the French psychoanalytic society and a dissident psychoanalytic group was created, uniting Lacan, a handful of loyal colleagues, and a substantial number of trainees (Miller 1976: 11). Throughout the 1950s and, indeed, throughout his entire career, Lacan refused to budge on the vexed question of the variable-length sessions, which, especially during the later years of Lacan's life, when his clinical practice expanded as exponentially as the audience attending his seminar, often developed into 'short sessions'. Reflecting upon his analysis with Lacan, the American scholar Stuart Schneiderman recalled: 'Short sessions

usually lasted only a few minutes. Their time was the time of a
dream, the few minutes of sleep eked out before the inevitable
awakening of the real; Lacan called it an exemplary instance of the
real' (Schneiderman 1983: 132). Schneiderman's testimony of the
short session tallies with that given by other analysands of Lacan (Rey
1989; Godin 1990; Haddad 2002), so one must not jump to the
conclusion that Lacan may have simply been challenging the popular
American belief that 'time is money'.

Quite remarkably, in none of these patient accounts does it tran-
spire that the short session was a form of 'cheap' clinical charlatan-
ism, which Lacan practised with the sole purpose of self-enrichment.
And although some of these testimonies were produced by people
who later committed themselves to the Lacanian cause, and are
therefore everything but neutral, others included in Roudinesco's
volume on the history of psychoanalysis in France (Roudinesco 1990
[1986]) strike the same tone of respect. Hence, if the psychoanalytic
officials brandished Lacan's technique as a totally unacceptable
instance of malpractice, his analysands seemed to accept it quite easily
as an appropriate analytic intervention, sometimes retroactively sat-
urating the act with Lacanian meaning. In Schneiderman's recollec-
tion, for instance, the short session had a clear relationship to the
experience of death:

> The gesture of breaking the session, of cutting it off, was a way
> of telling people to put things on the side, to move forward, not
> to get stuck or fascinated by the aesthetics of the dream. . . .
> There was something of the horror of death in the short ses-
> sions, in these psychoanalytic sessions whose time could not be
> known in advance, whose time was not counted by the ticks of
> the clock. . . . The combined pressure of the shortness of the
> sessions and the unpredictability of their stops creates a condi-
> tion that greatly enhances one's tendencies to free-associate. . . .
> Almost by definition the ego cannot be the master of the short
> session.
>
> (Schneiderman 1983: 133–134)

Lacan's own theoretical justification for the variable-length session
was much more prosaic: the analyst who manipulates the time of
the session operates with a supplementary, non-verbal tool of interpretation, since patients will experience the interruption as a punctu-
ation of their discourse (Lacan 2002a [1953]: 44). These temporal

scansions, Lacan continued, may also facilitate productive 'moments of concluding' in the analysand, and reduce the negative effects of protracted attempts at enhanced self-understanding (ibid.: 48).[8] Lacan never compromised on the legitimacy of this technique, yet it proved to be an insurmountable problem for the IPA.[9] After separating from the French psychoanalytic society, the renegade group of psychoanalysts attempted to reaffiliate with the official professional body, a fact which also proves that Lacan did not completely repudiate the latter's hegemonic status (Etchegoyen and Miller 1996: 48–49). The investigative committees took ten years to make up their mind, yet they eventually concluded that the 'French situation' was really a 'Lacan problem', and so they proposed that the group could be readopted on the condition that Lacan be excluded from his position as a teacher and training analyst (Miller 1977: 41–45). On the evening of 19 November 1963, a majority voted in favour of re-affiliating and accepted the condition, which left Lacan betrayed by his former allies, stripped from his teaching responsibilities and 'excommunicated', as he later called it, from psychoanalytic officialdom (Lacan 1994a [1964]: 1–13). Not for long, though, for within the space of a couple of months, Lacan found a new niche for his seminar—thanks to the support of Louis Althusser and Claude Lévi-Strauss— and a new, larger, younger and more devoted audience, who were less interested in the 'return to Freud' and more hungry for innovative critical knowledge. As was the case with the first schism in the French psychoanalytic community, this second schism again precipitated a new phase in Lacan's development of psychoanalytic knowledge. Once again, it is as if the implosion of Lacan's own group freed knowledge from its restrictive institutional setting and facilitated the emergence of an innovative epistemological enterprise. Opening up to this new generation of followers, and professing his allegiance to the fashionable doctrine of structuralism, Lacan's seminar also changed dramatically from an intimate reading group to a massive intellectual performance with little or no audience participation.

In June 1964, Lacan proceeded to create his own professional organization, the École freudienne de Paris, which set out with the overtly political aim of reconquering Freud's invention by denouncing 'the deviations and compromises that blunt its progress' (Lacan 1990a [1964]: 97). Yet instead of reclaiming the spirit of discovery in psychoanalysis through the reading and interpretation of Freud's texts, Lacan did not suggest a 'second return to Freud' but rather a meta-return or—as we called it in the previous chapter—a 'return to the return'. Whilst changing his conception of the unconscious into a linguistic, epistemic structure pervaded by the power of jouissance, he also launched an alternative constitution for the management of a psychoanalytic organization, a new set of institutional categories which avoid the classic distinctions between 'training analysis', 'therapeutic analysis', 'training analyst' and 'trainee', and a radical set of formal procedures for assessing the effects of training (Lacan 1995b [1967]). The most controversial amongst these procedures, for non-Lacanians and Lacanians alike, proved to be the procedure of the pass (Lacan 2001d [1969]), which demands that all members of the school who want to apply for recognition as Analyst of the School talk about their analysis to three other analysands (the 'passers'), who then each convey individually to a jury (the 'cartel of the pass') what they have heard, after which the jury decides whether the candidate has 'passed' or not. Less than five years after Lacan's creation of his own school, the pass constituted a thorn in the eye of many a member, some of whom at one point decided to leave the school and form their own organization, thus becoming 'Lacanians without Lacan' (Castoriadis-Aulagnier 1970).

In theory, the structures and procedures Lacan invented for the École freudienne de Paris were primarily designed as democratic alternatives to the rigid hierarchical stratification of the 'old' institutions. The school was meant to be open to anyone interested in the pursuit of its objectives. Nobody was forced to be in analysis, much less to practise psychoanalysis in order to contribute to its activities. Wanting to train as a psychoanalyst required undertaking one's own psychoanalysis, which did not differ from the psychoanalysis someone would start for purely clinical reasons. Applying for recognition by the school entailed an indirect judgement based on an evaluation of what someone was able to transmit about his analysis to people who were fellow-travellers along the psychoanalytic route, and therefore not in a position of authority. Rather than judging someone's capacity on the basis of academic qualifications, professional diplomas or general character, the school listened only to the nature of personal psychoanalytic experience. Lacan expressed the latter principle with the famous formula, 'The psychoanalyst derives his authorisation only from himself' (Lacan 1995b [1967]: 1), which has been misunderstood by many as a rejection of any type of professional regulation and a recipe for the proliferation of fraudulent practices. However, what Lacan tried to achieve, here, was an institutional framework in which psychoanalysis would flourish on the basis of social and professional equality, no member being by definition superior in terms of knowledge and power to any other member, and in which only one's personal psychoanalytic experience would condition access to the psychoanalytic profession.

In practice, the system proved to be a hotbed for growing narcissistic aspirations, pseudo-paranoid suspicions and acerbic rivalries. The main problem, it seems, is that Lacan's innovative procedure for organizing and verifying psychoanalytic training has often been interpreted as a radical challenge to the psychoanalytic establishment and therefore as an anti-institutional strategy which promises complete freedom from institutional chains. As a result, all attempts at institutionalizing the pass, including those undertaken by Lacan himself, have been perceived as a betrayal of the allegedly free, non-conformist ideology presiding over its principle. Yet with his invention of the pass Lacan did not seem to aim at a training procedure which guarantees the transmission of psychoanalytic theory and practice outside and against any form of institutional control. Instead, the procedure of the pass was a means to avoid the institutionalization of one-dimensional notions of freedom in the organization of psychoanalytic training and the transmission of psychoanalytic knowledge. More specifically, the pass allowed members of the École freudienne de Paris to apply for recognition as Analyst of the School *if they so wanted*, and thus provide 'evidence' of their 'analytic knowledge' in a non-academic way, without preventing others who had obtained recognition elsewhere (in a more traditional way) from also joining, and without stopping any member from trying to 'prove himself' as an analyst to the School through clinical presentations and theoretical reports.

Nonetheless, for members of the École freudienne de Paris and its successor, the École de la cause freudienne, the pass somehow failed to live up to its promises. Gradually, it acquired a new status as the ultimate litmus test of (Lacanian) 'analicity', whose outcome could literally constitute a matter of life and death—in March 1977, Juliette Labin, a younger member of the École freudienne de Paris and a renowned adherent of anti-establishment ideologies, committed suicide after failing to 'pass' the procedure of the pass. In a letter to Elisabeth Roudinesco, Lacan commented on the tragedy in the following words: 'I have said a psychoanalyst's authority comes only from himself. That's indisputable, but it entails a risk. I would add, however, that he's not obliged to run the risk involved in the pass. He undertakes that voluntarily' (Roudinesco 1997 [1993]: 383). Whatever the truth may be in the case of Juliette Labin, it is remarkable that despite thirty-five years of intense debate amongst Lacanians, a cornucopia of dissensions and a plethora of new institutional initiatives, the issue of the pass continues to devastate the Lacanian community until this very day—more than two decades after Lacan dissolved his school and a new one was created under the leadership of Jacques-Alain Miller.

Ever since Jacques-Alain Miller 'inherited' Lacan's legacy, the pass has elicited animosity and resentment, predominantly within the ranks of the Lacanian community itself, yet from time to time also externally, from representatives of non-Lacanian institutions. Amongst Lacanians it has given birth to suspicions that the vagueness of the criteria on the basis of which a candidate is accepted (or rejected)—a filtered narrative of psychoanalytic experience—is an excellent strategy for surreptitiously reinforcing analytic authority. Quite often, both the passers and the 'cartel of the pass' would know who the candidate's analyst is, so that the outcome of the pass would inevitably contain a judgement on the quality of the analyst. Given the fact that Analysts of the School are subsequently required to talk about their experience to a large forum, their analyst would then also be able to benefit, narcissistically if not financially, from the public exposure of his clinical achievements. In other words, the analyst of a successful candidate would invariably be regarded as an accomplished practitioner, and vice versa. If the analyst behind the candidate occupies, whether or not voluntarily, a position of authority within the school, the procedure of the pass can also be manipulated purely out of respect for the analyst, or the latter can throw the procedure into doubt whenever its outcome is unfavourable for 'his' candidate. Precisely such a suspicion of institutional foul play, amongst numerous other allegations of misuse of authority, triggered a massive crisis in the Lacanian community during the late 1990s, eventually leading to the defection of literally hundreds of analysts across the globe from Miller's World Association of Psychoanalysis (Soler et al. 2000).

More recently, Lacanian training procedures have also come under renewed attack from representatives of the IPA. In June 2001, Gilbert Diatkine, a member of the Sóciete psychanalytique de Paris (SPP), the oldest French psychoanalytic society and one of the two French groups currently affiliated to the IPA, published a paper in which he claimed that the Lacanian principle according to which the psychoanalyst derives authorization only from himself does not offer sufficient guarantees for protecting the public against 'wild' practitioners. As such, the accusation is everything but new. Indeed, Diatkine himself had already voiced similar concerns in a small book on Lacan published four years before the incriminating article (Diatkine 1997: 97–101). Yet when the editor of the SPP's journal decided not to publish Jacques-Alain Miller's reply to the allegations, the latter embarked on a large-scale public campaign explaining the stakes of the debate and attempting to reunite the numerous Lacanian factions against the new enemy (Miller 2002a). Echoing the French satirical magazine *Le Canard enchaîné*, who dubbed Miller 'Divan the Terrible', one may ask why a relatively minor incident should cause such a huge storm. Miller himself has not ceased underscoring the non-negotiable value of the 'right to response', yet from time to time he has also indicated that Diatkine's dismissive account of Lacanian training practices appeared at a rather unfortunate moment in French politics, when the government was moving towards a new regulatory system for the psychotherapeutic professions. What proves to be at stake, therefore, is much more than the 'right of response'; it is the demonstration of clinical and epistemological legitimacy vis-à-vis governmental regulatory bodies.

The delicate issue of the state regulation of psychotherapeutic practice, including psychoanalysis, has been on the European political agenda for many years and has intermittently stirred the psychoanalytic community since the mid-1980s.[10] It was mainly in response to imminent legal initiatives across Europe that, in December 1989, Serge Leclaire, one of Lacan's earliest associates and a key player on the French psychoanalytic scene, suggested the creation of an 'ordinal agency of psychoanalysts', to which the government could delegate the juridical, financial and social control of the psychoanalytic profession, as in the regulation of medical practice (Leclaire 1996). Leclaire's proposal met with strong resistance from various psychoanalytic groupings and was therefore never implemented. In response to the question as to why the École de la cause freudienne refused to endorse Leclaire's idea, Jacques-Alain Miller said: 'The IPA does not want to hear about it because it thinks that it is an Order in itself. The small groups of the Lacanian nebula [the numerous Lacanian groups existing outside Miller's school] don't want it because they know that they are not very presentable. . . . The members of the École de la cause freudienne don't want it because for essential reasons they are committed to the "pass" even when its practice has effectively not always been perfect' (Miller 1990a: 28).

It should not come as a surprise, then, that Diatkine's critical reading of the most cherished instrument for the verification of analytic training within Miller's school, as a 'not very presentable' procedure which potentially puts the public's health at risk, is perceived by Miller as an extremely damaging attack, requiring swift retaliation. Nor should it come as a surprise that Miller has taken the lead in the most recent debate over the state regulation of the psychobusiness in France, which could have put an end to psychoanalytic organizations implementing their own training procedures. On 8 October 2003, the French National Assembly voted unanimously in favour of an amendment (the so-called Accoyer amendment, after the person who promoted it) which gave the health secretary the right, by state decree, to define which types of psychotherapy are legally sanctioned and under what conditions its practitioners are entitled to exercise their practice.[11] Pointing out that the amendment was passed without any form of public debate and without any consideration of the possibility to deal with the existing risks to public health in a different way (Miller 2003), Miller took the lead in organizing a series of 'forums des psys', therein supported by such French public intellectuals as Bernard Henri-Lévy and Philippe Sollers, which eventually succeeded in 'extracting' psychoanalysis from the newly imposed regulations. The question remains, however, how psychoanalysts can legitimize their clinical practice and knowledge base, over and above these acts of resistance against the current ideologies of quality assurance and cost-effectiveness.

Seeking or believing?

Historically, Lacanian psychoanalysis started as a separate movement with a vehement dispute over the clinical legitimacy of Lacan's technical principle of the variable-length session, which defied the golden rule of the fifty-minute hour. Apart from justifying this principle theoretically with reference to psychoanalytically appropriate tactics of interpretation, Lacan subsequently disallowed his adversaries' moral right to situate themselves within the theoretical and clinical tradition of Freudian orthodoxy. Arguing in favour of a 'return to Freud', he constructed an architectural wonder of ideas, erected on solid Freudian foundations, and built with the same spirit of discovery that had animated the founder throughout his career.

With the introduction of the variable length session, Lacan of course favoured a technical principle which had not featured as such within Freud's original discourse, and this lack of Freudian justification no doubt contributed to his being perceived as deviating dangerously from a central aspect of psychoanalytic practice. Yet, as with so many of his 'innovations', including his famous marriage of psychoanalysis and Saussurean linguistics, Lacan would retroactively situate it back firmly within the intellectual scope of Freud's invention, adding that Freud himself had never really emphasized that a psychoanalytic session should always last fifty minutes.

Lacan's theoretical and clinical reappropriation of Freud's knowledge has always constituted a source of rivalry between Lacanians and non-Lacanians, especially representatives of the IPA. The same is true for Lacan's institutional initiatives—the creation of his own school, the implantation of a department for psychoanalysis at the university, the opening of a 'clinical section' (Lacan 1977b)—and for the associated procedures regularizing psychoanalytic training (the pass). Yet these initiatives have induced sharp divisions not only between Lacanians and non-Lacanians but also within the Lacanian community itself. It may be for institutional reasons (rather than for theoretical and/or clinical motives) that the first split occurred within the French psychoanalytic community, but it is definitely for institutional reasons that much dissension followed. At the same time, however, these institutional schisms cleared the path for Lacan's renewed revision of established psychoanalytic knowledge, including the knowledge he himself had professed. In this way, we could interpret Lacan's decision to dissolve his own school as a final attempt to protect his own knowledge against a type of doctrinal, structural, institutionalized representation that gives it the kiss of death.

After Lacan's own death, the Lacanian community has of course also been troubled by ongoing discussions over the legitimate ownership of his discourse—the transcription of the 28 volumes of his seminars and the copyright over his written texts—which prompted Jacques-Alain Miller to undertake legal proceedings, resulting in his being assigned the sole right to transcribe, edit and publish the seminars (Miller 1985). This ruling, however, has not stopped people from producing 'pirate versions' of the seminars and 'privately printed, not for resale' volumes of Lacaniana, nor has it encouraged Miller himself to take legal action against 'non-official' documents made available in French bookshops and over the Internet. Although many critics of Miller's version of the seminars have focused on his distortion of the original (École lacanienne de psychanalyse 1991), despite the fact that Lacan himself fully endorsed his pupil's work (Lacan 1973), the complicating factor, of course, is Miller's family ties to Lacan, which have put him in a position of intellectual, legal and genealogical authority.

This position of unassailable authority, attributed to, if not adopted by the leader and somehow initiated by Lacan himself during the 1960s, is for some psychoanalysts the reason why the Lacanian community has changed so radically since the early 1950s. Originally, during the good old days, Lacan's seminars were attended by seekers rather than believers; much like the early Christian movement, the Lacanian setting was originally characterized by diversity, multiformity and an intense desire to innovate. Gradually, diversity was replaced by a demand for conformity, formulated by a group of apostles cum Church fathers, which has reportedly led, in a Bakhtinian sense, to the disappearance of open debate and discussion and the emergence of dogmatism; discursive activity and dialogic exchange have given way to the reciting of dogma, dictated by the masters. In Lacanian psychoanalysis, so it is often heard, there are intellectual guides that do not possess guiding lights, but simply a strong desire to be recognized by the master; there are spiritual teachers who lack the ability to teach; there are prophets who do not even believe in themselves. And there are also heretics who refuse to recite the creed, and who are therefore persecuted, expelled and annihilated. Whatever the truth of these assertions, the religious metaphors here are quite inappropriate. Whereas a church, or a sect for that matter, generally welcomes new members but makes it extremely difficult and sometimes impossible for them to leave, anyone who has ever tried to become part of the Lacanian community will have had exactly the opposite experience: it is fairly easy to get out of, but excruciatingly difficult to get into.

Echoing Derrida in a memorable reflection upon his encounters with Lacan, one is tempted to exclaim: 'What wouldn't Lacan have said!' (Derrida 1998 [1996]: 39) What wouldn't a properly Lacanian, psychoanalytic outlook have been! Isn't psychoanalysis, the discourse of the analyst, a discourse in perpetual crisis precisely because it contravenes 'ownership' as such? Doesn't every attempt at 'owning' it (its knowledge, concepts, practice, history) fail to do justice to one of its essential principles, that is, that its knowledge (from which its practice emanates) is in a state of constant dispossession? In a seminal paper on the futility of applying psychoanalysis to literature, Lacan posited that psychoanalysis constitutes a 'knowledge in failure' (*savoir en échec*), which does not mean that it operates with a failed knowledge, nor that the analyst does not need to know anything, but that its knowledge is fundamentally unfinished, incomplete, non-totalized and non-totalizable (Lacan 2001e [1971]: 13–14).[12] But if psychoanalytic knowledge is by definition a 'knowledge in failure', isn't the crisis of legitimacy a necessary precondition, then, for the discourse of the analyst to sustain itself? Perhaps the only agency that could ever be in the position of owning psychoanalysis is the (unconscious of the) analysand, the Other of psychoanalytic discourse, who tests, directs, evaluates and (without any conscious knowledge whatsoever) advances psychoanalytic knowledge. The analyst may direct the treatment, but it would be the patient who paradoxically guides the applicability of psychoanalytic principles.

Legitimacy crises within Lacanian psychoanalysis and, indeed, within the psychoanalytic community as a whole, invariably revolve around the same old issues concerning the relationship between knowledge and truth, the installation and exercise of a particular social bond, the attribution and adoption of roles, functions and positions, and the delivery of a product whose surplus value is optimal, that is to say, neither exceedingly low nor excessively high, for the maintenance of the production process. As Lacan himself suggested, these issues do not merely constitute a central concern for the discourse of the analyst, but also feature high on the agenda of other discourses (Lacan 1991 [1969–70]). Regardless of the specific distribution of the relationships, the terms and conditions are exactly the same for the discourse of the analyst (analytical practice), the discourse of the master (ruling practice), the discourse of the university (educational practice) and the discourse of the hysteric (help-seeking practice). It is therefore to be expected that many of the instabilities underpinning the legitimacy crises within psychoanalysis, other than occupying psychoanalysis as such, are equally at work in the other 'impossible professions' (Freud 1925f, 1937c). Moreover, history has shown that the discourse of the analyst is by no means better equipped to recognize, solve and prevent these instabilities than any other, non-analytical discourses; on the contrary. The awareness of conflict, as a potentially productive experience, within psychoanalysis, and *a fortiori* within Lacanian psychoanalysis, does not guarantee better strategic plans for dealing with it. Or, to put it more provocatively, if the psychoanalytic community wants to preserve and guarantee its epistemological basis, as a knowledge in failure, it can do this only by avoiding the installation of a knowledge universe and by maintaining the existence of a knowledge 'multi-verse', yet the latter task is likely to imperil the subsistence of community life as such.

Part II

Less than knowledge: psychoanalysis and the economies of thought

Chapter 5

Reading *Seminar XVII*: from the desire to know to the fall of knowledge

> The sensibility of the professional common market is becoming
> more refined. What will become of the unconscious in all this?
>
> Jacques Lacan, *Preface to Anika Lemaire*, x
>
> The effect of truth is only a fall of knowledge.
>
> Jacques Lacan, *Seminar XVII*, 216[1]

Traumatic epistemology

Many people like to ponder the question of whether machines can be
made to think, or if animals already do. A more interesting question
is whether people think, and how they actually do it. Freudian psychoanalysis is founded on the claim that thinking is not a straightforward process, and that to be a subject is to occupy a field of
thought that is divided or split. The primary division within thought
that the subject of psychoanalysis introduces is the basis for Freud's
'first topography', which distinguishes between consciousness, the
preconscious and the unconscious, and also underpins his 'second
topography', which divides the 'psychic personality' into Id, Ego and
Superego (Freud 1923b).[2] One of the effects of this division is that
thought can appear to the thinker as an ongoing and organized
process that is also foreign, ungraspable and fundamentally 'Other'.
Human thought processes must therefore be considered as markedly
different from the fairly unambiguous cognition of a computer or a
cockroach.

As we demonstrated in Chapter 2, Lacan forged a link between the
Freudian split (*Spaltung*) and the Cartesian *cogito*. Descartes' courageous distinction between the commonality of thought processes
and the 'accidental' character of the individual mind, which enabled

him to define his own intellectual limitations with clarity and certainty, also cleared the way for the concept of the unconscious. Descartes took the first step towards conceiving of thought as divided into the occasional and fleeting nature of conscious apprehension, and a structured set of relations, a constant and uninterrupted movement of thought that is both impersonal and common to us all. Lacan argued, however, that Descartes was unable fully to approach the unconscious because of his insistence on retaining the existential 'I'. Indeed, Cartesian scepticism initiates a rift between knowledge and truth, but this rift is bridged by the existential 'I'. Descartes asserted that the certainty of knowledge is a thought process and that the certainty of thought process is the power of self-observation: 'I am thinking, therefore I exist' (Descartes 1985 [1637]: 127). Unfortunately, this same self-regarding 'I' reinstates the schism within the field of thought that it was supposed to resolve. Descartes lays the matter to rest only by introducing God as the invisible guarantor for the truth of our self-perception.

For the later Lacan, the relationship between knowledge and truth can only be understood as a rift within knowledge itself. A new distinction is made here between a conscious wish to know and unconscious knowledge, in which the 'I' appears as but one link, a single representation in an indiscriminate chain of relations linking past, present and future. There is no existential or divine agency at work in the unconscious. The way in which knowledge is experienced at the level of the unconscious changes from 'I want to know' and 'I know' to 'a knowledge that does not know itself' and 'a knowledge that does not know it knows' (*un savoir qui ne se sait pas*) (Lacan 1991 [1969–70]: 35). What characterizes a properly psychoanalytic approach to knowledge, then, is the abandonment of the Cartesian fall-back position, in which God underwrites the knowledge that confirms Descartes' existence and his philosophical method. The analyst offers no such epistemological guarantees to the analysand. Rather, she refers the analysand to the division between conscious and unconscious knowledge, by presenting him with his own knowledge in inverted form, that is, as 'a knowledge', a matrix of relations in which the 'I' weaves in and out.[3] The validation of what the analysand says in psychoanalysis, or the question of whether he is lying to himself or to the analyst, is not at issue. The analysand speaks the truth in the same way that he speaks words, as a chain of relations, 'a knowledge'. Only when we can conceive of 'a knowledge', and distinguish it from knowledge as message and content, can we establish a notion of the unconscious. Thus, the true legacy of Cartesianism is not rational thought, but a way of reasoning about thought that revokes every epistemological guarantee. The name for this way of reasoning is psychoanalysis.

The common ground of the unconscious is also distinguished by its stupidity. Not only is the unconscious 'a knowledge', but it is also 'a stupid', which, as Lacan argued in *Seminar XX*, may be used as the collective term for a network of signifiers: '[P]erhaps stupidity is not, as people think, a semantic category, but rather a way of collectivizing the signifier' (Lacan 1998b [1972–73]: 20). Stupidity is not defined, here, on a sliding scale of intelligence running from extreme cleverness (genius) to abject doltishness (idiocy), but is used to describe a universally familiar moment of inversion, when thought encounters itself as something Other, runs up against itself, or blocks its own progress. The unconscious thinks, but not in a way that the conscious mind can recognize—it is as foreign to us as a restaurant menu written in an unknown language.[4] This is expressed as an incommensurability of two different ways of ordering language: firstly as a conscious communication and secondly as an unconscious signifying chain. Lacan states that stupidity 'is a dimension of the signifier at work', because at the level of the signifier there is an operation of thought but an absence of communication (ibid.: 21). The paradox of the unconscious is that within its boundaries the relations of language continue, but sense fails or runs out. The signifier and its referent are no longer working in tandem.

In *The Psychopathology of Everyday Life* (Freud 1901b), Freud provides a gamut of examples of this traumatic encounter of thought and its Other as it appears in bungled actions, slips of the tongue, the forgetting of names and chance actions. What is common in all these examples is a moment of inversion: useful performance is suddenly transformed into useless action, or meaningful words are replaced with meaningless utterances. In the famous 'Signorelli' example (ibid.: 1–7), Freud provides a detailed analysis of such an inversion occurring within the act of forgetting, where a disinclination to remember something unpleasant (the suicide of an analysand), returns as the inability to remember something else (the name of the painter Signorelli). The key factor here is not the repression of memory in the wish to forget, but the return of repression (the intention to forget) in a form that negates and invalidates it: 'I wanted, therefore, to forget something; I had *repressed* something. What I wanted to forget was not, it is true, the name of the artist at Orvieto but something else ... I forgot *the one thing against my will*, while I wanted to forget *the other thing intentionally*' (ibid.: 4). It is not that the intention to forget is itself 'forgotten' or lost in the unconscious, but that when it reappears as the inability to remember the name 'Signorelli', it has undergone a sea change. The links that have stitched together remembering and forgetting are unbound in the repetitions of a signifying chain composed of a stream of art historical, sociological, biographical and anthropological elements. Within this chain, the shattered fragments of intention and will are borne along. In the Signorelli example, forgetting begins its journey as a mental 'something' that Freud might reasonably attain and returns to him as 'a nothing', an absence of mind and the erasure of the will.

It is the acceptance of absurdity and black humour, bound up with the encounter with 'a knowledge', that makes *The Psychopathology of Everyday Life* such an entertaining read. The book is a catalogue of mistakes, pratfalls, absurdities and errors, resulting in various degrees of trauma, including, *inter alia*, social compromise, unsought candour and sudden death. This also provides a clue as to what is at the source of the incommensurability of the conscious communicative act and the unconscious signifying chain. The unconscious does not answer our call to knowledge—indeed, it is 'an entrance one can only reach just as it closes ... and the only way for it to open up a bit is by calling from the inside' (Lacan 1995a [1964]: 267)—but in its very stupidity and senselessness, it reveals the fundamental impossibility of the desire to know. This is where Lacan's reading of Freud parts company with the Cartesian *cogito*. Whereas Descartes is happy to locate the subject of certainty within the continuity of thought processes, and in opposition to the quirks of the individual mind, certainty, for Lacan, is located within this opposition itself, in the 'fall' of remembering into repetition, self-sufficiency into stupidity, or knowledge into non-knowledge. As he put it in *Seminar XVII*: 'truth is only a fall of knowledge' (*L'effet de vérité n'est qu'une chute de savoir*) (Lacan 1991 [1969–70]: 216). The fall of knowledge alone is certain. Certainty only concerns the realization that a lack (or absence) of mind is at the root of that 'presence of mind' through which we dispose ourselves in the world. We are first alerted to this state of affairs by an alteration or denaturing of knowledge, a moment when it becomes unrecognizable. Stupidity is therefore not the opposite of cleverness. Instead, becoming stupid signals the very impossibility of 'being clever'.

Lacanian epistemology posits two moments of trauma. The first is the trauma of an encounter with stupidity, of knowledge as a 'thing', a *Lumpen*, an impenetrable Other. The second is a more radical moment of loss, which moves us from knowledge as something recognizable, to knowledge as something Other, and thence to knowledge as nothing at all. If one of the greatest merits of psychoanalysis is its clear insistence on the reality and intractability of trauma and suffering within the 'speaking body' that is exposed in the clinical encounter, one of the foremost accomplishments of Lacanian psychoanalysis is its model of a traumatic epistemology. Knowledge, far from being a promise of enlightenment underwritten by truth, is shadowed by the traumas of the speaking body, and thus by the forces of its own negation in stupidity and non-knowledge. Lacanian psychoanalysis radically inverts the infamous pop psychoanalytic moment of deep confession and sudden insight, in which the analysand starts to 'see the light' and receives new information about himself. Instead, it insists on the value of seeing the darkness that rests at the heart of the desire to know through an encounter with an unconscious knowledge in which we are concerned, but which does not concern us.

Knowledge post-mortem

In Lacanian psychoanalysis the analysand is guided not towards a moment of (self)recognition, as the culmination of a Socratic 'know thyself', but towards a practice of non-recognition in which knowledge appears as a foreign substance. Following this principle, Lacanian epistemology can be characterized as a set of operations conducted on knowledge 'as we know it'. These operations have a certain dynamic, because they redirect the communicative act (*connaissance/méconnaisance*) towards the symbolic network that supports it (*savoir*), and thence towards an encounter with the real/ impossible, as the primary division within the field of thought. In Lacanian epistemology, knowledge is systematically disaggregated, and its consistency as knowledge is consequently put at risk. Technically, this strategy follows the same path as that which leads to the common epistemological traumas whereby theories collapse, beliefs fall apart, and that which we thought we knew is revealed as deception and sham. It does so, however, in a controlled and ordered fashion. This order and logic of epistemological failure also has a specific purpose, which is to establish reference points for the discussion of knowledge *post-mortem*. For at the point of dismemberment and collapse, Lacanian psychoanalysis recovers knowledge once more, in the very form of its inversion. The death of knowledge is made concurrent with its truth; the fall of knowledge has a useful outcome, insofar as it locates a certainty.

It is interesting to note here that ex-Lacanians, when drawing up their accounts of the errors of Lacan's work, tend to elide the final stage of this dynamic in which the death of knowledge is accorded a positive and productive force. The traumatic shattering of what François Roustang has dubbed 'the Lacanian delusion' is often accompanied by a fervent wish to heal the wound through the construction of a new knowledge scenario:

> [H]is [Lacan's] seminar had become a spectacle, a show, and, if you did not always understand terribly well what he was propos-ing, you nevertheless remained spellbound . . . And how seduc-tive he could be when marvelling at some supposed discovery you had made . . . Being singled out in that way would make even the soberest man's head spin. But . . . what a long fall it was when he lost interest, and you abruptly found yourself back in the midst of collective stupidity!
>
> (Roustang 1990 [1986]: 3)

This new knowledge scenario is sustained, then, by the discovery and elucidation of the truth behind the façade of Lacanian cruelty and sophistry.[5] Roustang describes his intellectual seduction by Lacan, a figure he is now able to identify, in his post-delusional state, as an ill-tempered, badly dressed clown, who toyed with established know-ledge systems only to pick at their flaws. According to Roustang, one of Lacan's tricks of seduction was to hold out the possibility of a total system of knowledge under the sign of psychoanalysis: '[Lacan] gave the impression of his having produced, in an age of specializa-tions, what had only been possible in previous centuries, namely a synthesis of all forms of knowledge, the re-emergence of the man of real breeding' (Roustang 1990 [1986]: 5–6). Roustang is not simply in error in asserting that Lacan sought to establish himself as a Renaissance man in an age of specialists. Worse, he rekindles a form of opposition between 'free' and 'bound' knowledge that is totally alien to the project of Lacanian epistemology. This opposition informs the standard argument about what knowledge was and what it has become. The argument can be summarized as follows: know-ledge has moved from being the historical mark of an autonomous, aristocratic and cultivated mind to a contemporary situation in which it exists as a degraded, impersonal social product. In the following chapter, we will explain how this opposition collapses completely within the terms set by the role of free speech in a modern market place of ideas. For the moment, it suffices to note that from the Lacanian perspective 'free speech' is speech that has truth as its cause and not as its end in view. The blind, autonomous freedom of 'a stupid of signifiers' has nothing to do with the defence of an historically constituted notion of intellectual freedom against the contemporary hegemony of a knowledge economy.

Despite the radically different understanding of the relationship between knowledge and freedom offered by psychoanalysis, the opposition between academic freedom and the laws of the market continues to structure debates on the relationship between higher education and the world of goods. In these debates, universities either are seen to defend the individual pursuit of knowledge 'for its own sake' against the iron circumstances of modernity, or are encouraged to accept their place within the world of commodities. In *Seminar XVII*, Lacan takes the position that there is nothing more modern, pragmatic and impersonal than the pursuit of knowledge 'for its own sake', and nothing more metaphysical and nostalgic than the knowledge commodity. *Seminar XVII* is usually referred to as the seminar on the 'four discourses', because of the emphasis it places on the relationship between the discourses of the master, the university, the hysteric and the analyst—four types of relationship that can be distinguished within the symbolic structure of language.[6] Yet the word 'discourse' is somewhat misleading since Lacan's discourses account for the manner in which discursive or communicative action founders on the distinction between conscious and unconscious formations of knowledge and agency.

Following the terms Lacan develops in *Seminar XVII*, there is no distinction to be made between university knowledge and markets in knowledge goods. Both are conjoined in the impossible pursuit of an ideal economy of total knowledge that can support and guarantee functions of agency. The 'discourse of the university', as it presents itself in a clinical setting, draws on resources of speech and language from a number of sites, including actual universities. Moreover, Lacan suggests that the discourse of the university is in itself a function of the relationship of the discourses of the master and the analyst. The implications of this position are profound, since it nullifies any idea of an epistemological 'stand-off' between psychoanalysis and the university. Psychoanalysts are simply not obliged to consider what comes up for the count as knowledge in universities. What they are obliged to turn their attention to is how to create the conditions for the emergence of what Lacan termed 'the subject of science'. As we explained in Chapter 2, 'the subject of science' refers to a specific experience of thought that is marked by a central rift (splitting, division) between conscious rationality and unconscious reason. The coordinates of this subject were elucidated by Lacan's discussion of the Cartesian *cogito* in *Seminar XI*, and finally determined in 'Science and Truth', with its paradoxical statement that 'the subject on which we operate in psychoanalysis can only be the subject of science' (Lacan 1989b [1965]: 7). It bears repeating that the word 'science', here, refers to the Cartesian division of the field of thought, as well as to Freud's development of it, in which it is not the existential 'I' that is certain, but rather the field of the unconscious within which this 'I' is apprehended. The subject itself has no history and there is no history of the subject. In positing this subject, one simultaneously posits a fundamental division of all thought and all knowledge. The freedom Lacan accords to this subject of science is radical and its potential is revolutionary. In comparison, the ideal of 'knowledge for its own sake' is a variety of unfreedom and the 'knowledge product' merely constitutes the packaging of those constraints. When this subject enters the scene, philosophy and academic discourse in general appear as a 'harebrained lucubration', a halting commentary, on the fact that 'I, the truth, am speaking' (ibid.: 15).

Part of the uniqueness of *Seminar XVII* is its attempt to develop an epistemology outside an academic frame of reference, a project whose difficulty Lacan acknowledged throughout his development of the four discourses. The project required nothing less than the actual reconstruction of epistemology, not as a means of building knowledge and achieving truth, but as a means of segregating and dismantling all that traditional epistemological scholarship had held together as a set of relationships between knowledge and its referents, theory and reality, *doxa* and *episteme.* This seemingly perverse attempt at throwing epistemology into reverse gear was intended as a disclosure of the elided liberating potential pervading the radical separation of unconscious 'thinking' from conscious 'thoughts' which lay at the root of the Cartesian *cogito* and the development of modern science. The opportunity for a radically modern conception of knowledge had been missed, owing to the exponential growth of a technocratic form of social organization, in which science is placed in the service of industry. Lacan took issue with the 'desegregation' of knowledge in technocracies, relating it to the universal imposition of productive labour: 'Naturally, the refusal of segregation is basic to the concentration camp' (Lacan 1977a [1969]: xv, n. 3). Under capitalism, however, the rule is not *Arbeit macht frei* but rather the reverse: in our society, it is freedom that makes work, for scholars of mediaeval history and information analysts alike.

Lacan's alternative, 'segregated' definition of knowledge presents us with the daunting prospect of an epistemology which posits an inverted relationship between knowledge and truth, one in which only the failure of knowledge produces certainty. For this reason, Lacanian epistemology neither is *strictu sensu* theoretical, nor is it concerned with providing incentives for belief. It intervenes on the scene of knowledge in order to locate the position of the unconscious within discourse, by separating the order of the signifier, driven by desire, from a conscious order of signification, aiming at the communication of a message. The simplest way to put this is to say that Lacan developed an epistemological position in which a phallus need never refer to a penis.' This first separation of the chain of signifiers (*savoir*) from signification as an act of communication (*connaissance*) places a limit on knowledge, as the act of knowing encounters itself as 'a stupid of signifiers'. Further operations uncouple the signifying chain, revealing knowledge to be a field in which desire is at work. And finally desire is aligned with the impossible/ real that constitutes a topography of thought.

One might argue that Lacan's account of knowledge hardly deserves the name 'epistemology' at all, anatomy or butchery being more suitable descriptions. It would be more accurate to say that Lacan was concerned with the relationship between knowledge in the abstract and 'know-how' as a technique of intervention, misdirection and gaming within fields of knowledge, a practice that discloses the doubling of what he playfully and pointedly called *lalangue* ('llanguage') into its conscious and unconscious elements. Lacanian epistemology sets knowledge as an ethics of correct usage and timely intervention against that which obscures any liberating 'move' on existing relations of knowledge under the dead weight of historically sanctioned academic opinion.[8] Indeed, the unconscious that exists as 'a knowledge' does not multiply its products, but multiplies itself: 'The multiplication of loaves of bread is not the same as the collecting of loaves of bread. It is a matter of applying one of these relations to the other. You invent the algorithm. It starts to run wild in the world, according to little rules that have the air of nothing, but do not believe that the fact that they exist leaves you, any of you who are here, in the same state as before they emerged' (Lacan 1991 [1969–70]: 218).

Lacan emphasizes here that psychoanalysis is made possible by a scientific approach to knowledge, which divides the field of thought, rather than collecting thoughts into spurious wholes. In addition, he stresses that the intrusion of the 'subject of science' within a field of knowledge changes the internal relations of that field. The unconscious knowledge that is vigorously 'at work' must henceforth be distinguished from the work of knowledge in the production of representations, theories and beliefs. This lesson applies equally to the totalizing pretensions of science and the rigid dogmas of psychoanalysis.

In his own teaching, Lacan was at pains to separate the truth effects of the unconscious from the truth products of culture, while dreading his own reincarnation as founder of the Lacan industry. In his preface to Anika Lemaire's large-scale academic synthesis of his work, he wrote of 'texts faithful in pillaging me, but never deigning to pay me back. Their interest will be that they transmit what I have said literally; like the amber which holds the fly so as to know nothing of its flight' (Lacan 1977a [1969]: xv). This statement, which might seem to checkmate all forms of commentary on Lacan, should present no difficulty if we accept a fundamental distinction between truth effects in the psychoanalytic treatment and the sign of truth that is punctually produced by those citizens who are the successors to the exploited slave, 'those who are themselves products . . . *Consumer society*, we say' (Lacan 1991 [1969–70]: 35). In place of a knowledge with a force gathered from its historical foundations, Lacan gives us a 'weightless' epistemology, which aims to intervene at the right moment within the exchange of knowledge and the production of truth and belief.

This also provides us with a clue as to the exact nature of Lacan's 'structuralism', which is not concerned with articulating meanings or the systematization of phenomena, but rather with the possibilities of constructing a topography of thought. It is concerned with the conception of thought as a generative schema working across diverse levels, rather than as a process directed towards the ordering, categorizing and consolidation of meaning. In 'Science and Truth', Lacan already posited that 'the crucially important mark of structuralism' (Lacan 1989b [1965]: 10) accepts the conditions of trauma and division in a manner that is foreign to academic business as traditionally conducted. Yet Lacan's structuralism reverses the order in which *episteme* is used, from a knowledge designed to consolidate *doxa* (as exemplified, brilliantly, in the Lévi-Straussian figure of the *bricoleur*) to a knowledge revealing the divisions and antagonisms that structure the various systems of belief. Of course, the trajectory of post-structuralism, which took its first steps as structuralism under the sign of semiology, has taken a circuitous route from structure back to belief, through the incorporation of cultural marginalia and alternative epistemologies. It stands as a 'sexed-up' alternative to the perceived coldness and alienation of structuralism, yet it is therefore also in an excellent position to miss all the opportunities that structuralism has offered.

To Lacan, structuralism is useful insofar as it allows psycho-analysis to clarify its position as the field in which the unconscious knows, thinks and speaks, regardless of its source and origin. In *Seminar XVII*, Lacan argued that 'in order to structure a knowledge correctly one has to abandon the question of origins' (Lacan 1991 [1969–70]: 18). An account of knowledge as structure thus allows us to turn from the production of speech about the origins of the world, to a world that, at every moment, is being produced by acts of speech. We are used, indeed overused, to the idea that phenomena can be ordered and categorized in order to establish knowledge systems, whether these systems are those of zoology or the sociology of stardom. In *Seminar XVII*, Lacan works in precisely the opposite direction, moving from ideal orders of knowledge towards an epistemological scene in which these orders of knowledge are first dissolved and then reconstituted as a series of 'knowledge acts'. In such acts, the substance of knowledge lies not in knowledge itself but in *jouissance*, the perpetuation of enjoyment in speech as it traverses the real. This is the point where Lacan moves beyond the classic, Lévi-Straussian belief in the irrevocable power of knowledge structures and the intrinsic structuration of knowledge. Lacan sums up this position in his later *Seminar XX* (Lacan 1998b [1972–73]), in which he contrasts the 'exchange value' of knowledge goods with the 'use value' of a knowledge whose exercise is equivalent to its acquisition. The latter knowledge is voided as an accumulated, hoarded and tradeable 'stock', so that it can be understood as a logic of desire and a means of jouissance. Here Lacan establishes a typically para-doxical knowledge ethics. Insofar as it can be acquired within a knowledge economy, knowledge is utterly worthless. Its value can be assessed only through the personal 'cost' involved in its perpetual reconstruction as a means of jouissance: 'Knowledge is worth just as much as it costs, a pretty penny, in that it takes elbow-grease, and that it's difficult. Difficult to what? Less to acquire it than to enjoy it' (ibid.: 96). It can therefore be argued that texts offering a Lacanian 'primer', exegetical discourse, institutional doctrine or gospel narrative are completely missing the point of Lacanian epistemology. For this epistemology is directed not towards the construction of a 'Lacanian body of knowledge' but towards a (clinical) setting in which the subject emerges as such within the division of the knowledge field.

Knowledge and jouissance

Psychoanalytic epistemology is constituted in the analyst's relationship to the orders of technocratic and technological consciousness that dominate the world in which he has come to exist, and not through a contrast or comparison between the knowledge of the analyst and that of the academic. Lacan's arguments suggest that under the condition of modernity only the analyst, the scientist and the artist have the potential to treat knowledge in an unfettered, unconditioned state. Academics, for their part, are condemned to rationalization, knowledge accumulation and the maintenance of an epistemological *status quo*. For analysts, it is a condition of their practice that the totality of knowledge associated with it is always 'in play' and at risk. The death of psychoanalysis is therefore always a possibility, and the very realization of this mortal risk constitutes and maintains the analytic practice. Or, as Jonathan Lear has put it: '[T]he analyst lives with a lively sense of death' (Lear 2003: 54). For the philosopher and the academic scholar in the humanities and social sciences, the condition of their practice is that the totality of knowledge is never risked. Rather, its accumulated historical profits are continually reinvested in the continuation of the original enterprise. In time-honoured fashion, disciplines establish methodologies for addressing questions that serve the continuity of the discipline. Yet the question Lacan confronted in his impromptu at Vincennes in December 1969, 'What kind of world has psychoanalysts in it?', is less concerned with establishing a psychoanalytic body of knowledge, or conducting a sociological study, than with insisting on the dialectical relation of all knowledge to its social contexts (Lacan

1990c [1969]). His premise is that a world with psychoanalysts in it cannot be a world in which knowledge can be treated as a given. Insofar as it ushers in the certainty of failure, the subject of science is corrosive and fatal as far as a traditional understanding of knowledge is concerned.

Lacan's epistemological reconstruction should therefore be distinguished from those radical critiques of epistemology that have emerged from within philosophy itself. Indeed, philosophers announced the death of epistemology some time ago. We are not concerned with rehearsing these philosophical debates here, but with opposing Lacanian models of knowledge and discourse to the pragmatic, relativist and instrumentalist theories of knowledge that have emerged in the wake of Quine's attempt to 'naturalize' the philosophical model of epistemology (Quine 1969) and Rorty's attempt to bury it a decade later (Rorty 1979). These moves towards 'scientific' or 'real world' epistemologies are concerned with strengthening the social purchase or extending the cultural reach of academic definitions of knowledge, and thus with the repair of philosophical epistemology within a new means of totalization. Epistemological instrumentalism or pragmatism is but a means of retooling philosophy and is controlled by the aforementioned distinction between the 'cultivated mind' and the 'knowledge product'. The notion of the knowledge commodity seems to instrumentalize and pragmatize the functions of knowledge, even as the belief in 'knowledge for its own sake' appears to humanize it. In a Lacanian epistemological framework, these two change places. The freedom of thought embodied in philosophy is presented as the first step on the road to a technocratic social order, and the commodity is the illusion of human value built by this social order. The commodity is a compensation for alienated knowledge and deferred desire.

The way beyond the mass production of knowledge and its modern myths of value can only be marked by the refusal of a temporal order in which the work of knowledge is directed towards the end of truth. From a Lacanian standpoint, knowledge is newly understood as an effect of the primal cause of splitting (*Spaltung*), which delivers the subject into language and discourse. To understand Lacan's *Seminar XVII*, one needs to accept the fullest implications of the unconscious as 'a knowledge', and how this 'dark side' of knowledge is concealed from us by our own delight in the spectres of epistemological value and plenitude: knowledge goods displayed and catalogued for our collective benefit on television, the Internet and in galleries, museums and tourist sites. The manic accumulation and commodification of knowledge, the invention of new means of knowledge generation and distribution, and the constant thirst for new knowledge obfuscate the unconscious truth of the epistemological rift in the speaking body that is subject to the agency of the signifier.

Nowhere is the obverse of technocratic consciousness revealed better than in the discourse of the analyst, where the labour of knowledge and reason continues without the conscious intervention of the subject, disclosing the splitting of reason itself into conscious and unconscious elements. One of Lacan's major innovations in *Seminar XVII* was to provide an account of reason, by means of the structure of the four discourses, that could be used to understand both a subject's desire to know and its simultaneous exclusion from knowledge. As its title *L'Envers de la psychanalyse* suggests, *Seminar XVII* endeavours to look at psychoanalysis from 'the other side', that is, from the point of view of the world in which psychoanalysts have come to exist.[9] As we mentioned earlier, the labour of this *Seminar* is not towards a contextualization of psychoanalysis, but rather the unseating of the very epistemologies that might provide such a contextualization. A specifically Lacanian theme, developed in *Seminar XVII*, is that knowledge does not require a referential object, and is not commensurate with truth. In other words, knowledge is not what it seems to be. The knowledge that is at work in the unconscious is 'on business' for a jouissance that can only appear as purposeless to the conscious mind. In *Seminar XVII*, Lacan implicitly elaborates on the distinction between *tuché* (the intrusion of the real as primordial cause of the signifying chain) and *automaton* (the chain of signifiers), first staged in *Seminar XI* (Lacan 1994a [1964]: 53–62), within a more complex framework that accounts for the structures of an inwardly divided reason in which the subject is caught up in an approach to jouissance 'on the inverse scale of the Law of desire' (Lacan 2002f [1960]: 311). The epistemological series or relay of *Seminar XVII* constructs a single logic linking knowledge and non-knowledge together, and showing how the use of knowledge as a means to establish self-mastery is frustrated by the co-option of knowledge as a means of jouissance in which the reference points that guarantee selfhood completely disappear.

One of the paradoxes of *Seminar XVII* is that it places knowledge 'in the dock' (Lacan 1991 [1969–70]: 33), whilst affirming a view of psychoanalysis as the disavowed product of the rationalist ideologies of modernity. In the terms set by this *Seminar*, modernity can be defined as the perfection of a technocratic consciousness which reflects agency back to itself as all-powerful, enlightened and un-assailable. Under the sign of modernity, all forms of knowledge are co-opted to this task of making the world nothing other than the perfect self-signification of the principle of agency (the 'knowledge ego'). Yet this process also produces its own negation in the un-conscious, where a knowing agency is absent. Knowledge and non-knowledge are bound together in a single strand, and one cannot be understood without the other. This is why Lacan builds a framework of discursive dynamics within which the position of the analyst can be plotted at the extreme limit of modernity's dream of perfectibility. The analyst is the marginal figure who embraces non-knowledge, the inanimate loss of personhood and a latent, inchoate epistemology as the greatest gifts of technological consciousness. In this sense, the analyst who is concerned with the inward divisions of thought and reason can be described as being 'ahead of the game' of rationality that is played out under modernity. The discourse of the analyst confronts the technocratically mediated relationship of agency and knowledge directly, as that which produces its own inverted truth through the loss or absence of knowledge in the 'vanishing point' of the subject of science. By contrast, bureaucracies, universities or the media use knowledge as a means to rationalize and contextualize phenomena, thus concealing the reality of agency and mastery. This is both the secret of their power and the mark of their mindless submission to the rule, not of a particular master or agency, but of agency as such, made manifest in the accumulation of what Lacan termed 'knowledge-totality' (*savoir-totalité*) (ibid.: 35).

It will be clear by now that our own approach to *Seminar XVII* elucidates themes and motifs within it that are used to challenge epistemological orthodoxy, and which figure epistemological dis-course as an act of disaggregation. Despite the continuing vogue for histories of *les événements* of Paris 1968, we have thus chosen not to follow Sherry Turkle's approach, and contextualize this *Seminar* within the socio-political aftermath of the student riots and the general turmoil within French academia at the end of the 1960s (Turkle 1992). As with all of Lacan's *Seminars*, we feel that *Seminar XVII* needs to be understood on its own terms, and not on the terms set by Daniel Cohn-Bendit or Michel Foucault. While *Seminar XVII* has debts to Hegel, Kojève, Heidegger and Wittgenstein, among others, its true orientation is Freudian, and it stays true to the logic of the Freudian project in its emphasis on scientific and technological methodologies, whilst further deploying and modifying the theoretical paradigm of a split between the symbolic order and a jouissance 'beyond the pleasure principle'.[10] In *Seminar XVII*, this is first of all manifest as the alienation or cutting loose of jouissance by a symbolic order. The symbolic order perfects the rationalization of speech and language through the hegemony of the discourse of the university. Yet jouissance also remains 'under the skin' of those who are bound to this hegemony of rationalization, and this is why jouissance is also placed at the root of the rationalizing drive. Technological consciousness produces an unconscious, and modernity produces the psychoanalyst, as night follows day. This split is reproduced within knowledge itself, taking shape as an overproduction of knowledge in the form of explanation, contextualization and information, which conceals its status as knowledge begetting only knowledge itself. As such, the scandal of *Seminar XVII* is not that knowledge only serves itself, as 'knowledge for its own sake'. The real epistemological secret is that in serving itself, knowledge becomes a deferred, second-hand means of jouissance and therefore ultimately corresponds to non-knowledge rather than to truth. Both the 'cultivated mind' model of epistemology and that of the 'knowledge product' insist on a relation between knowledge and value. *Seminar XVII* dares to imagine epistemology otherwise, as 'a stupid' beyond value, operating outside the sway of academic reason. The new reason of the master (enlightenment, work and culture within the terms of the university discourse) is ultimately just as unreasonable as the old order of violent struggle and absolute domination.

Doing justice to the radical difference of the model of knowledge that Lacan constructs in *Seminar XVII* thus also requires attention to the manner in which its positioning of the discourses of the master and that of the analyst corresponds to a distinction between a technocratic social order and the liberating potential of an unconscious. This distinction is manifest in the dialectic of oppression and revolution that has characterized Western modernity. Psychoanalysis shares with Marxism the quality of taking modernity seriously, and of insisting on the intimate links between the product and its means of production. However, it also takes modernity's logic beyond reasonable limits, to the point where something unlooked for is 'produced' or developed out of the forms of social production themselves. For Marx, the 'secret product' of modernity is surplus value, extracted from the labour of the worker and concealed within class structures and divisions of labour. To Lacan, following Marx's terminology, the secret product is surplus jouis-sance, generated as a by-product of the technocratic orders of knowledge by which the subject is determined, and accessible in the analytic setting through a knowledge whose exercise corresponds to its acquisition. The discourse of the analyst, in which knowledge operates in the place of truth, corresponds neither to culture nor to its products and heralds the possibility of revolution and radical change.

The psychoanalyst as knowledge-worker

'*Keep going. March. Keep on knowing more*' (Lacan 1991 [1969–70]: 120). With these words, Lacan relayed the disembodied, motiveless command of the modern master. In *Seminar XVII* psychoanalysis is placed in the shadow of this insistent, all-devouring desire to know, an 'epistemological drive' (ibid.: 122) which possesses the analysand as much as it preoccupies any other subject divided by the symbolic order of language. In the master's command, the agency that issues the order to know and the actual agents of knowledge that are set to work by this order are bound inextricably together in the headlong pursuit of 'knowledge for its own sake'. However, rather than en-dorsing the psychoanalytic value of this command to know more, Lacan insists on the value of stupidity, ignorance, loose talk and bullshit—the disavowed waste products of the epistemological drive—and the manner in which this 'waste of knowledge' indicates the path from conscious knowledge (*connaissance*) to unconscious reason (*savoir*) and thence to jouissance.

Lacan's introduction of the discourses of the master, the uni-versity, the analyst and the hysteric is subsumed within a deeper logic, which juxtaposes the position of the analyst with the changing face, or increasing facelessness, of the master within modern forms of social life. The role of the 'master's discourse' is to mark the beginning of a dynamic of concealment and subterfuge, which the analyst's discourse exposes to scrutiny. Yet this same process of con-cealment, alienation and dissimulation has created the analytic func-tion itself. In the formulae of the four discourses, the discourse of the master and that of the analyst are two aspects of the state of know-ledge within modernity. Mastery survived, developed and dissimu-lated itself through the progressive and violent transformation of tacit and embodied knowledge into abstract social agency. In turn, analytic work occupies the sites of this process in the damaged bodies and psyches of modernity's subjects, identifying mastery's loci of control, its causes and its divisive effects. As such, embodied knowledge or 'know-how' is co-opted to mastery, which then resides as the hidden kernel of a self-perfecting technological consciousness. This technological consciousness ultimately conceals the weakness and infirmity of the classical master within a 'master function' that efficiently disposes of social products, bodies and fields of knowledge.

Psychoanalysis addresses the 'master function' by setting up camp in the very sites of epistemological division and the traces they leave in the organization of the self. This means that a psychoanalyst is a 'knowledge worker' of a very particular kind. The analyst draws up an account of the scattered 'reasons' of a localized epistemology. However, *qua* analyst, she cannot be accounted for according to descriptive or normative definitions of epistemological reasoning. It would be as difficult for a social epistemologist to say whether an individual analyst in the clinical setting possesses psychoanalytic knowledge, as it would be to say whether the psychoanalytic community and its institutions can be seen to guarantee their own knowledge domain.[11] It is also the case that the inability of university-based epistemologies to understand the particularity of psychoanalytic, and particularly Lacanian approaches to knowledge, is the cause of repeated misapprehensions concerning the relationship of academics to the social world, as well as a whole range of reactions, from outright hostility to uncritical embrace, that have characterized the academic reception of psychoanalysis. Lacanian discourse is not merely 'dense' in the academic sense, but actually blocks academic modes of understanding. Many people in the academic community are prepared to admit that Lacan is difficult; fewer will admit that all the difficulties of Lacan are actually in the possession of the academic, as a symptom of their particular way of being in the world. It is not just that Lacan is difficult and resistant to academic reason, but that his discourse lies below the horizon of that reason, taking its place instead among the circumstances of the world that is produced in speech.

The logic of misunderstanding that exists between academics and analysts is laid out in the dynamic relationship established by the four discourses. 'The university discourse' is another term for an apparatus of dissimulation and concealment in which the impotence of the master is disguised by the puissance and agency of knowledge itself, alienated into a social product that exists 'for its own sake' and for the sake of the master simultaneously. The name for this product is culture, the activity of acquiring and exchanging surplus jouissance. There are many paradoxes to be explored in Lacan's use of the word 'university' in *Seminar XVII*, but one which is immediately applicable to our present world of knowledge economies and knowledge transfer, is that 'knowledge for its own sake' is precisely what the technologically perfected and commercially savvy contemporary university is engaged in producing. Between the trite alternatives of 'business or cloister?' that are usually offered in debates on higher education, there lies the often overlooked question of knowledge as public work, and the relationship between the university as institution and the university as public speech. University research and well-educated students are valuable public goods which no businessman could afford to produce and distribute: public universities are designed to correct this failure by providing more education and basic research than the market would yield on its own; these are the fundamental roles of a university and the argument for government support. For a liberal sociologist such as Steven Shapin these words are a beacon of light in the encroaching darkness ushered in by the creeping commercialization of higher education, an affirmation of the university's 'central commitment to responsible teaching and free enquiry' (Shapin 2003: 19). In the terms set by *Seminar XVII*, however, the injunction to 'keep on knowing more', which also sets the university discourse in motion, does not guarantee an historical institution called the university. Rather, it contributes to the hegemony of a form of public speech in which every citizen becomes a student, trailing a slick of rationalizations, reflections, equivocations and explanations behind them in their progress across social space.

The consequences of this social hegemony of rationalization for the analyst's discourse are not hard to figure out: either the social being of psychoanalysis declines into an old and increasingly unfunny joke about 'phallic objects', or analytic practice submits to the dictates of the university discourse, and develops into one of the present-day legatees of ego psychology, such as cognitive behaviour therapy, the psychology of consumption, energy psychology, or various philosophies of self-knowledge and self-empowerment. The discourse of the university represents the point where knowledge as the 'front organization' for the agency of the master, and knowledge as the dirty secret of the master's tricks and ruses, are placed at the greatest distance from one another. Psychoanalysis, in its apparently morbid insistence on prolonged, intractable and irreducibly particular forms of suffering, will not let this dirty secret alone. This is one reason why the fantasy of agency offered by a 'knowledge economy', as exemplified in the rampant ideologies of the knowledgeable, politicized and discriminating consumer, seems socially purposive and epistemologically progressive next to the early twentieth-century trappings and quaint techniques of psychoanalysis, with its unhelpful and retrograde emphasis on trauma, dissociation and alienation. The university as institution, in its historically established role as arbiter and quality controller of the discourse of the university as a mode of public (and purportedly free) speech, is increasingly inclined to locate Freudian psychoanalysis and its legatees as an object of rationalization—a phenomenon to be contextualized, situated and defined within historical time (an absurd experiment never to be repeated)—or as a universal solvent for interdisciplinary adventurism. Psychoanalysis itself, in other words, can be employed to ensure that we keep on going and keep on knowing more.

'Applying' the discourse theory

This provides us with an excellent reason to revisit Lacan's theory of the four discourses, which returns rationalization to its roots in alienation. Along the axis set by the relationship of the master and the analyst, the discourse of the university marks an important moment of transition, isolating a powerful mechanism of control, but it must be unseated from its current position in debates on the social position and continuing relevance of psychoanalysis. Analysts, academics and analyst/academics have all contributed to a situation in which academic discourse contests, refutes, explains, adapts or contextualizes psychoanalysis. Lacan's theory of the four discourses makes clear that the truth of psychoanalysis is not academic and that the truth of academia is not academic either. This presents Lacan with the difficulty, which he acknowledges, of how to situate psychoanalytic work within a socio-epistemological scene, without falling under the shadow of academic labour.

In the third lesson of *Seminar XVII*, entitled 'Knowledge, a Means of Jouissance', Lacan noted that the very fact that he himself was speaking 'from the podium' carried with it 'a risk of error, an element of refraction, which means that some aspects of it will fall under the influence of the university discourse' (Lacan 1991 [1969–70]: 46). The form of academic speech is not primarily the issue here, but rather what one might call 'academic purpose' and the mediation of the master's will. Earlier in this lesson of the *Seminar*, Lacan mentioned that a person in Louvain (Anika Lemaire) 'has written a thesis on what they called, improperly perhaps, my work' (ibid.: 45) and that anyone with university training could not fail to reverse the meaning of his discourse in the very act of translating it. Lacan provided a concrete example of this process of the overturning of what he had said, as had occurred in 1960 at the hands of Jean Laplanche and Serge Leclaire. In an extensive report (Laplanche and Leclaire 1972 [1960]) that would subsequently gain notoriety for its theoretical astuteness, Laplanche and Leclaire replaced Lacan's statement, 'Language is the condition of the unconscious', with the assertion, 'The unconscious is the condition of language'—a revealing example of the academic insistence on defining the unconscious as an 'object of study'. Lacan went on to state: 'This thesis [by Anika Lemaire] retains its value nonetheless, its value as an example in itself, its value as example also by what it promotes to the level of distortion, in some way obligatory, of a translation into university discourse something that has its own laws (Lacan 1991 [1969–70]: 46). Lacan demonstrates a cruel, but logically impeccable twist here: an academic thesis on Lacan retains its value only as a symptom of the epistemological drive and its inability to encounter psycho-analysis. The academic can follow the master, but not the analyst. In his preface to Lemaire's book, Lacan put it even more bluntly: 'I saw a few members of this body [the university] being attracted by my pasture. I expected their votes. But they turned it into a schoolboy essay' (Lacan 1977a [1969]: xiii).

This presents the present-day commentator on Lacan with the unavoidable challenge of how to deal with Lacanian psychoanalysis as 'something that has its own laws', without straying into the aca-demic dissimulation of the law of the master. Lacan himself provides a clue. In the task of treating the laws of psychoanalysis, he does not take the unconscious as an object of study or research, but proceeds by accounting for his own position with respect to the existence of a world that has psychoanalysts in it. Accounting for the 'occurrence' of psychoanalysts carries with it the task of mapping out the con-tours of social life and the forms of social discourse, without thereby succumbing to the gravitational pull of sociology, ethnography or communication theory.

The importance of defining Lacanian discourse theory as a para-digm concerned with the social bond has been emphasized, *inter alia*, by Verhaeghe (1995) and Quackelbeen (1994), yet the even-handed treatment that both these authors give to each of the four discourses in turn, courts the danger of the kind of 'literal transmission' of his teachings that Lacan despised. Both Quackelbeen and Verhaeghe are keen to heap scorn on the fantasy of transparency that informs communications theory. Yet, strangely enough, Quackelbeen sees no problem with the incorporation of elements of a Lacanian theory of discourse into quasi-ethnographic methodologies such as action research, which is primarily concerned with the diagnosis and change of institutional difficulties and issues of practice. He even suggests that Lacan's discourse theory may provide a model for research into psychoanalysis itself: 'one can use it as a magnifying glass to question cases of "successful" and "unsuccessful" cures' (Quackelbeen 1994: 41). His 'suggestions for use' offer an ideal standpoint to the analyst/ethnographer, from where one can watch as the discourses of the master, the university, the hysteric and the analyst present themselves on a carousel within a given cultural, social or institutional example. Quackelbeen thus completely ignores, or fails to understand, Lacan's injunction that the four discourses are not abstractions to be applied to real situations, but are 'already inscribed in what functions as this reality' (Lacan 1991 [1969–70]: 13). The discourses are not to be used as keys to the meaning of speech, but as means of separating speech from meaning, thus isolating the reality of the unconscious from the real world as it is generally understood.[12]

Quackelbeen's epistemological optimism returns in Mark Bracher's remarks on applied psychoanalysis in his contribution to an edited volume on Lacan's discourse theory (Bracher *et al.* 1994). Bracher suggests that 'Lacan's theory can provide the means of determining the dialogical discursive structure of any given speech act, text or discourse, and on that basis, the means for gauging the psychological and (thereby) social-political functions it might serve for its producers, as well as the psychological and (thereby) social-political impact it might have on various types of receiving subjects' (Bracher 1994: 127). One feels entitled to ask, as with Quackelbeen: 'What position is this analysis accomplished from, and for what reason?' This is not to suggest that only analysts have the right to wield the four discourses, but rather that the ultimate reason for the separation of speech and meaning that they accomplish is provided by the analyst's discourse, which explicitly renounces its own rights to the determination of the structure of speech. In this sense, the four discourses are not free floating; they enter the clinical setting at a certain point in order to 'present' the unconscious in its relation to the contents of communicative speech. The four discourses usher in darkness and cast a shadow over knowledge. In an instructive passage from *Seminar XVII*, Lacan simultaneously introduces and obscures the infamous issue of 'the name of the father', but his words apply equally to the relationship of clarity and obscurity in the four discourses in general: 'I do not know whether you sense the import of this. It means that, if we say something in a certain way in this field, there will be another part of it which, by virtue of this saying itself, will become absolutely irreducible, completely obscure' (Lacan 1991 [1969–70]: 125). The discourses clearly articulate structure in order to effect the separation of speech and meaning, yet this same clarity of articulation produces and deepens obscurity, rather than dispelling it. The four discourses thus direct us to an increasingly tight spiral, linking clarity and brevity of articulation to that which is 'absolutely irreducible, completely obscure'.

This is, of course, the direction in which Lacan's later teaching developed, in one sense bearing out the accusations of those who said that he was deliberately and wilfully opaque. If one amends this accusation by adding that Lacan was also very clear about the irreducibility of the opaque and the obscure, one gets closer to the direction of his teaching. The lesson for anyone interested in extra-clinical applications of the four discourses is that they have an operative function, not an interpretative one. They reveal an unconscious that is present and at work, but they are not a means to describe and analyse the unconscious workings of discourse. Nor are they an ideal device, as Bracher would have it, for analysing the discursive structure of a speech act and its socio-political impact on a receiving subject. This distinction between what we have called an 'operative' and an 'interpretative' approach to the four discourses corresponds to the division between the traumatic loss of knowledge and the 'epistemological drive' to know more. The introduction of Lacanian discourse theory ought to have a limiting or circumscribing effect on knowledge itself. It should produce a better account of the irreducibly obscure and not be used as a means for producing a kind of hyper-academic knowledge out of a 'real world' situation.

None of the authors we have mentioned go as far in the straightforward application of the four discourses as Diane Rubenstein in her review essay 'The Four Discourses and the Four Volumes' (Rubenstein 1994). Rubenstein employs the four discourses as a labour-saving device, dispatching four volumes of Sage's 'Modernity and Political Thought' series in the following way: 'Lacan outlines four discursive positions in his Seminar XVII: L'Envers de la

Psychoanalyse [*sic*] . . . which are illustrated by the four volumes under review: the discourse of the master (Flathman), university (Dallmayr), hysteric (Connolly) and analyst (Schapiro)' (Rubenstein 1994: 1122).[13] Rubenstein's essay is simply the logical outcome of a general approach that turns the formulae of the four discourses into machines for generating knowledge, a universal key or a diagnostic 'kit'. Of the authors mentioned above, only Verhaeghe goes far enough in introducing the worm of doubt into his interpretation of the four discourses: 'In my introduction, I stressed the usefulness of this theory. Its formal character enables the theory to embrace many different particular instances. Nevertheless, in my experience, the greatest danger is that of reducing each discourse to one concrete implementation' (Verhaeghe 1995: 98). Verhaeghe remarks that any unitary application of the discourses is *a fortiori* a reduction, and warns of the danger of assuming, for example, that the discourse of the hysteric is always adopted by a hysterical subject.

If we turn our attention away from an idealist standpoint on the four discourses and proceed to examine, as did Lacan, the world in which psychoanalysts have come to exist, a radically different picture presents itself. Rather than being discernible simply as controlling elements of speech within a subject, an institution or a social bond, the four discourses can be seen to exist in a hegemonic or hierarchical relationship. This relationship is determined by the division between truth as cause of speech, and truth as an effect of meaning. This division creates an invisible wall that runs across each of the four discourses in turn.

One reason that we have laid such stress on the relationship of the master and the analyst is that it requires an effort to disentangle the relationship of these two discourses from the manner in which the master's discourse is secreted within, and occluded by, the discourse of the university. In *Seminar XVII*, Lacan illustrates this by borrowing the Napoleonic motto that 'every soldier carries a marshall's baton in his knapsack': 'The more unworthy you are . . . the better off you are. That really clarifies the recent reform of the University, for instance. Everyone, credit units—to have the makings of a culture, of a hell of a marshall, in your rucksack, plus some medals besides, as at an agricultural show, that when pinned on you will make you what people dare call masters' (Lacan 1991 [1969–70]: 212). The master signifier of the baton, hidden in the knapsack, can now only be discursively realized in a mediated form through the culture industries, with their rationalized and categorized desires expressed in sociological mores. To paraphrase Adorno, we could say that to speak of culture is contrary to culture, because it is to speak the language of the master. On the other hand, this same discourse of the master is nothing but a set of rationalizations, concealing what Lacan refers to as the secret shame of the master, his fundamental impotence. In contemporary Western societies, this hidden shame is discernible in the political symptoms and sympathies of trainee bureaucrats and cultural administrators who, at this early stage of their careers, tend to identify with the poor and downtrodden. This occlusion of the nexus of shame and mastery within a web of rationalizations and misidentifications also presents difficulties for the hysteric's discourse. The hysteric's address to the master is lost in a fog of received ideas and liberal popular opinion, generated by the educated classes and disseminated by the mass media. The dissent of the hysteric and the revolution of the analyst are sidelined by the manner in which the 'direct rule' of the social bond is replaced by the bureaucratic administration of short-term socio-political contracts and cultural service agreements. Difference, antagonism and the contours of power disappear in the fog of the knowledge economy. This situation produces academicized rulers and hystericized academics, and it condemns the discourse of the analyst to the margins of society. Here, the analyst is faced with three equally unwelcome options: to become an administrator of therapeutic remedies, to join the legions of hystericized academics, or to disappear.

Impossibility and impotence

One answer to this discursive hegemony and aggregation of forces is to highlight the structural importance of the functions of impossibility (*impossibilité*) and impotence (*impuissance*) in the four discourses. This emphasis takes us back to the model of a 'traumatic epistemology' with which we opened this chapter, insofar as it reveals the joints and seams within discourse, and the manner in which the discourses of the master, the university and the hysteric cement a relationship between *connaissance* and *savoir* by avoiding the implications of 'knowledge as a means of jouissance'. Two of the four discourses, those of the master and the university, stave off or prevent a moment of traumatic collapse. Another of the discourses, that of the hysteric, speaks from the place of confusion and disorder, yet reconstructs the master as an idol who is asked to provide an answer to the perennial question 'who am I?' Only the remaining discourse, that of the analyst, is satisfied with the condition of traumatic disorder, seeing it as a place to begin, rather than as a terminal point. The analyst's speech, precisely because it does not aim at truth, allows truth to assume a causal or initiating role for the analysand.

The first step towards understanding the role of impossibility and impotence in the four discourses is to grasp the paradox that the truth both is and is not spoken. The truth speaks, it drives and structures speech, but for that very reason the truth cannot take the form of a metalinguistic statement of 'the truth about the truth'. The function of truth here is causal. It sets discourse in motion through the action of the signifier on the body and the division of the field of thought. The unconscious truth that drives discourse and the conscious truth that is striven for initiate the shifting movements from one discourse to another. Conscious thought escapes from its causal determinations by altering its course from a discourse of mastery to one of rationalization, or from rationalization to hysterical dissidence. The four discourses thus represent four possible positions regarding the relationship between truth as an unconscious cause and truth as a consciously achieved effect. The manner in which the truth as cause sets discourse in motion is figured in the four relationships of truth, agency, Other and product within each discourse, which are always positioned in the same way:

$$\uparrow \quad \frac{\text{agency}}{\text{truth}} \quad \overset{\rightarrow}{/\!/} \quad \frac{\text{Other}}{\text{product}} \quad \downarrow$$

The relationship agency → Other represents the ideal of conscious speech, in which a speaker communicates with a receiver and produces a result. The wild card in this arrangement is the presence of truth as discursive cause at the bottom left-hand side of the diagram. The fact that truth as cause is inassimilable into the relationship agency → Other → product leads Lacan to posit two levels of communicative disjunction within his theory of discourse, as follows:

impossibility

$$\uparrow \quad \frac{\text{agency}}{\text{truth}} \quad \overset{\rightarrow}{/\!/} \quad \frac{\text{Other}}{\text{product}} \quad \downarrow$$

impotence

The upper disjunction, that of impossibility, concerns the failure of a metalanguage, the failure to 'tell the truth about truth'. The lower disjunction, that of impotence (sometimes called 'inability') takes us still further from the 'truth about truth', since it is evident that the *product* of the agent's speech, as delivered by the Other, is double-barred from access to the truth as *cause* of the agent's speech. Discourse is thus a one-way street, leading from the action of the signifier to the endless circuits of desire-in-language that it generates. The upper and lower levels of the diagram therefore posit an interpretation shadowed by its negation or, to put this another way, the relationship between *connaisance* and *savoir* is fundamentally attended by the demon of jouissance. Even before the staging points of the master, the university, the analyst and the hysteric have been introduced, we already have the two basic elements of Lacanian epistemology here, namely a desire to know (the epistemological drive) and a certain failure of knowledge, both conjoined in the speaking body as initiated by the signifier.

What is the foundation, then, of the epistemological drive, and the establishment of the modern, technocratic master? Correspondingly, what is the place of the unconscious in a technocracy? To address these questions, it is worth comparing the place of S_2 (unconscious knowledge, *savoir*), within the discourse of the master and that of the university in order to see how it maintains the primary alienation of truth as cause, from truth as a discursive product. In the two diagrams on the next page, we have highlighted the position of knowledge, S_2, within these two formulas.

The master signifier, S_1, occupies the position of agency in the master's discourse, but in the university discourse it takes the role of the hidden truth. Knowledge, S_2, is situated in the 'passive' place of the Other in the master's discourse, but assumes the site of agency in the university discourse. In the latter discourse, these machinations have the effect of expelling the (absent) subject of the unconscious, $, from the scene, and of constructing a hygienic barrier between $ and S_1, which limits the threat posed by $ in the place of truth in the master's discourse. The threat posed by the subject of the unconscious to the master concerns the revelation of the master's fundamental impotence, his self-undermining dependence on the Other to establish a sense of meaning. The discourse of the university is therefore a safeguard, a 'castling' manoeuvre; the master signifier is stowed away in the knapsack of the soldier/bureaucrat who rationalizes the exercise of power. Yet, most importantly, in the

Discourse of the master

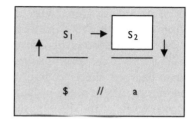

Discourse of the university

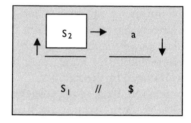

transition from the master discourse to that of the university, something also happens to knowledge, inasmuch as it has been abstracted from the other and delivered back to the agency:

> [I]n the initial status of the discourse of the master, knowledge is on the side of the slave. . . . [W]hat happens between the discourse of the classical master and that of the modern master, which is called capitalist, is a modification in the place of knowledge. . . . The fact that the all-knowledge [*tout-savoir*] has moved into the place of the master is something that, far from throwing light on it, obscures a bit more what is in question, namely, truth. Where does it come from, the fact that there is a master's signifier in this place? For that is well and truly the S_2 of the master, revealing the bare bones of how things are in the new tyranny of knowledge.
>
> (Lacan 1991 [1969–70]: 34–35)

In the structure of the master's discourse, the Other (or the slave, according to Lacan's Hegelian formulation) is dispossessed of knowledge, just as the worker in a capitalist economy is dispossessed of his labour. In the university discourse, 'the new tyranny of knowledge' into which mastery regresses and dissimulates itself, rationalizes these same products in an attempt to establish control over human resources, pleasures and desires. The slave is thus exploited twice, once as a member of the underclass and again as a 'student', an underclass subject to the tyranny of rationalization. Nowadays, a student is as likely to be someone attending benefit agencies, receiving computer training, and adopting the psycho-bureaucratic discourse of the television soap opera—'Let's talk it out!'—as someone paying for a higher degree of 'finish' at a university. One can sum this up by saying that the discourse of the university aims to make products (outputs, students) that also 'speak product' and thus intellectualize their alienation. As we suggested earlier, this phenomenon is by no means confined to actual universities—modern technocratic governments make students of all their citizens, without exception. This is another reason why the four discourses must be seen as a means of shutting down and foreclosing the possibilities of further knowledge, rather than opening them up for extra-psychological and supra-sociological adventurism. The fatal flaw of the discourse of the university is that its product, \$, the (absent) subject of the unconscious, merely reveals the vanity of the attempt to rationalize and streamline the production of human resources. As Verhaeghe puts it: '[T]he product of this discourse is an ever-increased division of the subject; the more knowledge one uses to reach for the object [object *a*] the more one becomes divided between signifiers, and the further one gets away from home, that is from the true cause of desire' (Verhaeghe 1995: 95).

The failure of the university discourse and its inevitable return to desire also indicate the trauma and the ultimate 'fall' of philosophy. In *Seminar XVII*, Lacan first of all traces the complicity of philosophy with mastery through a reading of Aristotle's *Politics*, in which, he argues, the slave's 'know-how' (his support of everyday life) is colonized by philosophy in the service of the master: 'The function of the episteme in so far as it is specified as transmissible knowledge . . . is, entirely, still borrowed from the techniques of the craftsman, that is to say of serfs. It is a matter of extracting its essence so that this knowledge becomes the master's knowledge. . . . Philosophy in its historical function is this extraction, this betrayal I would almost say, of the slave's knowledge, so as to obtain its transmutation as master's knowledge' (Lacan 1991 [1969–70]: 21–22). The advancement of the philosopher through the dispossession of the slave meets a barrier with the emergence of the 'subject of science'. The division between the action of the signifier and the effort of signification/communication, which, according to Lacan, was first introduced by Descartes, makes philosophy and nonsense interchangeable, because the signifying chain can generate multiple discourses, from the erudite to the foolish, quite independently of the body it colonizes. The psychoanalyst, who invites the analysand to say anything she wishes, accepts the reality of this division. The philosopher, who is locked into the drive for abstract knowledge, cannot. Lacan uses the example of Wittgenstein's discourse, a man possessed by a *férocité psychotique* (Lacan 1991 [1969–70]: 69) to illustrate the trauma of the philosopher whose work comes to grief on the distinction between the signifier and signification. He initially praises Wittgenstein for arguing that propositional statements structure and dispose their contents: '[A]n assertion announces itself as truth. . . . This fact, that "it is daylight", is only a fact by virtue of its being said' (Lacan 1991 [1969–70]: 41). What Wittgenstein cannot admit, however, is any divorce of proposition and fact, in other words any further atomization of knowledge that would create a division between an autonomous chain of signifiers and the world to which they refer. Wittgenstein, like all philosophers, 'wants to save the truth' (ibid.: 71) and, whilst admitting the notion of a world constructed by language, draws back from the radically disarticulated scene offered by Lacanian *lalangue* ('llanguage').

By contrast, the 'fall of knowledge' that the Lacanian epistemology aims at changes the historical trajectory that runs from the slave to the philosopher, by using 'know-how' as a means to disarticulate and dispossess abstract knowledge. It does so in the name of the possibilities introduced by the subject of science, as they are formalized in the structure of the four discourses. In this chapter we have argued that the four discourses must be seen as part of an operation conducted on knowledge which divides the signifier from signification. Furthermore, 'the signifier is stupid', and not only does the analyst encounter 'a stupid of signifiers' in the speech of the analysand but this same stupidity of the signifier is the very basis of his own discourse. This is the source of the 'horror' Lacan refers to in 'Science and Truth', namely, that the unconscious speech of 'I, the truth, am speaking' is as reckless, obdurate and inchoate as our own words are reasonable, rational and articulate. This point returns in *Seminar XVII*: 'Knowledge—I think I have insisted upon it sufficiently to get it into your head—knowledge is a thing that says

itself, that is said. Well then, the knowledge that speaks on its own—
that's the unconscious' (ibid.: 80).

The only epistemology adequate to this knowledge is an epistemology that encounters the horror of this 'speaking truth' head
on, as well as the traumas of the disarticulation of knowledge and
the loss of meaning that it introduces. A besetting problem of commentary on Lacan is that the danger of dismemberment and loss is
never worked through within the structure of the commentary, so
that the four discourses are treated as interpretative options, rather
than as four contingent solutions to the intrinsic collapse of the
communicative act into stupidity, non-knowledge and the circuits of
desire.

Chapter 6

Concluding the time for comprehending: the epistemological reversal of the knowledge at risk

> Life is impoverished, it loses in interest, when the highest stake in the game of living, life itself, may not be risked. . . . Thus the tendency to exclude death from our calculations in life brings in its train many other renunciations and exclusions.
>
> Sigmund Freud, 'Thoughts for the Times on War and Death', 290–291

> 'If it is any point requiring reflection,' observed Dupin, as he forbore to enkindle the wick, 'we shall examine it to better purpose in the dark.'
>
> Edgar Allan Poe, 'The Purloined Letter', 320

Feet for thought

In the previous chapter, we introduced two key elements of a psychoanalytic epistemology: the desire to know and the failure of knowledge. They are both at work in the operation of discourse, which simultaneously sustains the search for self-certainty and bears a desire that propels this search towards a moment of failure. In his 'Rome Discourse' of 1953, Lacan already expressed this inevitable failure, with regard to the dynamics of the communicative act within the psychoanalytic process: 'For in the work he [the subject, the analysand] does to reconstruct it [his being] *for another*, he encounters anew the fundamental alienation that made him construct it *like another*, and that has always destined it to be taken away from him *by another*' (Lacan 2002a [1953]: 42). The unconscious is the place occupied by the Other in our speech, not as a particular person who confronts us, but as 'the form of thought whose ontological status is not that of thought' (Žižek 1989: 19), a thought that is 'out of our mind'. For this reason, the categories that psychoanalysis has employed to account for this 'other thought' are neither those of personality psychology, nor those of individual psychology. Instead, psychoanalysis has consistently referred to myth, religion, jokes, kinship, social taboos and, more recently, mass entertainment and popular culture—things that are also the stuff our dreams are made of.

It is unfortunate that this preoccupation with 'thought out of mind' has been taken to mean that psychoanalysis offers a deterministic view of mental life, of the 'my mother made me a homosexual' variety. To avoid this misconception, it should be emphasized again that the subject of psychoanalysis is neither the mind nor the social world, but speech. In the environs of speech, the categories of mind, family, history and society all come into play, yet they are strictly operative as singular linguistic acts. One of the purposes of Lacan's 'return to Freud', as signalled by the psychoanalytic manifesto of the 'Rome Discourse', was precisely to oppose the determination of mind *by* discourse, through the foregrounding of a specific freedom available in the risking of mind *within* discourse. This risk depends on the abandonment of self-certainty and a paradoxical 'reliance' on the failure of the communicative act. The failure of communication indicates, firstly, the place that the Other occupies in our speech, and, secondly, the absence of a 'higher certainty' in this Other, of the kind that an analysand may expect from an analyst, or that the figurative homosexual may find in his mother. Only by abandoning the certainty of oneself and the certainty of the Other simultaneously, can the self be revealed as a discursive subject in the psychoanalytic scenario.

In psychoanalysis, the subject's 'I' is no longer 'in two minds' about its situation. Rather, the 'I' is in play within a situation where thought is real and where interpretation assumes an ethical and an effective dimension. This is, of course, very far removed from any hippy-ish 'forget your mind and be free' ideal, which assumes the existence of mind as a possession to be foregone, in a quasi-Franciscan manner. As we outlined in the previous chapter, the important distinction for Lacan is between knowledge that is acquired and that has mind as its unit of value, and knowledge that 'costs'. The latter form of knowledge is the terminus of a work of speech (the psychoanalytic labour), and not a unit of value that is traded solipsistically within speech ('my mind and I'). Its rhetorical form is encountered in the apparent epistemological absurdity that 'I, the truth, am speaking'.

The scandalous hubris of this statement is perhaps best understood by matching it with Lacan's equally notorious critique of cognitive psychology: 'We think we think with our brains; personally, I think with my feet. That's the only way I really come into contact with anything solid. I do occasionally think with my forehead, when I bang into something. But I've seen enough electroencephalograms to know there's not the slightest trace of a thought in the brain' (quoted in Roudinesco 1997 [1993]: 378–379).

Taken together, these two statements define unconscious thought as something that is at once more objective and less protean than the favoured image of the conscious mind. 'Thinking with one's feet', rather like thinking on one's feet, also refers to a cognition that is shaped by the circumstances pertaining to particular economies and environments of thought. This casting out of mind and the consequent encounter with the reality of unconscious thought does not concur with the static image of the mind/brain nexus offered by the electroencephalogram. At the core of this risking of mind in unconscious thought is the epistemological reversal that the title of this chapter presents. Under what circumstances and for what reasons could the act of knowing itself come up for judgement? And why on earth would scholarship, defined as a time set aside for comprehension and the development of the mind, wish to deny itself this luxury, and hasten to conclude its own operations?

A philosophical psychoid

The 'character type' of the philosopher is the constitutional embodiment of the self-reflecting and self-perfecting mind that feeds on the interrogation of the world of things. At the beginning of the twentieth century, a challenge to this self-image of the philosopher was offered by Freud's 'first topography', with its strict separation of the unconscious from consciousness and the preconscious.[1] In a famous passage from *The Ego and the Id* (Freud 1923b), Freud looks back on the difficulties that this basic distinction has presented for philosophical commentators. The source of this difficulty is the obstacle that the Freudian unconscious presents to a constitutive model of the mind. The roles of the unconscious and the preconscious had begun to be settled within models of the mind long before Freud invented psychoanalysis and they were generally designated as 'psychoid' stages of the fully conscious mind. Consciousness was thus perceived as a whole and properly psychical entity, with the unconscious as its primary (pre- or proto-psychical) stratum. The radical novelty of the Freudian model concerns its representation of the unconscious as an agency that is also fully psychical. It was Freud who introduced for the first time in history the concept of a thinking unconscious, and this idea challenged existing notions of an unconscious that is merely 'thought-like'.

The distinction is made clear as early as *The Interpretation of Dreams* (Freud 1900a), in which Freud introduces a division within the single psychological category of the unconscious, resolving it into a preconscious (*Pcs.*) that is admissible to consciousness, and an unconscious (*Ucs.*) that is constitutively inadmissible (Freud 1900a: 14–15). In *The Ego and the Id*, Freud unpacks some of the implications of this distinction for philosophical reasoning:

> The *Pcs.* is presumably a great deal closer to the *Cs.* [consciousness] than is the *Ucs.*, and since we have called the *Ucs.* psychical we shall with even less hesitation call the latent *Pcs.* psychical. But why do we not rather, instead of this, remain in agreement with the philosophers and, in a consistent way, distinguish the *Pcs.* as well as the *Ucs.* from the conscious psychical? The philosophers would then propose that the *Pcs.* and the *Ucs.* should be described as two species or stages of the 'psychoid', and harmony would be established. But endless difficulties in exposition would follow; and the one important fact, that these two kinds of 'psychoid' coincide in almost every other respect with what is admittedly psychical, would be forced into the background in the interests of a prejudice dating from a period in which these psychoids, or the most important part of them, were still unknown.
>
> (Freud 1923b: 15)

This Freudian paradigm, through which the psychical is first divided into conscious and unconscious elements, and in which the unconscious is subsequently accounted for by using a mixture of psychological, familial, mythical and anthropological categories, continues to trouble those who seek to reconcile psychoanalytic discourse with a philosophy of mind. In an essay that seeks to demonstrate a close similarity between Freudian and Kantian thought, Andrew Brook has remarked that Freud's rejection of philosophy in *The Ego and the Id* must be seen as 'surpassingly strange', in light of the popularization of a philosophy of the unconscious in the nineteenth century by von Hartmann and others (von Hartmann 1931 [1869]; Brook 2003). For Brook, the Freudian unconscious developed out of a pre-existing philosophy of the unconscious formulated by Schopenhauer, and the structures of the mind laid down by Kant: 'Freud himself saw his Superego as closely related to Kant's categorical imperative. As he once put it, "Kant's categorical imperative is . . . the direct heir of the Oedipus complex" ' (Brook 2003: 25). Brook completely misses the tenor of Freud's statement, here, in which it is suggested that the kind of philosophical deliberation in which one 'makes up one's mind' on an ethical issue is concurrent with the operation of a social bond. Freud is very clear on this point and insisted on it until the end of his life. In the posthumously published essay 'Some Elementary Lessons in Psychoanalysis' (Freud 1940b [1938]), he is still reminding his readers of what had been introduced in *The Interpretation of Dreams*, namely, that the equation of the mental and the conscious, as favoured by philosophers, has a decontextualizing effect, and is unable to encompass the contiguity between the psyche and the world (ibid.: 283). Freud also points out that this equation prevents any philosophical approach to the symptom, which is assumed to be caused by vaguely defined reciprocal relations between the body and the mind, precisely because the symptom presents difficulties for the equation of mind and consciousness. Freudianism therefore regards the symptom very differently, notably as the embodied evidence of a traumatic split between unconscious 'thinking' and conscious 'thoughts', a split that can be made bearable only by a certain realignment of consciousness. On these terms, the mind itself can be described as a symptom, the sign of a failed interpretation of relations between the psyche and the world.

As a result, it must be assumed that when Freud names the Oedipus complex as the ancestor of the categorical imperative, he is not claiming any 'close relationship' between psychoanalysis and philosophy. Instead, he is asserting the reality of thought across two different registers—one *of* the self and one *for* the Other. Freud more or less made the same point in *Totem and Taboo*, when he compared the nature of taboo to Kant's categorical imperative, 'which operates in a compulsive fashion and rejects any conscious motives' (Freud 1912–1913a: xiv). The overlap Freud observes, here, between a given social structure and a willed mental activity works to the detriment of any 'philosophy of the unconscious' that would define the unconscious as a property of mind. To this day, critics of psychoanalysis circumvent this problem by treating philosophy and psychoanalysis as if they were two academic disciplines contesting a single field of enquiry. Mikkel Borch-Jacobsen, for example, believes that 'psychoanalysis needs philosophers to help extirpate itself *from itself*, from this dubious philosophy of the unconscious we call "psychoanalysis"' (Borch-Jacobsen 1997: 211). He is also prepared to state that Lacan's rejection of philosophy was a 'denial', on the dubious grounds that nobody was more rigorously Cartesian than Lacan. Borch-Jacobsen wishes that psychoanalysis would either get itself included in philosophy to save its reputation, or realize that it was somehow always already there. Lacan, however, treats Descartes in much the same way that Freud treated Kant, as a means to explain a distinction between mind and thought which is encountered in the field of speech and discourse and which cannot be realized as philosophy.

The scandal is not that psychoanalysis sets itself up as a substitute for philosophy or as a rival to it. Much more radically, the very existence of psychoanalytic practice is the negation of a philosophy of mind. This may account for the 'dead but alive' paradox that haunts anti-psychoanalytic debates, which often picture Freudianism as a corpse that has been put to death by the progress of science and rationalism, but which nonetheless continues to corrupt academic and social life. In his richly immoderate book *Decline and Fall of the Freudian Empire*, the renowned psychologist H.J. Eysenck was at once able to claim that psychoanalysis was 'on the way down', yet making a last stand in South America, and to blame it for 'permissiveness, sexual promiscuity, decline of old-fashioned values . . . [and] ethical nihilism' (Eysenck 1985: 203). Either psychoanalysis falls or civilization does. *Decline and Fall of the Freudian Empire* is therefore quite a revealing text. It deals in essence with the tragic vicissitudes of the serious academic mind and with an attempt to master the place of the discursive Other. Eysenck's discourse is suffused with images of decline, disorder and corruption that trouble his psychological certainties and hard-won mental discipline. Even the extinction of the very last South American psychoanalyst could not have delivered him from this torment.

More recent critiques of psychoanalysis continue to circulate around a set of paradoxes generated by Freud's original divisions of unconscious, preconcious and conscious. In their recent collection of papers entitled *Psychoanalytic Knowledge*, Man Cheung Chung and Colin Feltham declare their interest in rescuing fragments of the psychoanalytic project for inclusion in contemporary debates in philosophy, psychology and neuroscience (Cheung Chung and Feltham 2003). The Other within speech is necessarily excluded from this mission, but familiar problems recur for the editors and contributors when 'Freud the neuroscientist' and 'Freud the philosopher' turn out to be fatally limited by 'the crude and misleading assumptions built in to ordinary language' (Livingstone Smith 2003: 70). The deadlock between philosophy and psychoanalysis, which Freud cheerfully described in *The Ego and the Id*, still stands and continues to inform the widespread perception among academics that psychoanalysis cannot be built on, improved or developed in a way that would make it useful to other disciplines.[2] In the following section of this chapter, we will provide an outline of how Lacanian psychoanalysis offers a contrasting approach which requires the abandonment of mind as a unit of epistemological value, and in which knowledge is constructed on risk and ambiguity, rather than on certainty.

Truth's conquering initiative

In Freudian theory, the philosopher is confronted with a fully psychical unconscious which results from an interplay of objective and subjective elements of reasoning. The unconscious thinks, but without deliberation or obvious evidence of mentation. It does not reflect, nor is it a reflex. For Lacan, unconscious thought is the field in which 'I', 'you', 'them' and 'us' are put into play by an act of speech. Lacan provided a well-known illustration of this principle in his essay on the 'prisoner's sophism' (Lacan 1988a [1945]).[3] A prison governor puts three convicts to the test by asking each to decide which disc, of a total set of three white and two black discs, he will be wearing between his shoulders. The prisoners are not allowed to converse or to mirror themselves. The first to guess correctly the colour of his disc and to provide an adequate explanation for his conclusion will be set free. The prison governor applies a white disc to each of the three prisoners, so that each of the three sees two white discs when looking at his fellow inmates. Each then works on the assumption that if one of the other two convicts were to see a black and a white disc in his field of vision, he would reason that if he himself were black, the remaining bearer of a white disc would already have left. Technically, the three convicts are thus in exactly the same position and if they follow the same type of deliberation they are bound to make a move at the same time, concluding 'I am white'. Of course, the certainty with which this conclusion is formulated cannot be guaranteed until the prison governor validates the statement as truthful, since the conclusion is purely based on the observation and interpretation of the other's hesitation.

In Lacan's interpretation, the 'moment of concluding' ('I am white') encloses two other temporal categories, an initial 'instant of the glance' (the observation of the other convicts' discs) and a 'time for comprehending' (the reasoning necessary for deciding whether one carries a black or a white disc). The longer the 'time for comprehending', the more one may be able to understand the nature of the situation, yet the more one runs the risk of a rival taking advantage of one's hesitation to draw a conclusion and to make a move. Hence, in order to win, it is crucial to ensure that one's own 'time for comprehending' is somehow shorter than that of the others or, in other words, to limit the time lapse between the 'instant of the glance' and the 'time for comprehending', regardless of the (lack of) certainty on which one's conclusion is based. Lacan argues that the 'aim of the game' is to 'reduce the moment of concluding the time for comprehending so as to last but the instant of the glance' (ibid.: 18).

Lacan's interest in this sophism turns on a dialectical relationship between the factors of the objective, the subjective, and the timely intervention of 'truth's conquering initiative', in which only the act of concluding can produce definitive knowledge and understanding, yet without certainty. Lacan identifies two kinds of logic at work within the sophism. The first works by a hypothesis concerning a set of transitive subjects A, B and C in which A, the subject who concludes, is constantly suspended. In the sophism, an answer to the question, 'Objectively speaking, who am I?' is permanently out of reach. Instead, the truth is made available only through another, assertive logic that 'takes on' the vacillating, transitive subjects of hypothetical reasoning. This second assertive logic puts the 'I' in play within a moment of concluding ('I am white') that takes account of *a failure to conclude* produced by the hypothetical reasoning about the positions of players A, B and C: 'Should he allow himself to be beaten to this conclusion by his counterparts, he will no longer be able to determine whether he is black or not. Having surpassed the *time for comprehending the moment of concluding*, it is *the moment of concluding the time for comprehending*' (Lacan 1988a [1945]: 12). Not only must the victorious subject of this sophism begin by accounting for the deliberations of the Other; the only way he can aim at truth is by 'stepping out' of the prison yard of deliberation entirely. The logical conclusion here is that logic must be concluded and that deliberation must stop if one cares at all about one's freedom. There is no objective answer to the question, 'Who am I?', but the truth speaks, nonetheless: 'I am white'. Lacan is at pains to point out that this 'subjective assertion' is 'the essential logical form (rather than what is called the existential form) of the psychological I' (ibid.: 14). The Oedipal subject that originally emerged from fruitless speculation about 'who is who' in the familial hierarchy thus acquires the status of a player within the drama of subjective freedom. Of course, becoming a player also means assuming the generational and social scripts and the signifying chains in which they are embedded.

If the first movement of assertive logic must be assumed personally, this same self-assertion is also what compels collective agreement. The prisoner's sophism is thus another way of addressing Freud's statement that Kant's categorical imperative is the direct heir of the Oedipus complex, since, as Lacan puts it, 'the truth of all depends upon the rigor of each' (ibid.: 18). Rigour does not mean the application of the trained mind, but rather the opposite: it is a question of identifying how and at what point unconscious thought works to conclude comprehension, and to frustrate the unity of mind and objective truth. It does so in the name of a collectively valid judgement from which the judgement of the individual mind is excluded. In Lacan's view, the precipitation of a subjective 'moment for concluding' the work of comprehension is also the moment of the greatest possible objectivity. The termination of a questioning process through the subjective (and fundamentally uncertain) assertion 'I am white' objectifies a process of abstract reasoning by introducing time as the dominant factor.

Lacan's work on the sophism foreshadows his later discussion of the desire to know and the fall of knowledge in *Seminar XVII*. It also sheds light on his insistence on the value of the short session, as a principle facilitating and accelerating the moment for concluding, notwithstanding Roudinesco's view of Lacan as the violent 'terminator' of the analysand's speech (Roudinesco 1997 [1993]: 390–397).[4] For the purposes of our own argument, we want to stress how the time factor in the prisoner's sophism, and especially the factor of haste, discloses a crucial interplay between knowledge and non-knowledge. 'Haste in logic', as it cuts through deliberation, precipitates the truth of desire at the root of abstract reasoning. In the sophism, desire enters the scene because of an epistemological failure, and is disclosed in a statement that bears both individual and collective truth. This is yet another way of defining unconscious thought. The deliberative mind has been recast as the Lacanian subject, bound by a causal truth which always arrives 'on time' in order to upset reflection on the question, 'Who am I?'

Lacan elaborated on this theme in his various commentaries on Edgar Allan Poe's story 'The Purloined Letter' (Poe 1988: [1844]), in which a truth is present and in plain sight yet for that very reason impossible to approach through abstract reasoning (Lacan 1972 [1956]). 'The Purloined Letter' also contains an excursus on the guessing game of 'even and odd', in which a schoolboy fools his companions by basing all his decisions for 'odd' or 'even' on those already taken by his rivals. Stanley Cavell has been quite content to describe this game as 'a contested play of mind-reading' (Cavell 1988 [1986]: 168), yet it would be much more accurate to say that the game of even and odd reveals that a true choice occurs 'in the light of the Other' and through a deliberate occultation of the power of one's own mind. The schoolboy in the game of even and odd does not 'read minds'; rather, he allows the mind of another to become the ground for his own. By contrast, the 'character type' of the policeman in 'The Purloined Letter' is accorded a scrupulous, but ultimately useless, dedication to method: 'They have no variation of principle in their investigations; at best, when urged by some unusual emergency—by some extraordinary reward—they extend or exaggerate their old modes of *practice*, without touching their principles. . . . What is all this boring, and probing, and sounding, and scrutinizing with the microscope, and dividing the surface of the building into registered square inches—what is it all but an exaggeration *of the application* of the one principle or set of principles of search . . . to which the Prefect, in the long routine of his duty, has been accustomed?' (Poe 1988 [1844]: 327).

In having recourse to his paradoxical 'principle of concealment' for hiding the incriminating letter, Minister D—— had taken account of the mental discipline of police work, but the reverse had not occurred. As Lacan argues, the difference is that which exists between the domain of exactitude and the register of truth (Lacan 1972 [1956]: 49), in which the letter can be regarded by the police as missing or 'out of place', but as perfectly placed by the person who conceals it. As in the prisoner's sophism, a mode of abstract reasoning works to keep a 'moment of concluding' in permanent suspension, as the epistemological drive of police work produces an accumulation of knowledge without the possibility of resolution. Furthermore, an approach to the truth occurs only after a renunciation of understanding, which is made in favour of this truth. The whole notion of activity and agency is shifted from the inner workings of a mind towards an action that is taken *against* its integrity. The 'insult to the intelligence' that is accomplished by hiding the purloined letter in plain view is the opposite of a passive accommodation of mind to society, or a simple determination of the human by discourse. Postmodern argot has been more than willing to situate 'the cultivated mind' within a socio-cultural matrix, but this nexus of self and society is not Lacan's business. In the prisoner's sophism, or the game of even and odd, success is not achieved by following a set of codes and rules, substituting one discourse or discipline for another, or by 'thinking outside the box'. Success is instead ensured in a 'game beneath the game', in which the mind is wagered against the goal of subjective truth, where what is true for one is also objectively true for all.[5] The darkness or 'death' of the mind becomes the light of the subject, through an act that aims at truth.

Two important aspects of the act that aims at truth are its absence of conscious will and its situation at a place of non-knowledge, where one discourse shifts into another. In his discussion of the death drive in *Seminar VII*, on 'The Ethics of Psychoanalysis' (Lacan 1992 [1959–60]), Lacan rejects a philosophical approach to the unconscious mind when he notes that the Freudian death drive is not comparable to the Schopenhauerian 'will' (ibid.: 212). In so doing, he distances himself from the casual assumption of philosophical precedence that still informs definitive statements such as 'the Schopenhaurian will was the ancestor to the Freudian id' (Taylor 1989: 446). The death drive is not self-will, but a will that challenges the integrity of the self. In Freudian terms, it is also dependent on the paradoxical recognition of unconscious thought as both fully psychical and fundamentally impersonal. Lacan captures both of these elements in his concept of a signifying chain, which can be set against the notion that mind is a unit of measure for personal worth. The psychoanalytic situation offers a different kind of measure, in which 'something . . . is presented as a measure of our action' (Lacan 1992 [1959–60]: 311). In other words, psychoanalysis gives us a chance to examine how far desire takes on an *effective*, an *ethical* and an *objective* significance in the unconscious. This objective significance is not available in the virtual reality of the mind and appears in the symptom only as an augury or 'hieroglyph' of the truth. The mind is thus a refuge or bolt-hole that excludes the one thing that makes life worth living, namely, thought that assumes the status of an act.

How does this shift in measure take place? In his reappraisal of the four discourses in *Seminar XX*, Lacan suggests that 'there is some emergence of analytic discourse with each shift from one discourse to another' (Lacan 1998b [1972–73]: 16). In other words, the discourse of the analyst introduces the possibility that a new bond can be forged between the individual and the collective, by means of an alteration in the positions that are currently held in discourse. This requires the analyst herself to stand at an unusual crossroads between knowledge and truth. As we pointed out in Chapter 1, Lacan advocated that the analyst employ *docta ignorantia* to forestall the production of knowledge as spurious information concerning the state of the analysand's mind. This refusal on the part of the analyst to identify with 'the supposed subject of knowing' allows the analysand to 'aim at truth' in his own discourse as something that is active, convulsive and collectively significant, but not historically determined or set in stone.

As we outlined in our previous chapter, the discourse of the analyst is the only one of the four discourses that renounces its claim on the determination of meaning:

Discourse of the analyst

$$\frac{a}{S_2} \quad \overset{\rightarrow}{/\!/} \quad \frac{\$}{S_1}$$

Far from revealing that the human being is a function of discourse, the discourse of the analyst reveals that discourse (about human beings or anything else for that matter) is a function of truth. The role of the analyst, who here occupies a transitional position as object cause (the object *a*) of the analysand's desire, is to allow the analysand to commit subjectively to the objective character of his own speech, and the manner in which it shapes and organizes his relationships with others. The analysand does this by confronting his own speech as an enigma, a thought from elsewhere that is bound up with unrealized desire, and by opening up the possibility of a reconfiguration. For this to occur, the knowledge of the analyst, concealed in riddles, proverbs and oracular statements, should never appear as the truth of the analysand. The analysand's question 'Who am I?' can then be replaced by the statement, 'I am known . . . in the precipitation of truth's conquering initiative'. The analyst as agent and object cause of desire is no mind-reader, nor is the analysand. Rather the analysand allows the analyst to lose her status as the great mind of his imagination and to become an impersonal matrix, a material framework for his own production of speech. The analyst's knowledge must therefore not become the certainty of the analysand. For knowledge, S_2, to occupy the place of truth (of unconscious certainty) it must be situated *hors de combat*. Unlike the philosopher, the analysand sees better in the dark.

The dread of certainty: Little Hans the philosopher

In the case of 'Little Hans' (Freud 1909b), Freud's critique of philosophy and philosophers is exemplified through a study of phobia in a small boy. Freud's discussion of the case turns on the collapse of Hans' theory of sexual identity (and thus of sexual difference), which is founded on the dubious proposition that all animate objects possess a 'widdler', whereas all inanimate objects do not. In this respect, Freud argues, Little Hans resembles a philosopher of the Wundtian school, who believes that all mental events have the property of consciousness.[6] Little Hans is unable to accept the fact that there is no sexual relationship just as the Wundtian cannot accommodate the notion that 'there is no mental relationship'; in other words, that thought encompasses both itself and its Other. Hans accommodates reality to his theory by surmising that little girls' 'widdlers' will get bigger one day. According to Freud, the philosopher does something similar: 'If now the philosopher comes across mental processes whose existence cannot but be inferred, but about which there is not a trace of consciousness to be detected . . . then, instead of saying that they are *un*conscious mental processes, he calls them *semi*-conscious. The widdler's still very small!' (Freud 1909b: 12, note). Earlier, in *Jokes and Their Relation to the Unconscious* (Freud 1905c), Freud had employed his critique of philosophy to establish a succinct and powerful definition of unconscious thought: '[T]he unconscious is something which we really do not know, but which we are obliged by compelling inferences to supply; they [the philosophers] had understood it as something capable of becoming conscious but which was not being thought of at the moment, which did not occupy 'the focal point of attention' (Freud 1905c: 162).[7] It is this theme to which Freud would return in *The Ego and the Id* (Freud 1923b) and 'The Resistances to Psychoanalysis' (Freud 1925e [1924]). In the latter text, he took particular issue with the philosophical concept of mind as an organically determined container for consciousness.

There is little doubt that Little Hans, and philosophers in general, are possessed by a desire to know. What requires examination is how they encounter the fall of knowledge. Thus far, we have characterized the fall of knowledge as a risking of mind in discourse which, although forestalled by abstract reasoning, can also be seen as bearing an ethical dimension, one which makes subjective thought contiguous with a collective act. The compulsive, intrusive nature of unconscious thought is also the function of haste in logic, the race for an effective truth. As such, it concludes the time for comprehending through the precipitation of desire. The collapse of Hans' speculative philosophical system is prevented by the onset of his phobia of horses, in particular his anxiety around seeing a large horse falling down. The phobia, in other words, manages to keep Little Hans' options open and forestalls a moment of concluding. Significantly, at the core of Hans' anxiety is his fear of a moment when, in his own words, '[I]t'll always be like this' (Freud 1909b: 49), that is to say, when his speculative flights are grounded by the certainty of the intrusion of unconscious thought. Anxiety, commonly assumed to be linked to a fear of the unknown, in fact strives to preserve endless rumination on the unknown. It does this in the face of a dread of certainty that calls a halt to individual deliberation on the nature of truth.

It is worth taking Freud seriously, and treating Little Hans as a model of philosophical consciousness. For this consciousness, an anxious mind is preferable to a mind penetrated by the desire of the Other, and the search for objective truth will always win out over the unconscious objectivity of the truth that is spoken. It may even be the case that, under the social hegemony of the university discourse, fragmentation and a 'mental breakdown' are preferable to the loss of a place within the epistemological drive. The epistemological drive produces an economy in which the formula of 'knowledge is power' is altered; instead, power is used as a means of generating knowledge. The mind becomes the metaphorical generator of knowledge in quantity and of quality. It is idealized as productive, and anything that calls a halt to this production is seen as personal tragedy and social waste.

A good example of this kind of idealization was recently provided by the film version of *A Beautiful Mind*, Sylvia Nasar's biography of the mathematician and game theorist John Nash (Nasar 1998). In the film, Russell Crowe stars as the brilliant scholar whose mind disintegrates with the onset of psychosis at the age of thirty, but who later partially recovers his sanity and his academic status. Nasar describes her book as 'a story about the mystery of the human mind, in three acts: genius, madness, reawakening' (Nasar 1998: 22). Akiva Goldman, the film's scriptwriter, constructed a slightly different arc of 'the genius, the schizophrenic break, the Nobel Prize' (quoted in Hawker 2002). Nasar presents a narrative of the cultivated mind, whereas the scriptwriter offers a story of the knowledge product. What both have in common is an assumption of concurrence between the 'recovery' of mind and the restoration of value. However, the diligent research that Nasar has done on Nash's mental illness and his partial recovery suggests a different interpretation. In a letter written in 1967, Nash described the topography of a psychosis rivalling that of Daniel Paul Schreber (Freud 1911c [1910]): 'He was covered with white stones representing Confucians and black stones representing Muhammadans. The "first-order" game was being played by his sons, John David and John Charles. The "second-order", derivative game was "an ideological conflict between me, personally and the Jews collectively" ' (Nasar 1998: 326). Nash set himself on the road to recovery by beginning to distinguish the political from the mathematical in these episodes: 'A key step was a resolution not to concern myself in politics relative to my secret world because it was ineffectual. . . . I began to study mathematical problems and to learn the computer as it existed at the time' (ibid.: 354). This suggests that, in a full-blown psychosis, Nash could no longer be said to possess an academic mind. In order to effect some kind of recovery, he was obliged to construct a mathematician *ex nihilo* from the elements of the psychosis. It can thus be argued that there is no continuity of mind 'from genius to madness to re-awakening' in Nash's story. Instead, it reveals a strange collusion between the unbroken certainty of psychotic knowledge and the speculative circuits of the academic mind, in headlong pursuit of objective truth. Lacan noted that the unanchored, uncensored yet petrified language of psychosis is characterized by the absence of belief: 'This solidity, this mass seizure of the primitive signifying chain, is what forbids the dialectical opening that is manifested in the phenomenon of belief' (Lacan 1994a [1964]: 238). Philosophical and academic speculation, on the other hand, maintains the *episteme* of objective knowledge, but does so at the price of a blindness to the moment of termination latent in unconscious knowledge. As such, psychosis prevents and philosophical speculation forestalls the moment that Little Hans dreaded, the moment when 'It will always be like this', when the alien 'thing' of unconscious thought is most fully experienced. For mid-period Lacan, this moment of concluding is signalled in the social bond of the 'Name-of-the-Father', which provides access to the possibility of a subjective assertion that is both personally significant and collectively recognizable (Lacan 2002a [1953]: 66). In the case of Little Hans, this point of access appears under the totemic and culturally potent sign of the horse, and it is at once the site of Little Hans' deepest fears and his most fervent desires.

Free speech!

Little Hans' statement 'It will always be like this' does not refer to the force of familial or social circumstances, but to the alien and intrusive character of unconscious thought, whose psycho-social mass far exceeds the weight of Hans', or anyone else's, mind. It is the source of the problem that psychoanalysis presents to philosophers and academics, a problem Freud had isolated and analysed in *The Interpretation of Dreams* (Freud 1900a). It also produces a sharp divergence between the psychoanalytic and philosophical definitions of freedom of speech. In psychoanalysis, freedom of speech is strictly equivalent to the right of the analysand to talk bullshit and still be listened to attentively: 'The life of a psychoanalyst . . . isn't rosy. The comparison that can be made between the analyst and a rubbish dump is justified. All day long in fact he has to endure utterances that, surely, are of doubtful value to himself and even more so to the subject who communicates them to him' (Lacan 1993 [1955–56]: 29).[8] Of course, the analyst's waste collection contract is undertaken on condition that what is really at stake are those moments when the bullshit machine breaks down . . .

For the academic, on the other hand, free speech is the condition of an Augean labour in search of a truth that, for the analyst, is always present 'in bulk', if not easily accommodated. Paradoxically, the speech of the academic in pursuit of truth is far more free than that of the profligate analysand, who can say the first thing that comes into her head, but who is always bound to speak the truth. The ethic of psychoanalysis is the assumption of this obligation by the analysand as well as the analyst. By contrast, since Mill's discussion of the free productive engagement of truth and error and his association of truth with social utility (Mill 2003 [1869]: 86–93), a modern ethic of the quest for objective truth has remained intimately connected with the notion of a market place of ideas. In *On Liberty*, Mill values minority opinion and the notion of truth as proven in the contest and free exchange of ideas, rather than through habit and consensus. However, his position is informed by an argument in which free exchange finds its justification in truth, and truth is proven by being subject to exchange. This truth must remain provisional, subject to further exchange, and all doctrines must be regarded as amenable to debate, with a view to the production of useful and partial truths in the long run (ibid.: 112–113). What is ultimately 'true', here, is the constant engagement of many minds in the search for truth. Margaret Jane Radin has commented that the commitment to an idealized yet endlessly deferred 'end-state truth', produced by the exchange of ideas, has ensured that government regulation of the free trade in goods has not been matched by a corresponding regulation of free speech (Radin 1996: 165). Radin's argument reverses the usual logic of debate on academic freedom. Rather than freedom guaranteeing truth, the pursuit of truth has become the exceptional condition for the free expression of ideas. Truth is assumed to be the product of a free market in which a thousand schools of thought collide; it has become a 'contested commodity'.

Radin posits that several forms of alienation are currently associated with this state of affairs, including objectification (ideas are detached from the individuals that have them), fungibility (one idea is as good as another) and commensurability (ideas are ranked by their level of acceptance). Of these three, only the issue of fungibility, or equivalence of value, might seem to trouble the psychoanalyst. In fact, every theory the analysand advances about his condition is as *worthless* as any other, basically because its claim to truth is not at issue. This is not the case in the market place of ideas. Even the 'dumbing down' that allows Proust to be recast as a self-help manual, or Lacan to pair off with Hitchcock, is dependent on the cherished ideal of end-state truth—the truth of oneself, of Lacan, or of Hitchcock. By contrast, the provocation inherent in the statement 'I always speak the truth' (Lacan 1990d [1974]: 3) is that the use value of speech must not be confused with Lacan's own fluctuating exchange value, or the fate of psychoanalytic ideas in knowledge markets.

When Lacan compares the speech of his analysands to rubbish, he seems to be showing contempt for the sincerity of their traumas. In fact, the statement is part of an argument concerning truth and value, whereby Lacan goes on to say that while the analyst must learn to overcome his negative reaction to the analysand's bullshit, he cannot be so generous towards analytic literature that is saturated with errors and contradictions. Why is it that the analyst must be blind to speciousness and error in the analysand, but nonetheless become a merciless critic of faults in the analytic literature? A crucial point is that the analysand's speech should not be seen as being of lesser value than any other. Instead, it must be regarded as invaluable, since the knowledge it bears is constituted by paradox—it is a common knowledge that can nonetheless not be acquired within the market place of ideas. Psychoanalytic literature, on the other hand, is part of this market place, and may therefore be constituted by a free exchange of knowledge whose ostensible goal is public understanding of 'the clearer perception and livelier impression of truth, produced by its collision with error' (Mill 2003 [1869]: 87). The market in psychoanalytic literature sits oddly with the aims of analysis; insofar as it 'sells itself' to other parties in the market place of ideas, it fails to accord with a psychoanalytic ethic. This is the source of Lacan's concern with the effects of *poubellication* (waste-basket publishing). In an address given at the University of Milan in 1972, he noted that there is much scope for confusing 'making public' and 'making waste' (Lacan 1978a [1972]: 34).

If the unconscious 'publicizes' desire, why should the partisans of psychoanalysis desire publication? Might it be possible to address this question under the terms set by the fall of knowledge and its judgement? What is 'on sale' in this chapter is a set of terms applicable to the *conclusion* of the search for objective truth in the environs of intellectual freedom. Having outlined the importance of a 'moment of concluding', as well as some features of a philosophical resistance to it, we will now go on to say why we believe that this moment of concluding has lately become necessary to any examination of the ethics of academic life, including the publication, dissemination and social status of academic knowledge. The necessity of this move bears upon the disappearance of the academic mind.

The disappearing mind

We referred earlier to the disappearance of the academic mind in the psychotic episodes of John Nash, and his subsequent reconstruction of it, prior to receiving the symbolic mandate of the Nobel Prize. In his 'Rome Discourse', Lacan defined psychosis as 'negative freedom of a kind of speech' (Lacan 2002a [1953]: 68). The extravagance and obscenity of a psychotic delusion and the complexity of its *Weltanschauung* are conditions for its inability to find an anchor in the world. As Lacan puts it, psychotic speech has 'given up trying to gain recognition' (ibid.: 68); it is richly decorated but socially groundless. Academic speech, on the other hand, supposedly partakes of a privileged exception: its freedom attains a distinctive socio-political significance in the pursuit of 'end-state truth'. However, the fact that academic freedom is a product of the market place of ideas exposes it to various forms of alienation and contradiction. Foremost among these is the problem of objectification. Radin frames this problem as one of conceptual detachment and disinterest; the buyers of knowledge goods do not particularly care how ideas are produced and who made them, nor does it matter who buys knowledge and for what reasons. 'It is as if buyers—people's minds—could be constituted wholly apart from the ideas that they are willing to buy from time to time' (Radin 1996: 167). The contradiction for the academic is obvious: market rhetoric (the contest of ideas in pursuit of truth) is threatened by the creeping realization that there may be no market for truth at all. In this way, one of the supporting planks of academic consciousness is removed. 'Knowledge for its own sake' becomes just that, a free-floating product without any link to the ethics and responsibilities of the producer.

The dream offered by the discourse of the university is one of infinite expansion, of the absolute rule of knowledge over material and human resources. Its concrete, and less appealing, reality is the reduction of knowledge to abstract agency. As we have suggested, the formula of the epistemological drive is not that 'knowledge is power', but that 'power makes knowledge'. To be in possession of a freely producing creative intellect is now a civic duty, not a historical right accorded to scholars and researchers alone. Every commercial, governmental and educational establishment worth its salt has developed, adapted or borrowed protocols for turning the embodied knowledge of its staff into the agency of competitive advantage and the phantom jouissance of 'dress down Friday' (Herschel *et al.*

2001).[9] 'The cultivated mind' is another name for necessary labour, and 'the knowledge product' is the form in which this labour is consumed. The most friable and flaky opinions and the most banal pseudodoxia can be grouped and focused for the purpose of running countries, or selling films. Opinion gains in stature and becomes knowledge, whilst knowledge reduces in value to become function and agency. In such a situation, politicians treat knowledge as a means to an end and yet fear the verdict of popular opinion, whereas citizens are encouraged to place an exaggerated value on their own opinions, despite being unable to distinguish between the reasons and the functions of power.

Occasionally, the crisis of academic knowledge under these conditions is clearly revealed. A recent example of the link between the hegemony of the university discourse and the disappearance of the academic mind was provided by the British government's notorious 'dodgy dossier' on Iraq's weapons of mass destruction, published in February 2003. This document, which has now disappeared from official websites, was partly plagiarized from an article by Dr Ibrahim Al Marashi published in the *Middle East Review of International Affairs* (*MERIA*) (Al Marashi: 2002). In this case, the marshall's baton, in the form of the drive for war, was clumsily concealed within the foot soldier's knapsack. The ruler spoke in the voice of the scholar, the purveyor of disinterested knowledge and the seeker after truth. Al Marashi's position in this affair was that of the slave or Other in the university discourse. His academic autonomy was disposed of by a government that had staked its claim to 'intelligence' as one element of the public fantasy of the empire of knowledge. The *Middle East Review of International Affairs* was caught between admonishing the British government for the theft and using it as an occasion to promote the quality of the journal's academic wares: 'We are pleased that the high quality of MERIA Journal's articles has made them so valuable to our readers, who now number 20,000 people around the world, including many government officials, as well as diplomats, journalists, scholars and students. As noted on the masthead of each issue and all our publications, however, we do appreciate being given credit. The fact is that the articles by Mr Marashi and our other authors are highly accurate, insightful, original and extremely timely' (Rubin: 2004).

This statement reveals the contradictions at the heart of the search for 'end-state truth' in the market place of ideas. If no one wants to buy the truth as such, it can at least be advertised as a well-made

product that can even be delivered on time. It also shows the futility
of maintaining a distinction between the cultivated mind and the
knowledge product, on which the modern fantasy of the university
has been built. All human knowledge, from a polished article in a
refereed journal to the results of a shopping survey, can be subject
to the same process of separation into abstract agency and useful
product that places it at the service of the epistemological drive.
'Ibrahim Al Marashi' became one element of the drive for war in the
name of knowledge, and end-state truth was shifted to the elusive
search for weapons of mass destruction.

A Lacanian perspective on the 'dodgy dossier' affair will not tell
us anything about the meaning of the speech acts of the British
government. What it can do is introduce the possibility of separating
speech and meaning, and distinguishing knowledge and truth in the
market place of ideas. The desire for knowledge about weapons of
mass destruction, the search for 'the truth about the truth' which has
guided advocates and critics of British state policy alike, is the very
mechanism of contemporary machine politics. Unlike the machine
politics of the nineteenth century, there is no longer any need to
threaten or offer material incentives to an electorate. The key incen-
tive for citizens within the contemporary political sphere takes the
form of a seductive knowledge totality (*savoir-totalité*): 'the idea that
knowledge can make a whole is ... immanent to the political as
such' (Lacan 1991 [1969–70]: 33). The concrete form of this enticing
image of society moulded into a politico-epistemological totality is
the stark functioning of knowledge as a pure principle of order or
administration, the function of agency within the university discourse. The price that is exacted for the administration of knowledge, in payment for the dream of 'society made whole', is the
further divorce of the knowledge that is acquired (the market place
of ideas) from the knowledge that 'costs' (the psychoanalytic ethic).
The middle term between these two poles is the historical privilege
accorded to the academic producers of end-state truth, who seem to
provide the market with some kind of ultimate *raison d'être*. However, if the higher commodity of 'truth' is devalued or loses its significance, the academic becomes a kind of institutionalized pervert,
reduced to the rhetorical inflation of his epistemological symptoms,
as an alternative to the attainment of collective significance (Lacan
1994a [1964]: 206). In general, perverse thinking is exemplified by the
difference between the symbolic mandate 'Hitler is an Austrian' and
the rhetorical statement 'Hitler is Germany'. What was 'perverse'

about a figure such as Hitler, was his morbid insistence on compelling others to accept his own bile, the fruit of bitterness and exclusion, as the panacea for their ills. The pervert's knowledge always constitutes a *Weltanschauung* and his intellectual ambition is at least as exuberant as that of the author of *Mein Kampf*. His speech is free only insofar as it insists on his personal right to the reconfiguration of the world in the image of its own insufficiency. Perversion thus delivers a phantom symbolic order, which stages segregated and marginalized enjoyment in exclusion in the guise of universal knowledge. The hegemony of the university discourse is an incitement to this kind of perversion, an acting out of exclusion by means of academic posturing.

At this point, it is worth examining particular instances where academics have responded to the threats of objectification and commodification, in order to isolate the peculiar insufficiency of these responses, as well as a general inability to find a vocabulary appropriate to the situation. The Internet is one arena where academic knowledge can be found competing for attention with other kinds of intellectual goods. Occasionally, this can be seen to reflect directly onto the constitution of the academic mind. In 2000, Bernard Porter, currently emeritus professor of history at the University of Newcastle and an acclaimed scholar of the British Empire, wrote an article for a British national newspaper describing his reaction on discovering that notes from his visiting lectures at Yale had been posted on the Internet without his consent (Porter 2000). His *cri de cœur* was one of a number of polemics directed at American companies such as 'Versity.com', 'Study 24.7.com' and 'Studentu .com' that, riding the first dot.com wave, employed students at $8–12 a session to take notes in lectures, which were then offered free on websites funded by advertising revenue.[10] Porter stated that the non-consensual posting of his notes made him feel that 'what I had been offering as personal interpretation, attached to me, had been transmuted into general, objective truth, a kind of impersonalised commodity' (ibid.: 12). Porter makes the link between truth and commodity, which is appropriate to the historical model of the market place of ideas, but in describing this truth as an unmediated generalization he signalled the occurrence of an important conceptual shift. If truth appears as a ready-made and instantly available product, it cannot embody the higher value of 'end-state truth', the outcome of freedom of debate and expression. Academic debate can of course continue, but it no longer has any social meaning, even for primary consumers such as students. Liberty and its product, useful social truths, have become dissociated. It may be that Porter's trauma is bound up with the realization that this has always been the case, that there never was any necessary connection between academic freedom and socially significant truth. He concludes his article in the following manner: 'If I had known that my lectures were to be distributed so widely . . . I would have given them differently. There would have been no speculation, improvisation, experiment; nothing I wouldn't want to be committed to, or could be taken the wrong way; probably no jokes. If lectures are public property, that is how they will become. It is difficult to see what will be the special point of them then' (Porter 2000: 13). Where Porter observes a reduction from academic knowledge to commercialized product, there is in fact the uncontrolled replication of his own productive efforts in a domain where there is nothing but knowledge (as information), the 'hive' of the Internet. From a Lacanian point of view, Porter has discovered that he is a worker bee in a collective enterprise, namely, the construction of the edifice of *savoir-totalité*, a labour in which 'knowledge is its own reward'. The relation between the lecture on 'British Imperialism from 1815' Porter delivered at Yale on 23 June 2000 and the notes and subsequent term papers that were subsequently produced is one of similarity, not difference.[11] In fact, the only difference between Porter and the students who bought the notes from his lectures is that he still works with a notion that they do not subscribe to—that of the cultivated mind.

It is of course one of the tragic vicissitudes of all academics to discover that their audience lives a reality that excludes them, and to compensate for that difficulty by acting out the hand-me-down jouissance of academic freedom. It may be more difficult for these academics to accept that the enjoyment in exclusion that goes by the name of academic freedom may be part of a historical discourse on the relationship of mind to truth, staged in the market place of ideas. What has changed in this market place, is that we have learned that the academic mind can disappear, whereas the knowledge product remains visible. In the future, battle lines will have to be redrawn, and the fruitless opposition of philosophy and psychoanalysis will be recast as a contest between the social production of knowledge and those moments when this production encounters a moment of estrangement or conclusion. The following chapter will address this issue through an examination of the epistemological vertigo of the hoax and its connection with 'the Lacanian game'.

The game beneath the game: logical aspects of the artifice, the dummy and the hoax

> The ideal game of which we speak cannot be played by either man or God. It can only be thought as nonsense. But precisely for this reason, it is the reality of thought itself and the unconscious of pure thought.
>
> Gilles Deleuze, *The Logic of Sense*, 60

The critical power of artifice

In our discussion of 'the prisoner's sophism' in the previous chapter, we at one point introduced the notion of 'the game beneath the game'. In this paradoxical formulation, the occlusion of the existential self is wagered against the goal of subjective truth. The vacillations of the existential self are reconfigured as a certainty, within what Lacan refers to as 'the essential logical form of the psychological I' (Lacan 1988a [1945]: 14). This chapter will examine how this 'game beneath the game' is played out in such a way that psychoanalysis can be seen to function as public ethics, 'a measure of our action' (Lacan 1992 [1959–60]: 311). It may seem fatuous to combine the idea of game playing with the austere issue of ethics, but the notion of the game is used in this chapter to differentiate between an ethic of action in psychoanalysis and 'ethical discourse' as democratic debate. In addition, there is also a clear distinction to be made between Lacan's thinking on the game, which places emphasis on artifice but eschews intersubjective relations, and the popular use of games as models for social life—a simulated contest of agents, positions and values.

Two important consequences follow from our refusal to define 'the Lacanian game' as a model, representation or virtualization of social and intersubjective 'non-games'. The first is that the distribution of options and values and the control of possible outcomes are not being employed in order to map conventional knowledge frameworks onto social realities. For this reason, psychoanalysis can never be satisfactorily applied to, or adapted within, normative social theories, although it may be brought to bear on the question of a 'politics of the model' through which such discourses are maintained.[1] Secondly, the breakdown of the conventional relationship between model and reality and the emphasis on artifice in Lacanian psychoanalysis (on what Deleuze has called 'pure game') implies that a Lacanian conception of the ethical act is radically distinct from that which determines the application of ethical guidelines to 'real-world' situations. In fact, those aspects of Lacanian psychoanalysis that appear most artificial, capricious and unrepresentative of common experience or common sense are precisely the elements that carry the greatest ethical force.[2] These kinds of connections have been recognized by both Alain Badiou and Slavoj Žižek, yet both these writers tend to confuse the power of the artifice with the tyranny of the regime. Their fertile reconstructions and misreadings of Deleuze and Lacan are fatally compromised by their too-faithful readings of Lenin and Mao. Nonetheless, neither Badiou nor Žižek commits the cardinal error of Elisabeth Roudinesco, for whom almost every Lacanian theory appears as a model or representation of a stage in Lacan's life history (Roudinesco 1997 [1993]).[3] Roudinesco's tactics of contextualization and debunking disregard one of the central elements of the Lacanian project, notably that in psychoanalysis the subject of certainty and the search for truth never coincide. The 'proof' of Lacan's theories is that they maintain this distinction, and thus cannot be satisfactorily applied or mapped onto real-life situations.

If you choose, you lose

In Deleuze's 'Tenth Series of the Ideal Game', included in *The Logic of Sense*, the game as model, a distribution of rule-governed possibilities determining action and delivering fixed results, is replaced with a game in which a distribution of results occurs as the consequence of an act (Deleuze 2001 [1969]: 60). The game as model establishes a representation of the present by situating the action of rule-bound agents within a field of play. It is replaced with a concept of the game that is determined by the dimension of the event, stretching before and beyond a field of actors. In the second case, a 'virtual' schema containing actors is exchanged for an unconscious dimension of the act, which comes close to 'the Lacanian game' and to Lacanian ethics. As Lacan's discussion of the prisoner's sophism shows, the game synthesizes past, present and future. It is not a field of abstract possibilities modelled on a present situation, but a configuration in which risk is 'totalized' rather than divided across a set of possible winning and losing options. Deleuze also suggests that the structure of rules, variations, winners and losers in conventional games indicates that their ultimate referent is 'another type of activity, labor, or morality, whose caricature or counterpart they are, and whose elements they integrate in a new order . . . [T]he moral model of the Good or the Best, the economic model of causes and effects, or of means and ends' (ibid.: 59). Deleuze contrasts this with 'an ethic of effects' in the pure game, one that disturbs the usual relationships between games and reality.

In an ethic of effects, ethical action does not follow ethical reflection. Instead, the radical artifice of the pure game discloses the role of standard ethical models, in the service of the distribution and minimization of risk, and the deferment of desire within a closed system of choices and options. A 'democratic model', for example, is another name for a way of theorizing the present as a field of play in which there is a multiplication of agents and choices and a corresponding reduction of risk. It necessarily imposes a rather limited notion of social agency, compensated for by a frenzied, globally distributed 'activity of alienation' within the production of knowledge and other social goods. In this scenario, a detailed knowledge of the field of possible choices is affirmed, while the dimension of the act is repressed (along with a concomitant ethic of effects), since it threatens the very consistency of this field. It is one of the ironies of modernity that it opens up a 'knowledge without relations of knowledge' and the dimension of the pure game, while negating the possibility of this artifice in the production of knowledge 'for the choosing'.

This state of affairs exposes a central paradox of the knowledge economy, which structures the field of knowledge as a representation of general economic life. Within this field there are knowledge 'winners' and knowledge 'losers'. The winning or losing of knowledge, however, dwindles in importance in a game where the real end is not personal triumph, but the multiplication of agents and the even distribution of risk. Democracy is a game where what counts is not winning, but increasing the number of players and versions of the game. As we argued earlier, the epistemological drive to 'keep on knowing more' is less about the iron circumstances of the economy than about the transition from a 'state of alienation' (non-production) to an 'activity of alienation' (production), in which every citizen becomes a 'student', a neophyte in the game of knowledge. This knowledge has become a generally available social product, rather than the mere means of fulfilling the master's will. Clustered around it is a class of knowledge specialists and knowledge managers (academics, bureaucrats, philosophers) dedicated to the development of methodologies, models and tools for knowledge production. For this reason, as Lacan suggests in *Seminar XVII* (Lacan 1991 [1969–70]: 68), a philosopher such as Wittgenstein can accept the notion of language as a construct, but cannot abandon the belief that language is something that 'works' in relation to the real world. What Lacan calls Wittgenstein's wish to 'save the truth' can also be described as his wish to preserve his language game as a model of learning and communication. The more radical, Lacanian position is that the truth can be made out of anything. For Lacan, the truth is not proved by the grip on real-world situations offered to us by a philosophical model, but by the gap between language as pure artifice and language as model, a gap opened up by the dynamics of psychoanalytic practice.

The gap between artifice and model also expresses a division between two kinds of ethic: an 'ethic of the act' and 'an ethic of the model'. As Deleuze emphasizes in *The Logic of Sense*, the former exposes the status of the latter in its representative relationship to capital and labour. To elucidate the difference between these two positions, we shall introduce the notions of the dummy and the hoax as problems or tests for the 'democracy of knowledge', since they enforce a separation between an ethic of the act and ethical discourse. The cruel game of the hoax presents itself as a regressive or inhibitory moment of the desire to establish a democratic polity. The hoax can be defined as a test, because it strikes against the very notion of relations of knowledge within democratic discourse. In a hoax, an apparently honest, rational choice is perversely linked to the initiation of an unforeseen, shameful catastrophe. Distributed risks are converted into totalized risks, with the possibility of losing more than one bargained for. Choosing becomes concurrent with not knowing. In a hoax, if you choose, you lose. This is the opposite of the democratic model, in which choice is entirely linked to participation and knowledge acquisition.

What unites psychoanalysis with the hoax is that in the hoax an ethic of the act is linked to an interruption of the labour of knowledge, or a withdrawal from this labour. The hoaxer achieves this by direct action against the mechanisms of knowledge production, dissemination and reception. Likewise, psychoanalysis opposes the accumulative labour constructing a body of knowledge and favours the renunciation of knowledge in the act that aims at truth. In psychoanalysis, one aims at truth by directing a shot away from knowledge accumulation, achieving a conclusion only by terminating questions of being, meaning and self-interpretation. There is a temporal aspect to this deliberate 'misfire', which bears upon the difference between the existential 'I' and the 'I' of the unconscious. In the unconscious, 'it thinks', and so 'I am known', deflecting the progress of the question, 'who am I?', which always arrives too late for an answer. The existential 'I' is homeless, cut adrift, because it tries to produce an ontological answer out of itself, attempting to attain certainty by an inconclusive process of speculative reasoning. It proceeds by acquiring a body of knowledge and constructing a model for action towards the goal of truth. By contrast, the 'I' that is at home in the unconscious is not in search of truth and so achieves certainty. The attainment of certainty is only available by passing through the 'dead zone' of the unconscious, where the presence of the subject is merely logical (as opposed to ontological) and where the normative operations of knowledge are invalidated. The unconscious, in other words, is the logical form of existence.

For this reason Lacan argues in *The Ethics of Psychoanalysis* that ethical action is inscribed in tragedy, which 'functions in the direction of a triumph of death' (Lacan 1992 [1959–60]: 313). A psychoanalytic conception of the ethical act accepts the inexorability of a collectively valid logic over and above an ethic in the service of property, goods and the stability of the state. There is a crucial difference, therefore, between the logical collective of a 'stupid of signifiers' and the common discourse established by the mutual exchange of goods. An ethic of the service of goods links the discourse of the master to the discourse of the university, whose injunction is 'keep on going, keep on knowing more'. As Lacan points out, this labour continues even though the name of the master changes: 'What is Alexander's proclamation when he arrived in Persepolis or Hitler's when he arrived in Paris? The preamble isn't important: "I have come to liberate you from this or that." The essential point is "Carry on working. Work must go on." . . . The morality of power, of the service of goods, is as follows: "As far as desires are concerned, come back later. Make them wait" ' (Lacan 1992 [1959–60]: 315).

In recent British history, Margaret Thatcher's famous statement, 'there is no such thing as society', provides us with a perfect equivalent of this Alexandrine/Hitlerian injunction (Thatcher 1987). Thatcher's phrase, which actually means, 'there is such a thing as work', situates the supposed hedonism of the free market as a sentence of hard labour imposed on the citizen by the state, with no remission. In an ethical act, on the other hand, it is not the contracts of labour between the citizen and the state, but the relations of the subject to the logic of the unconscious that provide the measure of our action. In Lacan's famous and endlessly discussed treatment of Sophocles *Antigone* in *The Ethics of Psychoanalysis*, he is at pains to point out the anti-social and 'atrocious' character of the heroine's sacrifice. She does not partake of an intrasocial debate on ethics and responsibility. Instead, she renders ethical practice itself into something uncivilized and 'unspeakable'. Also significant in Lacan's account of *Antigone* is his distinction between the ethical act and the service of goods: Antigone's brother, for whom she is willing to die, cannot be exchanged for another. A husband or a child, on the other hand, can be so exchanged. Indeed, the market for husbands has long been a commonplace of the novel, and every day newspapers carry stories of the market in children. Antigone's allegiance to her dead brother falls outside an ethical discourse that relies on the exchange of goods or ideas. The logical form of ethics does not recognize such exchanges and debates.

The unconscious is a game without players

In Lacan's account of the ethical act, a strange transition is taking place from a discursive field of play, in which intellectual goods are exchanged, to the field of the unconscious, in which the 'I' is registered, but without players, agents or vested interests. The logical time of the unconscious can be described as 'a game beneath the game' because it establishes a continuum in an ethical practice between being a player in discourse and the disappearance of the player/agent in the unconscious. In the ethical act, one always proceeds by a strategy of discursive refusal and withdrawal of agency, in order to reveal the disequilibrium of a discourse. Following the game to its logical conclusion requires a break with the play of the existential 'I' and its tactical manoeuvrings of personal agency and individual choice, which never reach a conclusion. As such, it can be suggested that the only game worth taking part in, and in which there are real winners and losers, is a game with no players—an anti-game which voids the rules of all the others. In Lacanian psychoanalysis, the most obvious instance of this deliberate negation of discursive rules is Lacan's statement, 'I always speak the truth' (Lacan 1990d [1974]: 3). This wilfully dumb *bon mot* was hardly likely to get Lacan taken seriously. As a discursive gambit, it is absurdly hubristic; one wouldn't bet on it. Furthermore, it has no purchase in any field of enquiry or research other than the extensive corpus of literature on the follies of (Lacanian) psychoanalysis.[4] And yet the statement, 'I always speak the truth', is an ethical act. What sounds like an absurd and narcissistic claim to agency on Lacan's part is in fact a withdrawal of agency. It ensures that two orders of signification, conscious and unconscious, appear within knowledge and discourse, whereas before there seemed to be only a single order of communication. The ethical act aims to expose the divided aim of the order of communication, which moves in one direction towards the deferral of desire in the service of goods, and in another direction towards the satisfaction of the drive in the realization of desire. As far as desire is concerned, goods must be spent and used up. Lacan's ultimate proposition for an ethic of psychoanalysis is: 'There is no other good than that which may serve to pay the price for access to desire' (Lacan 1992 [1959–60]: 321).[5] This foreshadows Lacan's later assertions that knowledge in the place of truth is knowledge that costs rather than something accumulated and exchanged. In the ethical act, knowledge is shaped for use, and as such one 'gets the point' of knowledge through using it in order to produce desire and not to reproduce more knowledge. This is perhaps another way of defining the role of the analyst: someone who uses his knowledge in order to produce desire in another, rather than to *reproduce* therapeutic discourse through the exchange of information, insights or wisdom.

The Lacanian concept of the game we are advancing here can be understood as a process in which the whole notion of 'playing the game', as it is commonly understood, is deliberately misrecognized and one is 'playing through' the game of discourse in order to aim at desire. This idea was shaped in the work Lacan accomplished during the late 1940s and early 1950s. Lacan's interest in game theory initially enabled him to develop models of the unconscious as the field of the Other, a set of networked relations of the signifier. Revisiting his work on the prisoner's sophism and the concept of logical time in

Seminar XI, Lacan subsequently employed game theory to define a logic in the unconscious that is independent of the stratagems and manoeuvres of a subject (Lacan 1994a [1964]: 39–41). Lacan emphasized here that the certainty of the unconscious is present in the hesitations and misrepresentations of the subject. In game theory, he now discerned the possibility of separating the decisions of agents with regard to the rules from the calculus of the game itself, within which the agents have the status of possibilities or variations within a pattern of signifiers.

The difference between an outcome pertaining to the agent and a logical variation pertaining to the field of the unconscious is also exemplified in 'the prisoner's dilemma' (not to be confused with the prisoner's sophism), a classic of game theory developed by Melvin Dresher and Merrill Flood at the Rand Corporation in 1950, as part of an enquiry into nuclear warfare strategy. In the prisoner's dilemma, police officers arrest two partners in crime suspected of robbing a bank and place them in separate cells. Both prisoners are told, 'You may choose to confess or keep silent. If you confess and your accomplice remains silent, we will drop all charges against you and use your testimony to ensure that your accomplice gets a lengthy sentence. If your accomplice confesses but you remain silent, he will go free and you will get the lengthy sentence. If you both confess we will obtain two convictions, but you will both receive a light sentence. If you both remain silent, we will convict you of a lesser offence.' What establishes the 'dilemma' in this case is that *no matter what each prisoner chooses to do*, each considered alone would be better off if he confesses. Yet taken together, both would be better off if neither confessed. Thus, there is a hidden consequence of individual choice, which is nonetheless not a consequence of personal agency. This factor is clearly underlined throughout Freud's *The Psychopathology of Everyday Life*. In one of the more dramatic reversals cited in the book, a woman's decision to get married precipitates her unacknowledged desire for death (Freud 1901b: 186, n. 1). In this instance, an intersubjective contract is cancelled by fidelity to desire. It is important to note that what Freud describes in such examples is not the famous 'law of unintended consequences', which refers to the secondary effects of particular decisions, but rather the immanent consequences of unconscious law.[6]

The logical architecture of the prisoner's dilemma raises some of the same issues Lacan studied in the prisoner's sophism and Poe's game of even and odd, in which the schoolboy successfully plays his opponent, precisely by not playing at all. Instead of 'making a move', he makes an account of the total field of moves already played, a calculation which becomes the cause of his next move. The key issue is that in the unconscious the notion of consequence should be understood as logical and determinate, yet immaterial and unrealized. As Lacan says in his treatment of *Antigone*: 'Involved here is an invocation of something that is, in effect, of the order of law, but which is not developed in any signifying chain or in anything else. Involved is an horizon determined by a structural relation: it only exists on the basis of the language of words, but it reveals their unsurpassable consequence' (Lacan 1992 [1959–60]: 278).

Nowhere did Lacan articulate the clinical significance of the connection between the fall of knowledge and 'the game beneath the game' more forcefully than in 'The Direction of the Treatment and the Principles of its Power' of 1958 (Lacan 2002d [1958]). In this text, he uses a discussion of the role of the 'dummy' partner in the game of bridge, in order to establish a contrast between the rivalry and competition that characterizes intersubjective game playing and position taking on the one hand and 'the stakes of the game in analysis' on the other hand (ibid.: 219). In a similar fashion to the schoolboy in the game of even and odd, the analyst leads the treatment by absenting or abnegating his own agency, and enlisting 'the aid of what in bridge is called the dummy [*le mort*, the dead]' (ibid.: 218). By conducting the treatment in this way, the analyst does not lead or seduce the analysand, as a demanding, suggestible or competitive subject. Instead, she directs the transference towards an encounter with what we have described as the 'dead zone' of the unconscious. The dimension of the game is present insofar as the psychoanalytic encounter is a deliberate artifice, rather than a representation of 'how things really are' in the troubled life of the patient. Yet the aspect of the game as a field of interpersonal rivalry or competition is completely absent. In his emphasis on deliberate artifice, the tactical and strategic aspects of the psychoanalytic encounter and the concept of the analyst as a director of the action, Lacan is careful to retain some characteristic elements of game playing. However, he also insists on distinguishing the structure of a game from the agency of its players—the analyst in particular must learn to employ the dead in order to direct the treatment.

'The Direction of the Treatment' does not yet develop the notion of the analyst's mandatory 'dis-being' (*désêtre*), whereby the necessity of a relationship with the analyst as Other is reduced to the utter

contingency of an encounter with the analyst as a replaceable, partial object (object *a*) (Lacan 1968a [1967]: 59). Yet the notion of
'action by withdrawal', in which the analyst absents himself from the
terms of an intersubjective encounter, does already look forward to
the notion of the ethical act as elucidated in *The Ethics of Psychoanalysis*, with its emphasis on refusal and negation of the social
contract and the service of goods, and thence to the distinction
between the discourses of the analyst and the master in *Seminar
XVII*. In 'The Direction of the Treatment', transference is consequently reconstituted in a radical theorization of the act. The shift
from intervention to withdrawal on the part of the analyst directs the
transference in the analysand, who is therefore unable to substantiate
a 'supposed subject of knowing' what it is that troubles him. Knowledge is unseated from its privileged position as something worth
having or possessing and transmuted into something worth losing
in its very form as a promise of distinction and value.

Within everyday intersubjective encounters, knowledge, value and
exchange are intimately linked. The artifice of the psychoanalytic
situation suspends these relations and interactions, and as a consequence knowledge immediately loses value—it can neither be possessed by the analyst, nor gained by the analysand. If psychoanalysis
were a representation or staging of the reality of the analysand, this
loss of value would not occur. Analysis would then be a 'changing
house' or a 'laundry of value', in which old values would be discarded and new ones embraced with a view to the analysand becoming a more effective social agent, a better 'player'. To avoid becoming
such an institution, the psychoanalytic setting must assume the
characteristics of a game, but without the struggle over value that
competitive gaming and intersubjective contest normally bring
about. For example, the question, 'Why do I always lose (in the game
of life, love, work, etc.)?' directed at an analyst is a question perform-
ing its own answer, by preselecting the analyst as the victor, the
'person supposed to know'. It assumes a logic of value based on the
socio-cultural distribution of winners and losers in the game of
knowledge, and the abstract sphere of speculation concerning right
or wrong choices: 'if only I had known . . .' As in the prisoner's
sophism, the game of existential speculation, where 'if you choose,
you lose', is countered only by direct action against an apparatus for
the production of any answer whatever to the question, 'Am I black,
or am I white?' To direct the treatment, the analyst must radically
alter the scenario in which having or losing knowledge is a matter of

agency and disposition in 'the game of life', towards a moment in which losing knowledge is concurrent with attaining certainty. In the place of a culturally established distinction between the 'haves' and the 'have nots' of knowledge, the analyst directs the analysand to a distinction between knowledge and truth, which derails his mission to be 'in the know'. At the level of the unconscious, the analysand is always 'in the know'; that is, he is located by the terms of 'a knowledge of signifiers'.

Thought is real

Much of the time we operate according to schematic semblances of what we ourselves are like and match these semblances with theories about the nature of reality, of 'how things are with the world'. On this basis, and with the assistance of numerous discourses from astrology to management theory, we try to figure out our position within the game of life, guided by the Baconian assumption that, in this case above all, knowledge is power. The paradox Lacan develops in 'The Direction of the Treatment' is that the only way the analyst can avoid contributing to the general deception of life as a game with men and women as players is to perpetrate a set of egregious hoaxes on the analysand—enlisting the dead, being blind, playing dumb, acting deaf. It is only through this artifice that the supposed onto-logical consistency of the game of life can be dissolved and the logic of the unconscious exposed. Fourteen years after presenting 'The Direction of the Treatment', in his discussion of knowledge and truth in *Seminar XX*, Lacan remarked that unless the unconscious as object is allowed to intrude between reality and model within the analytic situation, the logical time of the yet-to-be-born (*encore-à-naître*) will run aground in *l'encorné* (getting horns)—a process in which one is cheated of the truth through its very pursuit (Lacan 1998b [1972–73]: 95). In *Seminar XX*, Lacan is ready to state that the function of the analyst is to put 'object *a*' in the place of semblance; in other words, to replace a discursive machine for the generation of self-images in 'real-world' situations with the stupid, factitious and contingent encounter between the analysand and the cause of his desire. This is not simply a reversal of roles, but the destruction of all role playing, including the illusion of the game of life itself. The agency of the analyst and that of the analysand are replaced by the agency of the signifier, the matter of language within which questions, answers, meanings, fantasies and semblances are for ever dispersed and leaking (in the barrel sense!). What remains after the removal of intersubjective agency from the scene is a stupid of signifiers, a particular artefact made of *lalangue* ('llanguage')—the term to be interpreted here as an indication of substance, as in 'made of wood'—which has been isolated through psychoanalytic technique. The analytic process accomplishes nothing except this 'gear shift' from the search for a referent ('who am I?') to a production of 'llanguage' ('I is being made of this'). The analysand is in a position, then, to reconfigure a question, such as 'Why do I always lose?' by uncoupling the referents of the question, which are basically concerned with scales of value and the assignation of agents within the game of life, and situating the issue within 'the game beneath the game', in which acquisition and loss are links within the order of a signifying chain which follows the business of jouissance. The question itself bears the truth that knowledge is not the answer. Instead, knowledge is the distribution or scattering of the question across a field of 'losses' and 'wins'.

Ed Pluth (2004) has recently offered an interesting commentary on this issue in a discussion of Lacan's treatment of the famous '*Fort/ Da* game', in which Freud's grandson transformed the experience of his mother's coming and going into a game of absence (*Fort*) and presence (*Da*), alternately casting away and reeling back a small object (Freud 1920g: 14–16). As Pluth comments, this game must be seen as act and artifice, and not as the representation of a traumatic event: 'What is peculiar about the Fort-Da game is that in it there is an excessive, irresolvable tension coming from within the child himself. The child undergoes the trauma of his mother's departure, but then repeats this trauma in a game. This means that in the playing of the game an excessive tension keeps returning in the child, and not from an outside source . . . the game is a part of the very tension that it is supposed to be resolving' (Pluth 2004: 24). Crucially, the game is not 'therapy' for the child. As Pluth points out, it accomplishes a shift from the 'affective tension' of a real-world trauma to a 'signifying tension', which does not include intersubjective relations or a discourse of demand between a child and a mother, but which does create its own mad jouissance of creation and destruction. Pluth argues that the attempt to 'bind' and resolve trauma by giving it symbolic form is countered in the *Fort/Da* game by a perverse strategy in which the inexplicability of the traumatic occasion becomes an opportunity for the disproportionate and excessive expression of desire. Furthermore, the time of the mother's departure and the time of the game are incommensurable. Trauma is not being retold or represented; instead, it is being 'recycled' as the base element of an artefact constructed by an unconscious process.

If, as Pluth argues, the *Fort/Da* game depends on keeping the 'unreadability' of tension and trauma in play, then it makes no sense to try to understand the affective tension from within the form of its cancellation as signifying tension, any more than it would make sense to try to understand the life of Isidore Ducasse by reading the work of the Comte de Lautréamont. As in Ducasse's *Songs of Maldoror* (Lautréamont 1987 [1868–69]), *Fort/Da* is a game of horror, for instead of trying to resolve the enigma of betrayal and loss, it redoubles and extends it within a new dimension. In *The Ethics of Psychoanalysis*, Lacan compares *Maldoror* with Sade's *Justine* and *Juliette*, defining them as examples of works of art that are also experiments with the psychosocial consistency of the mind of the reader (Lacan 1992 [1959–60]: 201). These works, therefore, are not just to be understood as horrible tales, but as attempts to 'de-explain' trauma through a process of recycling, inversion and variation, which has nothing to do with the life history of a subject: '[W]e see emerge in him [Sade] . . . the idea of eternal punishment. I will come back to this point, because it amounts to a strange contradiction in a writer who wants nothing of himself to survive, who doesn't even want any part of the site of his tomb to remain accessible to men, but wants it instead to be covered with bracken' (ibid.: 202–203). Lacan sees Sade's experiment on the reader, which is designed to cut the subject free from his psychosocial moorings, in the writer's own self-obliteration. This is also why Lacan argued that one can speak of 'Kant with Sade', since both the philosopher and the writer converge on the issue of an ethics that is purged of particular interests, and which is, for this very reason, incommensurable with an ethic in the service of goods (Lacan 1989a [1962]). The Lacanian game is ethical because it has been designed, like the experiments of Ducasse and Sade, to dissolve the ontological consistency of the game of life, and counter it with the game of desubjectivized creation, destruction and re-creation that emerges in the death drive, and of which *Fort/Da* is a primitive form. In the psychoanalytic setting, the withdrawal of the analyst as Other, that is, as a 'person supposed to know' the meaning of the analysand's tension and trauma, exposes the analysand to the ways in which the affective, historically located traumas that he speaks of are in the process of being transformed and re-created by desire. The analysand, in other words, needs to encounter the asocial and desubjectivized dimension of his speech through the analyst's absence from the scene of knowledge and the failure of an intersubjective relationship. It is not just that the psychoanalyst must play with the dummy for the analysand; the entire psychoanalytic setting is a kind of suspended animation in which the game of life fails to proceed according to its usual rules, and where representation is replaced with construction.

Freud affirms this position in one of his last contributions to psychoanalytic technique, the paper entitled 'Constructions in Analysis' (Freud 1937d). Describing the process by which an intersubjective encounter, bound by the rules of truth and error, is replaced by an artifice built from elements of unconscious logic, Freud deemed the truth-in-practice of analytic construction more vital than the correct interpretation of past traumas. Freud begins by situating the problem of truth and error in psychoanalysis within a familiar deadlock of interpretation in which, if the analyand says 'Yes' to an interpretive move the interpretation is deemed correct, and if he says 'No' the analyst is also in the right since refusal is a sign of resistance. Freud's answer is to move away from the game of correct or incorrect interpretations, assessed on an individual basis, towards a position in which the subjectivities of the analyst and the analysand are subsumed within the collaborative production of a logic that exists outside the possibility of interpretation: 'The analyst finishes a piece of construction and communicates it to the subject of the analysis so that it may work upon him; he then constructs a further piece out of the fresh material pouring in upon him, deals with is [sic] in the same way and proceeds in this alternating fashion until the end' (Freud 1937d: 260–261). The 'truth' of this process is only ensured in the certainty of further production. In Lacanian terms, a construction is incorrect only if it does not bring about desire, through connecting the subject to the reality of the unconscious process. This process is not something that is bound up with the knowledge of the analyst or the responses of the analysand.

In 'Constructions in Analysis', Freud also compares the work of the analyst to that of an archaeologist reconstructing a vanished ruin, with the proviso that the analyst has the advantage of working with material that is still 'live'.[7] Paradoxically, in order to treat this live material, the analyst must refuse to participate in everyday discourse, behaving as if both he and the analysand are 'dead' to thought, another unconscious thought being animated in their stead. The game of life stops, so that the game of the unconscious process can begin. Psychoanalytic construction intervenes in this game of life by making space for a kind of quasi-delusional structure in which unconscious truth can find a home. In Chapter 6 of *An Outline of Psycho-Analysis*, Freud would return once more to the theme of construction and the exchange of knowledge between analyst and analysand (Freud 1940a [1938]: 172–182). He begins by stating that the analyst must neither refuse to intervene nor seek to impose his knowledge on the analysand ('we never fail to make a strict distinction between *our* knowledge and *his* knowledge') but must allow his own interpretations to precipitate unconscious effects: 'On that particular matter *our* knowledge will then have become *his* knowledge as well' (ibid.: 178). The latter statement makes it clear that Freud privileges the construction of the psychical artefact, whether 'delusional' or not, over and above the personal truth of either of the individuals involved in the psychoanalytic encounter.

Delusion is a key factor here precisely because it is not simply a representation. In his essay on 'Negation' (Freud 1925h), Freud posits representation as something that confers a pernicious intellectual freedom on human beings, allowing them to see the unconscious as a matter of choice, rather than necessity. By introducing a form of thought whose function is to negate another, such as 'I didn't think that' or 'I never think such things', we can both parse unconscious material and assert that it is not our concern. Negation is the very signal of the unconscious, since it separates thought itself into internal and external elements, in which the 'internal' thought attempts in vain to represent and select from the unconscious. It is the epistemological form of repression, 'a kind of intellectual acceptance of the repressed, while at the same time what is essential to the repression persists' (ibid.: 236). Nonetheless, the refusal that is present in negation also signals a shift from a mere representation to an actual threat to the integrity of consciousness. We constantly find that thoughts we deem 'unthinkable' possess all the characteristics and qualities of thought. Our response is to intellectualize them and treat them as external objects that our mind merely represents.

The division of thought into representation and object is the foundation for normative mechanisms of interpretation and for the game of truth in which there is the possibility of a 'yes' or 'no' answer. Conversely, 'we never discover a "no" in the unconscious', and so, at the level of unconscious, the whole notion of selection and choice is invalidated (Freud 1925h: 239). Unconscious certainty can be approached only by procedures that direct interpretations towards construction, treating the unconscious as 'another thought', and not, therefore, as an object to be thought of. In 'Constructions in Analysis', Freud links construction to delusion, because both allow unconscious thought to dictate its own terms, replacing the false logic of negation with the certainty of the division of thought: 'The vain effort would be abandoned of convincing the patient of the error of his delusion and of its contradiction of reality; and, on the contrary, the recognition of its kernel of truth would afford common ground upon which the therapeutic work could develop' (Freud 1937d: 267–268). Here Freud claims that a construction or artifice can contain the productions of a constant, temporally dispersed truth which the conscious mind is unable to grasp, and which is not recognized within its orientation to reality. It follows that only by means of an artifice will the analyst be able to direct the analysand beyond the relationship of self and other, with its attendant anxieties over the disposition of truth, knowledge and value.

Psychoanalysis is less concerned with applying its model to reality than with revealing the radical artifice at the heart of all the models the analysand attempts to apply to his own situation. Even in the act of representing his trauma in order to negate it, the analysand discovers herself reproducing, extending, decorating and finessing it. The function of the analyst is to reveal these mechanisms of production and reproduction at the heart of the analysand's desire to know the truth about her essential nature. The analyst does this by directing the analysand away from those interpretive models that are designed to elicit answers: 'It is true that we do not accept the "No" of a person under analysis at its face value; but neither do we allow his "Yes" to pass' (Freud 1937d: 262). It is not the case that either as 'yes' or as 'no' the answer is wrong, but that the idea of 'answer' as such is inapplicable. The unconscious is not an object for investigation that will produce a positive or negative result. In 'Constructions in Analysis', we see Freud building a strategy in which the function of truth as the finished product of a standard interpretive model is reassigned to the process of production itself. Or, as Deleuze would have it: 'We do not seek in Freud an explorer of human depth and originary sense, but rather the prodigious discoverer of the machinery of the unconscious by means of which sense is produced always as a function of nonsense (Deleuze 2001 [1969]: 72). In this passage from *The Logic of Sense*, Deleuze compares the Freudian revolution to the innovations of structuralism. He argues that both structuralism and Freudianism have shown that the search for truth and the mechanisms through which human subjects interpret and recognize it may be better conceived of as a truth process, a logic from which sense proceeds. Indeed, for Deleuze, truth is not the end product of careful reasoning, but a process which has 'sense effects'. Through such a process, one of the key aims of psychoanalysis can be identified: making thought real for the analysand. This task is undertaken in spite of all tendencies to make thought into the means through which reality is represented, interpreted and judged, and non-thought into the zone of external reality. Making thought real implies a loss of subjective and interpretive potency. It invalidates the investigative questions of the analyst as well as the responses of the analysand, both of which depend on a gap between thought and reality mediated by models and theories.

Psychoanalysis applicable and inapplicable

In a sense, the problem of clinical interpretation and the problem of applied psychoanalysis are exactly the same: how to avoid 'aiming at truth' and thus negating the reality of thought once more? As we have argued in Chapter 3, in the clinical situation the deliberate direction of interpretation away from truth as end result may involve the use of 'dummy' tactics, such as deliberate mishearing or misunderstanding of the analysand's words, in order to provoke desire. The equivalent of the 'dummy' in applied psychoanalysis is more difficult to determine, mainly because an economy of intersubjective relations determined by a free market in ideas and the service of goods imposes a set of interpretive terms and conditions on the particular interpretations of the psychoanalytic 'applicant'.

Nowhere is this problem more manifest than in the work of Slavoj Žižek, a writer who has found himself bound to the production of interpretive truths in ways that his valiant textual manoeuvres fail to escape. The clearest instance of it can be found in his book *The Fright of Real Tears: Krzystof Kiéslowski Between Theory and Post-Theory* (Žižek 2001a), in which he clearly and explicitly attempts to 'play the dummy' as a tactic of de-interpretation. While apparently pursuing an ethical discourse on the difference between 'real theory' and its degraded imitations, Žižek perpetrates an unobtrusive hoax, which radically undermines the rigorous relationship between psychoanalytic interpretation and its objects (films, literature, world events) that has characterized his own philosophico-psychoanalytic method. He sets up the hoax by affirming his disgust at his own interpretive position:

> Some months before writing this, at an art round table, I was
> asked to comment on a painting I had seen there before for the
> first time. I did not have any idea about it, so I engaged in a total
> bluff, which went something like this: the frame of the painting
> in front of us is not its true frame, there is another, invisible
> frame implied by the structure of the painting, which frames our
> perception of the painting, and these two frames do not over-
> lap—there is an invisible gap separating the two. . . . To my
> surprise, this brief intervention was a huge success, and many
> following participants referred to the dimension-in-between-the-
> two-frames, elevating it into a term.
>
> (Žižek 2001a: 5–6)

The extraordinary thing is that much later in the book Žižek inserts
his own spoof of the 'dimension-in-between-the-two-frames', word
for word, into an apparently serious discussion of paintings by
Malevich, Hopper and Munch! (ibid.: 130). This attempt to use a
hoax in order to undo the mechanisms of applied psychoanalysis is
faithful to a Lacanian ethic of the radical act, in the same way that
the bridge dummy is used to misdirect interpretation and response.
Yet its critical potency vanishes here, because it does nothing to
change the relations of 'The Žižekian field' that secured him a place
at the art round table in the first place, nor does it alter relations
within the market place of ideas in which the public discourse on art
and psychoanalysis is contained.

The insignificant hoax Žižek perpetrates in *The Fright of Real
Tears* perfectly illustrates the dilemma of applied psychoanalysis,
which is unable to reply to every demand for interpretation with a
systematic process of misunderstanding that would enable a psychoanalytic construction. Žižek's response to this problem is to turn
interpretation into a taunt that stretches credulity to breaking
point (David Lynch is the key to understanding Kant; the war in the
Balkans is structured like Hitchcock's *Rear Window*, etc.), whilst
issuing intermittent demands for a 'Terror' that might provide an
emancipation from the task of interpretation. However, both of
these solutions are purely rhetorical. The key lesson of Freud's
'Constructions in Analysis' is that interpretation cannot simply be
turned against itself. Rather, it must be turned *towards* construction,
through the methodical employment of misunderstanding, opacity,
fabrication and delusion. The Freudian assertion of the reality of
thought against the negation that would deny it can appear in Žižek's

discourse only as an appeal to the value of material production over symbolic exchange (Žižek 2001b: 137). Unfortunately, this brings us no closer to a truly psychoanalytic understanding of the artefact, which depends on a notion of production that is neither material nor symbolic, but logical.

The very distinction between material and symbolic, or reality and thought, is refused in a Freudian notion of construction, where thought exists as a chain of consequences and effects, and not as an apparatus of judgement and interpretation. In all fairness, we need to point out that Žižek does state that the Freudian notion of construction 'has the status of a knowledge which can never be subjectivized' and which exists as 'a purely explanatory logical proposition' (Žižek 1998: 210). Yet the hoax employed in *The Fright of Real Tears* is by no means incorporated within a systematic mode of production that would yield such explanatory logical propositions. Here, Sade and Lautréamont prove themselves more methodical than many practitioners of applied psychoanalysis. In order to release the subject from its psychosocial moorings, their texts intervene violently, yet systematically within the contract of recognition, understanding and the exchange of ideas that is set up between the writer and reader, instituting a new mode of production in its place.[8] What prevents the delusional systems of these writers from establishing a socially viable way of approaching the reality of thought is their very existence as works of art, within what Lacan calls 'the order of experimental literature' (Lacan 1992 [1959–60]: 202–203). This order assigns them a place within the service of those goods that are labelled daring, experimental or transgressive.

Any application of psychoanalytic ideas outside a clinical context thus faces the 'Žižek or Lautréamont?' problem. Neither of these alternatives can undo the intersubjective dialogue and the ethics of free exchange that structure the market in knowledge goods. Lacan's solution of this problem was largely to reject publication as a useful strategy, in favour of a psychoanalytic practice where his own *lalangue* would not suffer the same pigeon-holing as that of Sade and Lautréamont. Žižek's approach is much more contradictory, since his texts appeal for the demise of the democratic order that sustains them: 'The only "realistic" prospect is to ground a new political universality by opting for the impossible, fully assuming the place of the exception, with no taboos, no a priori norms ("human rights", "democracy"), respect for which would also prevent us from "resignifying" terror, the ruthless exercise of power, the spirit of sacrifice. . . . If this radical choice is decried by some bleeding-heart liberals as *Linksfaschismus*, so be it!' (Žižek 2000: 326). The problem is that the 'choice' offered here is not radical at all, no matter how much Žižek wants us to believe that his position is revolutionary: it is just a readily available synthesis of political neo-brutalism and standard academic practice. A better strategy might be to reveal these modes in their contradiction, a tactic which Žižek employs only fleetingly in his hoax in *The Fright of Real Tears*, where he raises the tentative possibility that his entire oeuvre might be merely a cruel joke on the reader's desire for intellectual satisfaction. It may very well be the case, of course, that only the clinical encounter allows us to envisage a systematic approach to the direction of inter-pretation towards construction. Outside the clinical domain, the Rimbaldian project of 'rational disordering' that Lacan saw in Sade and Lautréamont might be consigned to the study of literary avant-gardes. In any case, Žižek's appeal to Leninism as a 'total and final solution' for the particular methodological problems associated with the psychoanalysis of culture remains quite unpromising.

The specific problem of the role of the 'dummy' and the hoax in applied psychoanalysis is linked to a problem of hoaxes in general, which always move from a particular fall of (public) knowledge towards a (public) knowledge of the fall. The problem concerns the translation of the particular economy of the hoax into the wider sphere of culture. The hoax that begins as a 'game beneath the game' of an existing pattern of intersubjective relations may then take its place within new forms of intersubjective rivalry and competition, as it begins to transcend the conditions of its own perpetration. If one compares the highly effective Trojan Horse tactics employed by Alan Sokal in his original hoax of the cultural studies journal *Social Text* in 1996, with the *ad hominem* approach of the book *Intellectual Impostures* he later wrote with Jean Bricmont, this failure of transla-tion is clear (Sokal 1996; Sokal and Bricmont 1998). Sokal's first intervention in the 'Science Wars' went some way towards identify-ing and locating elements of a desubjectivized academic economy at work beneath the supposed 'interdisciplinary dialogues' of cultural studies.[9] On the other hand, *Intellectual Impostures*, with its cata-logues of particular errors, took no account at all of the artifice of the original hoax on which it was built. In his original hoax Sokal constructed a kind of 'Protocols of the Elders of Cultural Studies', whose origins lay in the recipe for 'Theorese' offered by the scientists Paul Gross and Norman Levitt in their book *Higher Superstition*

(Gross and Levitt 1994).[10] Gross and Levitt had described a process of textual assemblage (a little Marxism, a little sexism, a little deconstruction, a bit of Afrocentrism) that was followed by Sokal in the construction of his interventionist device. It is vital to note that the editors of *Social Text* (Bruce Robbins and Andrew Ross), in their turn, were more concerned with getting a Left-credentialled scientist on their side in the 'Science Wars' debates than they were with the status of Sokal's article as sense or nonsense. Thus, there was deception on both sides; while both Sokal and the editors of *Social Text* pretended that an interdisciplinary, intersubjective exchange was taking place, subjectless academic knowledge was being produced. To use Freud's words in 'Constructions in Analysis', Sokal's 'bait of falsehood had taken a carp of truth' (Freud 1937d: 261). The truth in this instance has nothing to do with the mathematical and scientific credentials of Lacan, Deleuze and Kristeva that Sokal and Bricmont attacked in *Intellectual Impostures*. It has more to do with the manner in which the 'Sokal affair' showed how construction and the artifice can be directed to appear from within the search for 'end-state truth' that supposedly guides academic reason. Unfortunately, none of the parties involved had any means to proceed on this basis, and map the delusional mechanics linking Gross, Levitt and Sokal to Robbins and Ross. Years later, even pro-Lacanians are wont to frame the debate with references to the 'discipline' of psychoanalysis and the supposedly inalienable knowledge attached to it.[11] This shows that few lessons have been learned from the violence of Sokal's initial intervention and the 'game beneath the game' that it exposed at the heart of academic labour.

The ethics of critique

If there is a useful legacy of the Sokal affair, it is to be found in its fundamental challenge of the idea that free exchange finds its justification in truth, and that truth is proven by being subject to exchange. Neither of these Millian precepts was valid for the inter-disciplinary exchange of knowledge that occurred between Sokal and the editors of *Social Text*, despite the adoption of a Left-leaning critical stance by both sides. The conceptualization, submission and acceptance of Sokal's postmodern verbiage disclosed the frightening possibility of academic speech without academic subjects to speak, receive, or understand it. The logical outcome of this disclosure was Andrew Bulhack's notorious 'Postmodernism Generator' website, first established in 1996 (Bulhack 1996a). The site took its cue from Sokal's realization of a 'Protocols of the Elders of Cultural Studies', but recast it as a representation of the disappearance of the academic mind in the circuits of the epistemological drive. The Postmodernism Generator neatly reverses the logic of academic production by presenting truth as continuous, not teleological. Every time a link on the website is opened, the 'Dada Engine' (Bulhack 1996b) produces a few pages of gibberish using recognizable keywords, rhetoric and famous names, extending the hand-crafted core of pure nonsense in Sokal's original article into the efficient production of a seamless, endless stream of unmeaning. In this way, Bulhack's project revisited a familiar 'bad dream' of the discourse of the university. Indeed, already in 1988, the cultural studies scholar Meghan Morris had fantasized that somewhere there must be a publisher's vault from which 'thousands of versions of the same article about pleasure, resistance and the politics of consumption are being run off under different names with minor variations' (Morris 1988: 15). In the terms Lacan employed in *The Ethics of Psychoanalysis*, Morris' 'master disc' is the symbolic order in the service of goods, deferring desire within a dizzying array of intellectual, material and political options. Morris was anxious about the ethics of critique in the face of global capital, and recent critical fashion has shown that she was right to be concerned.

In 2000, Flamingo published Naomi Klein's *No Logo*, a text about pleasure, resistance and the politics of consumption, which proved that the production and distribution of cultural studies style capitalist critique had now 'gone global' (Klein 2000). While offering an energetic *tour d'horizon* of the machinery of capital, this book also consolidated a style of knowing, and became a guide to the manners and rules of critique. Although driven by the honest desire to unmask the economic inequalities underlying consumer consciousness, the difficulty of Klein's approach is that the commodity does not 'mask' inequality, or replace it with a simulation of social reality. It both produces and consumes inequality in the form of 'commodity relations'. Whether those relations happen through the wearing of trainers or the consumption of radical critique is neither here nor there. By the same token, the consumer is not the person who makes up his mind to buy an iniquitous product or an ethical one. In this instance, the consumer is a relation between otherwise unrelated or merely generically linked products, one of which is ethically 'bad' and the other 'good'. This relation ('the consumer') can be used to make speech and to express a social understanding of the difference between 'badness' and 'goodness'. The unconscious of consumption cannot therefore be reduced to the essentially preconscious or implicit realization that our shoes are produced under sweatshop conditions. Instead, it is located in the purely formal acknowledgement that the public discourse on ethics is now conducted by *talking about shoes*. The corollary of this is that when we are known as the consumer, we may discuss ethics. If we are not known as the consumer, we may lack the vocabulary and the authority to do so. Once again, the unconscious comes from the Other as a set of relations from which speech may be generated, and not from the Other as exploited labourer or exploiting capitalist whom we could use to reflect our perfected ethical consciousness. Klein's text enables us to perfect this ethical consciousness, and thus to ignore the connection between Meghan Morris' 'master disc' for the production of discourse on the politics of consumption, and the ideal of end-state truth in the market place of ideas. Like any book of manners, *No Logo* teaches us how *not* to fall out of knowledge and discourse. It follows that a truly ethical position advocates a fall from discourse, with its goal of truth, into the logic of the unconscious, whose end is desire. This is the ethic of psychoanalysis as Lacan understood it.

The psychoanalysis of culture is uneasily poised between the service of this ethic and the service of goods. Engineering the fall of knowledge in the contract between writer and reader is of course very different from the direction of the psychoanalytic treatment. The psychoanalytically inclined critic may become acutely aware of this problem and suggest extreme, politically radical solutions. Yet the problem of whether and how to deal with the fall of knowledge is one that all critical analyses of culture and society must encounter, whether they draw on psychoanalysis or not. When the sociologist Pierre Bourdieu submitted one of his last reports on the impossible task of critique in his book *Pascalian Meditations*, he made a significant choice of an exit strategy from the charmed circle of academic life:

> Being convinced that Pascal was right to say that 'true philosophy makes light of philosophy', I have often regretted that academic proprieties prevented me from taking this invitation literally: more than once I have wanted to fight the symbolic violence that is exercised, firstly on philosophers themselves, in the name of philosophy, with the weapons most commonly used

to counteract the effects of that violence—irony, pastiche and parody. I envied the freedom of writers . . . or of the artists who from Duchamp to Devatour, have, in their own artistic practice, constantly subverted the belief in art and artists.

(Bourdieu 2000 [1997]: 2)

Yoking together Duchamp and Devatour may actually obscure what Bourdieu is aiming at in Duchamp here, namely a logic-based approach to the fall of knowledge.[12] As is well known, in 1917 Duchamp successfully hoaxed the Independents' Show in New York, an open submission exhibition in which anyone paying six dollars was entitled to exhibit, by submitting a urinal under the pseudonym 'R. Mutt'. Thierry de Duve has argued that the purpose of Duchamp's gesture was 'the testing of the Independents' liberalism' by showing how a discourse on freedom prohibited its actual expression (de Duve 1998: 117). The subsequent embarrassment over the urinal exposed the difference between the Independents' own historical critique of previous, less open submissions, and the implicit restrictions imposed by this historically founded notion of progress. The urinal is manifest as the future that has been forestalled by the supposedly forward-looking and liberating historical reflection; it appears from within this historical notion of progress as its unconscious possibility—its failure, in fact, to be progressive. In a similar way, Bourdieu struggles with critique's failure to be critical as it takes its place within a general economy of knowledge governed by the precepts of the maximization of agents and the minimization of risk. Yet his chances of 'doing a Duchamp' or 'doing a Sokal' are limited by the scrupulousness of his analysis of academic life. This analysis is premised on Bourdieu's own position as an 'oblate', a person of modest origins who owes his attainments and material prosperity to the *skholè* (academic leisure and school) that has severed him from meaningful links with other modes of life.[13]

In *Pascalian Meditations*, Bourdieu relies on himself as oblate to gauge his own social truth as a fully fledged academic, by means of a reflection on the process of his habituation to scholastic reason, and thus to a process of renunciation or forgetting of the world. The figure of the oblate, which is intended to mediate between the intra- and extra-academic in Bourdieu's critique, is in fact just another sociological category that he sees himself as having occupied. The oblate is someone posited by what Bourdieu has become; one cannot reverse this process and posit a social actor who remembers how he became an oblate. Bourdieu's critique of the institution thus delivers the institutional object, along with its means of representation. In *Pascalian Meditations*, he also wonders whether his critical work is not 'a little perverse' in creating a schism between himself and his fellow academics: 'When he simply does what he has to do, the sociologist breaks the enchanted circles of collective denial [of the social world by academics]. By working towards the "return of the repressed", by trying to know and make known what the world of knowledge does not want to know, especially about itself, he takes the risk of appearing as the one who "gives the game away"—but to whom, except those with whom, in so doing, he breaks ranks..?' (Bourdieu 2002 [1997]: 5). Despite Bourdieu's use of psychoanalytic language to indicate epistemological radicalism, one is entitled to ask whether Bourdieu gives the game away at all, since a little perversion goes a long way towards confirming the limits of that particular brand of freedom that is recognizably and distinctly academic.

As Duchamp's hoax proves, a true 'return of the repressed' does not reflect an institution or a discourse as it is in terms of its internal and external dispositions and historical trajectory, but inversely, as a thing which it *cannot* be on those terms. This is also the function of the construction in the analytic scene, which is to stage an encounter between the analysand's search for 'the truth about the truth' and the unconscious logic that this search forestalls. As we demonstrated in this chapter, the staging of this encounter depends on an operation that can separate the game as an artifice of language from 'the game of life', with its contest of agents in the service of goods.

Chapter 8

Epistemological regression and the problem of applied psychoanalysis

> Now let us, by a flight of the imagination, suppose that Rome is not a human habitation but a psychical entity . . .
>
> Sigmund Freud, *Civilization and its Discontents*, 70

Making interpretation stupid

We closed our last chapter with Bourdieu's appeal for 'another critique' that would deliver his life's work from its complicity with institutional power. A preceding discussion of applied psychoanalysis also showed that the general problem of social critique and the particular problems of the psychoanalysis of culture and society are one and the same. Both are caught up in the ideal of freedom embodied in the search for end-state truth, situated within a market place of ideas. This chapter does not offer a conclusion to this discussion, nor to our book as a whole. Rather, it looks again at the relationship of psychoanalysis to the conditions of knowledge in which it has come to exist, and the critical necessity of a moment of epistemological regression, of becoming (and staying) stupid. In this chapter of our book, the moment of regression is located in Freud's development of an archaeological knowledge without relations of knowledge, within what is disarmingly referred to as his 'archaeological metaphor'. Freud's regression towards something less than archaeological knowledge accompanies his development of the technique of the analytic construction, in which the status of the knowing subject and the object of knowledge are fundamentally altered. If archaeology is a 'metaphor' for anything in psychoanalysis, it is a metaphor for this epistemological regression.[1]

What is the connection between going stupid and becoming

critical? How does what is 'less than knowledge' connect with what is 'more than (mere) interpretation?' Lacan gives a clue concerning this issue in *The Ethics of Psychoanalysis* (Lacan 1992 [1959–60]), in which he presents an extended panegyric on Freud's *Civilization and its Discontents* (Freud 1930a [1929]) and its discussion of the characteristics of the death drive. In defining Freud's text as 'indispensable' and 'unsurpassed', Lacan is careful to avoid the implication that *Civilization and its Discontents* is the work of a psychoanalyst playing at philosophy or social theory, stating that Freud was concerned with a primary ethical demand at the heart of both social life and psychoanalytic practice (Lacan 1992 [1959–60]: 6–7). If we are inclined to accept Lacan's position that Freud was not offering second-rate sociology or misplaced psychoanalytic theory, we must therefore be able to identify how Freud's text can be distinguished from garden variety applied psychoanalysis.

This key epistemological difference can be located in the famous passage where Freud employs his 'archaeological metaphor' in order to imagine a Rome in which all time periods exist simultaneously, and where nothing has passed away (Freud 1930a [1929]: 70). This recasting of the city state in the image of the unconscious voids Rome of its population and its intersubjective qualities, and fuses it into a single artefact, 'a psychical entity': 'In mental life nothing which has been once formed can perish—that everything is preserved and that in suitable circumstances (when, for instance, regression goes back far enough) it can once more be brought to light . . . an entity in which nothing that has once come into existence will have passed away and all the earlier phases of development continue to exist alongside the latest one' (ibid.: 70). In pursuing this idea, Freud is brought up against an inherent limitation: neither the object world, nor its associated systems of representation can adequately encompass the psychical object: 'There is clearly no point in spinning our phantasy any further, for it leads to things that are unimaginable and even absurd. If we want to represent historical sequence in spatial terms we can only do it by juxtaposition in space: the same space cannot have two different contents. Our attempt seems to be an idle game. It has only one justification. It shows us how far we are from mastering the characteristics of mental life by representing them in pictorial terms (ibid.: 70–71).

Freud is quite open here about his use of metaphor as a way of demonstrating lacunae rather than parallels. The unconscious is compared to the city in order to demonstrate the limitations of this comparison. What we are left with in this 'unreal city' is the unconscious, a primary thought process without an intersubjective dimension. The task of interpretation is now faced with two routes or options. The first takes interpretation back to the 'real city', the site of human interaction and the accumulation of knowledge goods', whereas the second directs it towards the fall of knowledge in the unconscious. These two alternatives do not just pertain to the clinical situation, but also co-exist within the textures of everyday life, institutional operations and human interaction. They do not require the application of psychoanalytic theory to make an appearance, but a psychoanalytic understanding of the knowledge process evinces this distinction (between epistemological accumulation and epistemological fall) most trenchantly.

When a psychoanalytic approach to knowledge occupies itself with other discourses such as archaeology, anthropology or sociology, it tends to expose this distinction between accumulation and fall in some way, however limited the effect might be. This subdiscursive or subdisciplinary aspect of psychoanalysis, in which the host discourses may be fractured or disarranged, should be seen as distinct from the problematic status of an applied psychoanalysis. The operators of applied psychoanalysis function as correspondents between a supposed body of psychoanalytic knowledge and established literary or cultural discourses, and as such they do not pose a threat to the knowledge fields with which they trade. Moreover, applied psychoanalysis is often used in a last-ditch attempt to 'save' interpretation where other interpretive strategies have failed. The Freud of 'Constructions in Analysis', on the other hand, asks us to think carefully about the distinction between, firstly, the furthering of an interpretation, and, secondly, the use of construction to address a deadlock of interpretation itself, at the point where it is seen to lack validity and a claim to truth.

The notion of the psychoanalytic construction tells us that there is a world of difference between psychoanalytic theory applied to archaeology, and archaeological knowledge as it was deranged and altered by Freud. Freud the collector and accumulator of objects is also the person who presented us with the notion of the psychical object. The epistemological status of this object seems to depend on an opposition between intention and interpretation on the one hand, and cathexis and the generation of effects on the other. Here we confront the 'force versus language' dilemma that Paul Ricoeur identified as the central question of Freudian epistemology: 'How can the economic explanation be involved in an interpretation dealing with meanings; and conversely, how can an interpretation be an aspect of the economic explanation?' (Ricoeur 1970 [1965]: 66). The solution for Ricoeur is to see psychoanalysis as a 'higher hermeneutics' of desire, which is of course not the direction Lacan took after 1965. Whereas he was still willing to entertain the possibility of a marriage between psychoanalysis and hermeneutics at the beginning of *Seminar XI*, by the end of it he defined the aim of interpretation as 'reducing the signifiers into their nonsensicality (*réduire les signifiants dans leur non-sens*') (Lacan 1994a [1964]: 192, translation modified).[2]

This regression, or 'making stupid', of interpretation lies at the heart of the violence that Freud enacts on archaeological method in 'Constructions in Analysis'. Uncritical references to the Freudian 'archaeological metaphor' have failed to take account of Freud's introduction of the psychical artefact alongside the archaeological one, and the epistemological disturbance that is thereby produced. What Freud does with the relationship of knowledge and the artefact in 'Constructions in Analysis' locates the position of psychoanalytic knowledge in the world more precisely than any Freudophile excursus on books, films or cultural phenomena. When a scholar such as Marcia Cavell claims that there is no general epistemological problem created by the collapse of the division between subject and object in psychoanalysis, and that the issue pertains only to the clinical situation, she ignores the precise manner in which psychoanalysis has colonized and reshaped existing patterns of thought (Cavell 1993: 101). We can refer here to the manner in which Freud's typically bohemian-bourgeois 'addiction' to an ethnographic fantasy of ancient and exotic artefacts ran parallel to his work on the psychical object, which exposes this fantasy in its relation to the unconscious.[3] This has allowed Lacan to see an individual compulsion towards the desired object, and the object so desired, as two elements of a single psychical artefact, built from signifiers.

Our examination of the critical effects of the analytic construction allows for a reconsideration of Bourdieu's appeal for 'the subversion of belief' in the practice of critique. Any such subversion will not consist in the simple replacement of interpretation with construction, or of fact with fantasy. Construction is not the opposite of interpretation, but a methodical misdirection or redirection of interpretation towards an encounter with the consequences of the reality of (timeless, subjectless) thought in the unconscious. Both in the

clinical encounter and in its institutional forms, Lacanian psychoanalysis assumes the discursive conditions set by the service of goods
through untying the bonds that link forms of interpretation and
analysis to psycho-social reality. This creates a paradox, because
Lacanian psychoanalysis works in close proximity to the 'manners
and rules' of discourse, solely in order to mark out a gap between the
artifice and representation that are inherent to discourse and speech.
Of course, this gap may be exposed without the aid of any psychoanalytic misdirection, as was shown when the 'Sokal affair' revealed
that the exchange of nonsense made perfect academic sense. However, psychoanalytic practice is the only form in which the distinction
between 'a knowledge' and 'the truth' is approached seriously and
systematically. Problems occur when this distinction, as established
through psychoanalytic practice, is applied to social reality, within
the contractual conditions set by the service of goods. The root cause
of these problems can be easily stated: in applied psychoanalysis
various possibilities, figures or representative ways of thinking about
social and cultural issues usurp the reality of the unconscious thought
that might undermine them. In this way, applied psychoanalysis
becomes just another interpretive option in the market place of
ideas. In this chapter we claim that the 'backward step', or moment
of epistemological regression, which psychoanalysis introduced from
its inception, offers a way to negotiate this impasse.

The consequences

Not only are the lessons of psychoanalytic intervention and its penetration of other discourses relevant to the current practice of discourse, but they have never been more urgently needed. The current
conditions of knowledge production are increasing the number of
players ('students') and varieties of knowledge goods, while making
the enlargement of the knowledge field into an end in itself. In a
situation where the law of 'more agents, fewer consequences' applies,
psychoanalysis is uniquely devoted to an understanding of consequence without agency in the unconscious. Perhaps the most
urgent issue that can be addressed from a psychoanalytic perspective
is that of the development of an understanding of consequence
itself, as it falls under the shadow of self-reproducing agency. It is
not simply that discourses do not possess an adequate language with
which to understand the failure or fall of knowledge, but that they
are increasingly hampered by their *inability to fail* and their tendency

to transform every trauma into a rationalization, from which 'lessons will be learned'. For many forms of knowledge, consequence itself is abolished. This is the problem that exercised Bourdieu, as he found his scathing institutional critiques to be part of a larger narrative of institutional success. Hence Bourdieu's recourse to Duchamp in his search for a weapon of critique that could actually engender a moment of institutional failure. Duchamp's gesture is exemplary, because it made the fall of the institution a direct consequence of its own institutional fiat; in other words, the instructions for sub-missions to the Independents' Show became the death warrant of the Society of Independent Artists.[4] The crucial point here is that the organizers of the exhibition assumed that the multiplication of agents ('anyone can exhibit') dispensed with the consequences of the artistic act; in other words, that democracy guaranteed ineffectuality. 'R. Mutt', on the other hand, was not one of these agents: he was nothing other than the appearance of 'the consequences' for the committee of the Independents' Show.

Duchamp's action in 1917 and that of Sokal in 1996 both take their place within a set of instances where 'the consequences' reappear from within forms of discourses that had sought to cancel out consequence entirely. At both these points, the forward march of 'artistic freedom' and the unstoppable progress of enculturation are halted in their tracks, and thereby revealed as institutionalized projects for the recruitment of agents and the production of goods. However, these instances of what Bourdieu describes as a fight against symbolic violence with its own weapons do not resolve them-selves into a coherent method of institutional critique, nor do they establish an alternative mode of knowledge production. In 'Con-structions in Analysis', on the other hand, Freud offers just such an alternative to the analysand. The 'suspended animation' of the psy-choanalytic construction, in which normal discourse is systematic-ally rebuilt with unconscious logic to the fore, replaces a process for the production of truth with a process for the production of effects and consequences: 'The "Yes" has no value unless it is followed by indirect confirmations, unless the patient, immediately after his "Yes", produces new memories which complete and extend the construction. Only in such an event do we consider that the "Yes" has dealt completely with the subject under discussion' (Freud 1937d: 262).

There is no equivalent of this process for a critique of the institu-tion, whether or not that critique is psychoanalytically informed.

Lacan's own battles with the psychoanalytic institution never assumed the status of a generally available anti-institutional methodology. His 'challenge to the psychoanalytic establishment' did not guarantee freedom from institutional chains; instead, it responded to the institutionalization of one-dimensional notions of freedom. In his address to students at the experimental University of Paris VIII-Vincennes, on 3 December 1969 (Lacan 1990c [1969]), which was concurrent with the development of *Seminar XVII*, Lacan was keen to point out his own 'regressive' position on the question of anti-institutional revolt. Instead of engaging with the particular contents and historical reference points of anti-establishment discourse, Lacan focused on the horizon of production within which the contemporary critique of power was contained. In his view, there was no intersubjective contest of 'us' and 'them' within the walls of the institution. The 'game of war', which had reached its apogee in 1968, was being supplied with combatants by the university itself, defined as a process without subjects: 'You are the products of the University and you prove that you are surplus value. . . . You come here to turn yourself into units of credit [*unités de valeur*]: you leave here stamped "Units of Credit" ' (Lacan 1990c [1969]: 121).[5] The university discourse is thus a procedure for the 'accreditation' of all citizens as players in the game of knowledge and as partisans in the struggle over truth. The subject is 'valued' in two senses here: as the agent who is provided with a piece of the action, and as the bearer of the act itself. The psychoanalytic challenge to this discursive establishment follows the logic of the Freudian construction, which directs relations of subjects in search of knowledge towards an unconscious knowledge without intersubjective relations, that is to say, towards the non-relational stupidity of the knowledge that contradicts itself. In this way consequence comes to the fore and the pursuit of (political, social) truth recedes into the background. In addition, Lacan's address at Vincennes employs a distinction between what is inside and what is external to the institution, whilst refusing to couch this difference in terms of intersubjective relations. The discourse of the university produces its own 'insides' and 'outsides'. Lacan reinforced this point in a comment during an exchange between two members of the audience, in which he situated the Other of university discourse as a mere function of 'university speech'. When one of the students advocated a Situationist-style occupation of the university by workers' councils, emphasizing that his role as a student was to incite others to abandon the institution, Lacan replied: 'Ah! You see . . . everything is there, my friend, in order to get them to go out, you come in . . .' (Lacan 1990c [1969]: 125).

Lacan's 'impromptu' at Vincennes suggests a reversal of the usual direction of critique, away from the enlightenment of agents of radical action, towards an understanding of how the enlightenment of the revolutionary subject coincides with the cancellation of the force of the revolutionary act. Lacan was fully aware that such a reversal could appear only as retrograde and conservative within the heady atmosphere following the events of 1968: 'I am a liberal, like everyone else, only in so far as I am anti-progressive. With the single modification that I am caught in a movement which deserves to be called progressive, for it is progressive to see the discourse of psycho-analysis achieve its foundation in so far as it completes the circle that might perhaps allow you to situate what precisely is at stake, what it is that you are rebelling against' (ibid.: 128).[6] Here, as so often, Lacan's stance appears arrogant and hubristic. His 'return to Freud' is held to offer more opportunities for change than does the over-throw of those in power. It stands as a direct refutation of the idea that 'pathological social structures can only be changed politically' (Torney 1994: 145), since political change is itself being posited as a pathological and illusory response to the need for changes of a more fundamental kind. In 1969 Lacan advocated a return to Freud as an antidote to this pathology, and it remains something current approaches to the analysis of institutionalized freedoms might directly benefit from.

Nonetheless, Lacan's thoughts on institutional critique do not amount to a fully worked out methodology. There is as yet no way to recognize a psychoanalytic construction outside the clinical situation, nor has applied psychoanalysis managed to generate distinctive approaches to the direction of the knowledge process. Most applied psychoanalysis is just 'more knowledge', which does not take part in the reshaping and redirection of knowledge production. However, on the basis of a reassessment of the Lacanian approach to knowledge that our book has tried to take forward, some of the characteristics of analysis beyond the clinic and the psychoanalytic establishment may be suggested, taking account of the problems of applied psychoanalysis that have already been described. Differentiating a form of knowledge without intersubjective relations from 'applied psychoanalysis' as such is not about splitting hairs, for if we wish to look at knowledge without relations of knowledge, psychoanalysis is the only approach available. If, on the other hand, we wish to study politics, culture or art, psychoanalysis is one of many discourses that we may apply in search of answers.

For this reason, a strategy for the regression and the 'making stupid' of knowledge does not aim to found a new orthodoxy in the psychoanalysis of culture and society. It is instead addressed to a specific and current problem of analysis and practice, namely, how can an all-inclusive 'discourse without consequences' encompass the fall of knowledge? This is the question hidden within Bourdieu's appeal for a way to set violence against (symbolic) violence, and it deserves an answer that does not involve his distinction between academic probity and the play of artistic subversion. Whereas Bourdieu names the violence of parody and pastiche as a remedy for the impotence of self-reflexive academic critique, we prefer a psychoanalytic approach highlighting 'the stupid of signifiers' for setting the compass of discursive freedom. This approach points to the necessity for an epistemological schema that can bridge the gap between the no-risk, all-inclusive approaches to knowledge that dominate the current scene and the grotesque consequences that these approaches tend to generate. It also points to another lesson of the Sokal affair, notably that none of the players involved were in the possession of a vocabulary and criteria with which to explain the epistemological contradictions that the affair exposed. The affair ensured the conduct of academic business as usual and consigned Sokal's article to the annals of parody.

The psychical object

The starting point for an analysis of the gap between the desire to know and the fall of knowledge is the identification of two sets of differences. The first difference occurs between ordinary discourse and the suspended animation of the psychoanalytic construction. The second difference is situated between the 'psychical object' that has been constructed and the artefact to be interpreted. In his comparison of techniques of reconstruction in psychoanalysis and archaeology, Freud noted that 'psychical objects are incomparably more complicated than the excavator's material ones' (Freud 1937d: 260), possibly because, unlike drinking bowls or ceremonial headdresses, they are not exactly built to human scale.

As Lacan went to great lengths to show in *Seminar XI*, the psychical object denatures the normal relationships between objects, bodies and space we use in order to negotiate our way within the world

(Lacan 1994a [1964]: 67–78). The intrusion of the gaze as psychical artefact within the field of vision, for example, makes it impossible for us to 'put ourselves in the picture' (ibid.: 85–90). The most quoted example here is the anamorphosis in Holbein's *The Ambassadors*, which bisects the 'walk-in' space of the painting, only to be revealed as a distorted image of a skull, the symbol of a violent terminus for the act of perception. More recently, artists have deliberately attempted to collapse normative relationships between material objects, institutions and systems of classification, often with a critical end in view. A key work of this type was 'The Department of Eagles', curated by the Belgian artist Marcel Broodthaers at the Städtische Kunsthalle in Dusseldorf in 1972.[7] The 'Department of Eagles' was an exhibition of three hundred images of eagles from the Oligocene era to the present, each labelled 'this is not a work of art'. It was part of an ongoing project, the *Musée d'art moderne*, which had an inaugural exhibition in Broodthaers' own home in 1968. By curating the 'uncuratable', Broodthaers constructed a kind of anamorphosis of museological and archaeological knowledge, in which material and historical facts are assembled in a deliberately 'dumb' fashion. According to Michael Compton, Broodthaers' construction was less a critique of the institution than a parody of such critiques: '1968 was the year of student revolutions during which the intelligentsia had focused on the idea of the worker (student) taking control of the institution in which he worked. . . . The 'Musée d'Art Moderne' . . . must be his reaction, both joining and subverting the vogue as always. . . . Although he said that this was a parody of art in terms of politics, the intention of the work is not finally to parody the museum; it might rather be to parody the sociologist of the museum' (Compton 1980: 18–19).

It can therefore be argued that Broodthaers supplies the kind of epistemological schema that the students of Vincennes would have required in order to discover, in Lacan's words, 'precisely what is at stake' in their act of rebellion. 'The Department of Eagles' renders the institution as 'a knowledge' without a knowing subject. It offers a certain logic of desire in search of completion (in psychoanalytic terms, a fantasy) and a mindless game extended to a potential infinity. In so doing, it pokes fun at the critical sociologist's intention to examine and intervene in the institutional landscape of intersubjective power/knowledge relationships, while ignoring the unconscious relations of knowledge that determine his activity. The sociologist of the museum thus fails to understand his own role in the eagle collection business, in the same way that the students of Vincennes do not realize their true place in a system for the accreditation of the autonomous, enlightened and radical subject.

In Broodthaers' art, 'museum type' artefacts, ripe for interpretive solutions, are instead used to construct a psychical artefact ('The Department'), which occupies both the institutional site of the museum and the consciousness of its spectators. In order to accomplish this transition, a process of desubjectivization must take place. The act of interpretation must be directed away from the search for museological truths and cultural choices towards the stupid, non-relational character of the unconscious production of knowledge. This marks another difference Freud noted between analytic (re)-construction and the archaeological variety, namely, that 'for the archaeologist the reconstruction is the aim and end of his endeavours while for analysis the construction is only a preliminary labour' (Freud 1937d: 260). For the archaeologist, reconstruction is the primary end in view, insofar as she wishes to build an approximation of vanished intersubjective relations out of inert shards of pottery and scattered fragments of bone. The task of the psychoanalyst is almost exactly the opposite; that is, to employ construction in order to expose the lack of a cognitive destination and an intersubjective dimension for unconscious knowledge.

Following the elucidation of differences between archaeological and psychoanalytic reconstruction, 'The Department of Eagles' provides a means to differentiate the material culture artefact from the psychical artefact within a single set of objects. It also fulfils some of the criteria of 'the other side' of academic critique, to which Bourdieu appealed in *Pascalian Meditations*. It does this by revealing the subjective refinements of the ethnographic imagination to be a perpetually unsatisfied yet all-consuming mania for completion. However, it is unlikely that Bourdieu would have been able to admit Broodthaers to the inner circle of sociological criticism, because rather than using his skills to make sense of cultural and social phenomena, the artist was employing them to redirect the relations of sense towards the effect of nonsense. This creates an impasse Bourdieu himself recognizes: the forms of critique the sociologist needs most are also those that would place the sociological field at risk. This last point is fundamental and relates directly to Lacan's evocation of a 'regressive' path of critique in his address to the students at Vincennes. Against the notion of the psychoanalyst as cultural hero, who can still come up with an interpretive solution when everyone else has failed, any critique based on a Lacanian reading of the knowledge field must work in the opposite direction, producing nonsense and epistemological failure where sense 'cannot fail'. Failure and the fall of knowledge are thus the necessary and unwelcome contribution of psychoanalysis to the spirit of epistemological enquiry.

If such a redirection of knowledge 'spoils the game' in a way that standard reflexive critiques are unwilling or unable to do, and if it deliberately refuses to contribute to the better functioning of an interpretive methodology, what use is it? The answer can only be that an apparently negative or spurious critical act, which seems to invent problems where none exist, or which fails to respect the wish for knowledge to 'move on' in search of the latest epistemological trends, is precisely what is needed in order to link knowledge to its effects. The 'backward step' of psychoanalysis discloses how socio-cultural models of knowledge are built upon a series of negations, which establish relationships between methodological habits of thought and their external objects of study. As Freud argued in his essay on 'Negation' (Freud 1925h), representation provides temporary immunity from the object of the unconscious. The 'no' of discrimination, judgement and scholarly probity is a defence against the absence of a 'no' in the unconscious. The psychical object cuts across these divisions between representations/interpretations and their objects, and reveals that the unconscious is made of thought as well. However, this other thought of the unconscious possesses none of the defining characteristics of intradiscursive activity; instead, it resembles a 'thing', a blockage or obstruction, a mass of uncategorizable, unreadable material. Admitting this lumpen mass of thought within the boundaries of discursive practice can be seen only as a mistake, as the 'Sokal affair' has shown.

Nonetheless, more recent cultural criticism has made significant efforts toward the reclassification of unthinkable discursive objects as elements of an unconscious thought process. In *The Philistine Controversy*, Dave Beech and John Roberts have sought to demonstrate how the philistine, as a figure of cultural blindness, inertia and regression, features as a contiguous stain or flaw within the fantasy of completion that informs both the aesthetic subject and its contemporary variant, the enlightened, inclusive subject of culture (Beech and Roberts 2002).[8] Their work positions the 'stupid' philistine as an integral element of refined aesthetic thought, and not as an anti-aesthetic Other or as the object of an enlightened rescue mission. Beech and Roberts' work was not carried out within an explicitly psychoanalytic framework, yet it does demonstrate the need for methods that can counter, firstly, the refusal to acknowledge an unconscious dimension to knowledge within traditional academic disciplines, and, secondly, the incorporation of the unconscious as another interpretive option within postmodernist criticism.

Freud's regression

In his metapsychological essay on 'The Unconscious', Freud stated that unconscious processes become 'cognizable' only when the higher functions of the preconscious system undergo a moment of regression, when they are 'lowered' or 'set back to an earlier stage' (Freud 1915e: 187). In order to understand the epistemological implications of this moment of regression, it is worthwhile comparing Freud's discussion of archaeological method in the Dora case (Freud 1905e [1901]) with his later and fuller treatment of archaeology in 'Constructions in Analysis' (Freud 1937d), where the archaeological metaphor is incorporated within a testament of analytic technique. In the earlier work, Freud designated psychoanalytic and archaeological reconstruction as the best approximation of the truth: 'I have restored what is missing, taking the best models known to me from other analyses; but, like a conscientious archaeologist, I have not omitted to mention in each case where the authentic parts end and my constructions begin' (Freud 1905e [1901]: 12). Here, the purpose of excavation and restoration is still to serve an intentional consciousness and the act of interpretation. By 1937, however, the persistence of the archaeological metaphor disguises the fact that Freud has definitively parted company with archaeological knowledge. In 1937 there is no longer anything 'archaeological' about Freud's archaeology, despite his constant references to images of excavation and recurrent comparisons of the unconscious to a buried city.[9] Perhaps the best evidence of this is that Freud first asserts that archaeological and psychoanalytic construction 'are in fact identical' and then proceeds to show exactly why they are not. The analogy of an investigation that proceeds to the lower depths is overruled by a procedure in which knowledge itself is lowered or regressed, to a point where neither an archaeologist, nor any other self-respecting scholar can follow. As we have argued above, this epistemological 'point of no return' is the one that Bourdieu both dreams of and cannot accept, since it involves the radical transformation of knowledge itself into a thing or an object, which in Bourdieu's opinion can be symbolized only by the object of art. The example of Broodthaers' 'Department of Eagles' has shown that the question of the work of art is less important in this case than the way in which the psychical object is bound up with the 'fallen state' of knowledge in the unconscious.

Contra Ricoeur, the whole problem of Freudian epistemology is not a question of meaning/interpretation/language (hermeneutics) versus energy/power/cathexis (the economic principle). Instead, the core epistemological problem is how to direct a procedure in which knowledge is disclosed as a psychical artefact through the procedures of construction. There is a stark distinction to be made between this artefact and the relations between subjects of knowledge and their own knowledge products. The aforementioned example of Bernard Porter and his lecture notes provides a good illustration of how to differentiate individual epistemological alienation from the alienation of knowledge in the unconscious. Rather than simply existing as 'Porter commodified', the lecture notes are simultaneously 'less than Porter' and 'more than Porter', so that the location of Professor Porter himself within this new knowledge artefact becomes difficult to define. Academics may rail against the product that they have become, but they have no language with which to encounter the artefact that their knowledge always was.

It is also worth noting, in turn, that partisans of the psychoanalysis of culture and society may treat psychoanalytic epistemology itself, and its moment of regression, as just another product. In an essay from the early 1990s, James Donald quotes a key question formulated by Shoshana Felman, 'How can I interpret out of the dynamic ignorance I analytically encounter, both in others and myself?', endorsing her sentiment that psychoanalysis can teach us only to 'learn from our ignorance' (Donald 1991: 1). Although their appeal to ignorance might initially seem to resonate with the theme of this book, Donald and Felman still contribute to a general situation in which knowledge becomes impervious to failure, and in which cultural and social interpretation can always grow and flourish, even within the 'philosophy of ignorance' that psychoanalysis has engendered. Psychoanalytic regression is recruited to a progressive task, here, notably to delimit the space of 'the good'. In this epistemological situation, knowledge is unable to experience the fall that resides at the heart of Freud's technique of analytic construction. Through his particular approach to this fall, Freud was able to connect the act of interpretation to the provision of an analytic solution. Psychoanalysis, in other words, gave interpretation an effective dimension.

This effective dimension of knowledge is now gradually being written out of our lives. When Lacan addressed the students of Vincennes in 1969, his appeal to Freud as an alternative to political change appeared as extremely old-fashioned and reactionary. Since that date, however, we have become accustomed to the idea that neither political action nor 'theory' can effect any meaningful change. Knowledge regimes have become expanded, consolidated and refined, whereas change can only be imagined as a rudimentary fantasy of global disaster or terrorist catastrophe. The challenge that Freud and Lacan continue to offer to the contemporary knowledge establishment stems from a unique characteristic of psychoanalysis within the world of goods: it embodies a systematic approach to a type of knowledge which is 'less than knowledge'. The name for this 'less than knowledge' is the unconscious. In a situation in which the injunction to keep on knowing more shows no signs of losing its grip on our collective consciousness, it is the 'less' of psychoanalysis that is required in order to sustain an ethical link between interpretations and their effects.

Coda: Conceptualizing the rigorous hole

Less than 48 hours after a void appeared in the New York skyline, two different sources in completely different parts of the world sent out an electronic message to various discussion lists, containing a document in which Slavoj Žižek cast his critical eye on the impact of the terrorist attacks within our late capitalist consumer society. Implicitly relying on Lacan's notion of the fantasy as a psychic protection against the traumatic intrusion of the real, Žižek argued, amongst other things, that the events of 11 September 2001 managed to create such a devastating shockwave precisely because America was suddenly faced with a scene it had already visualized numerous times in its Hollywood disaster movies. Less than a week after Žižek's statement had been forwarded, another message was sent out, again from various sources, in which the collapse of the WTC was also dissected with the conceptual tools of Lacanian psychoanalysis. The second message was a composite text comprising an article by Eric Laurent, president of the École de la Cause Freudienne, an abridged translation of a paper by Abel Fainstein, president of the Argentinian Psychoanalytic Association (associated with the IPA), and the transcription of an interview with Jacques-Alain Miller, president of the World Association of Psychoanalysis, on the validity of the viewpoints expressed in the two previous texts. Laurent claimed that the Twin Towers had been attacked neither as symbols (of prosperity and pride, but also of banality) nor as functional entities (office blocks for the financial world), but as objects of a jouissance extracted from market globalization by the Wall Street moguls. Fainstein, for his part, conceded that the terrorist onslaught defies understanding and that the destruction of symbolic points of reference, like the WTC and the Pentagon, was bound to shatter people's psychic coordinates, leaving them perplexed and traumatized. In his comments, Miller first endeavoured to reconcile the two ostensibly contradictory interpretations with reference to the two sides of Lacanian theory—that of the signifier and that of the object—and then decided to postpone his own opinion, on the grounds of mental slowness and a general lack of information.

However thought-provoking these psychoanalytic readings of the terrorist attacks may seem, they elicit important questions about the contemporary status of psychoanalytic knowledge. There is no doubt a category of people for whom the level of expectation generated by every new Žižek release is similar to that sustained by each new album of one's favourite rock band. Žižek's idiosyncratic amalgamation of Lacanian psychoanalysis, pop culture, (not so) dirty jokes and austere political philosophy is simultaneously entertaining, disconcerting and inspiring, however disrespectful it may be for the serious-minded mainstream critic (elucidating some of the worst world conflicts via the stakes of Hollywood cinema?). Moreover, the views of self-identified Lacanian psychoanalysts on one or another of the current debates ripping through our comfortable social fabric, be it the issue of homosexual marriage, the controversy over the free choice of surname or, indeed, the global ascendancy of terror and violence, generally attract limited public interest, yet they are often sufficiently trenchant to deserve some serious attention. And why should we disapprove of the creation of a Lacanian press agency and the deep concern of psychoanalysts (Lacanian and other) with sociopolitical events outside their immediate, clinical sphere of influence? Although it is doubtful whether the psychoanalysts in question would be happy to admit it, it seems that the psychoanalytic comments on the events of 11 September bear witness to the fact that psychoanalysis, as Jacques Derrida put it in a high-profile intervention in July 2000, is indeed the 'only discourse that can today claim the thing of psychical suffering as its own affair', and that it is therefore the responsibility of politics to take account of psychoanalytic knowledge (Derrida 2002 [2000]: 240).

However, the speed with which psychoanalytic knowledge was brought to bear on the carnage in New York's financial district may also give us some serious reasons for concern. Isn't the swiftness with which psychoanalytic ideas are being employed to unearth the hidden motives of radical terrorists and to enlighten the obscure sociopolitical configurations of their acts indicative of how psychoanalysis, contrary to Freud's aspirations, has indeed become a new *Weltanschauung*—a trendy meta-theory whose notions are so powerful that they enable us to explain everything and anything, from the unexplained to the unexplainable? Doesn't the psychoanalyst, or the psychoanalytically inspired cultural critic, prove to be the last remaining cultural hero, so impervious to intellectual discomfort that he can still come up with a thoughtful intervention when thought itself has been shattered? Hasn't the psychoanalyst, in his inexhaustible desire to produce comforting rationalizations for the traumas that affect our lives, become the last unshakeable vestige of our knowledge economy? And isn't the popularity of the psychoanalyst in the socio-cultural field, across the disciplines, inversely proportional to his acknowledged value within a clinical setting? One might feel inclined to defend the ongoing significance of psychoanalysis, against the ever-looming threat of the fanatic Freud bashers, by saying that Freud's work is impossible to divorce from contemporary society since it has become a staple of postmodernism, feminism, deconstructionism, and gender-, culture- and women's studies, not to mention comparative literature, film studies, law, political science, religious studies, queer studies, sociology and anthropology. Yet the momentum psychoanalysis has gained over the past twenty years within and across the social sciences, cultural studies, the arts and the humanities, is also a reflection of its moribund state in the area of specialization for which it was originally invented, namely the clinical treatment of people suffering from a variety of mental and physical symptoms. A wealthy member of an anti-psychoanalysis terrorist organization could not do better than fund as many psychoanalytically inspired multi-, inter- or cross-disciplinary projects as possible, since this strategy would definitely contribute to wiping psychoanalysis off the map as a theory of a particular clinical practice.

Derrida's claim (and the implicit message conveyed by the psychoanalytic readings of 11 September) that it is the responsibility of politics to take account of psychoanalytic knowledge encompasses an even more pressing danger than the gradual disappearance of psychoanalysis as a theory of clinical practice. For psychoanalysis runs the risk, here, of being solidified into a self-contained and self-governing body of ideas, whose wide array of applications serves not only the meaningful unravelling of objects outside its boundaries but also the fortification of its own subsistence as a global explanatory doctrine. Externally fruitful yet internally sterile, constructive across many disciplines yet autodestructive in the progressive sclerosis of its own foundations, psychoanalytic knowledge is unlikely to benefit from its penetration of and dissemination across the disciplines.

Reading the collapse of the Twin Towers along the dual lines of Lacan's conceptualization of the symbolic order and the object of jouissance principally strengthens our belief in the value, if not to say the truth, of this conceptual distinction. Yet we can reasonably assume that Lacan did not have in mind the singular status of an American tower block in the murderous fantasy of a fundamentalist Muslim when talking about the object of jouissance. And what do psychoanalysts in general really know about terrorism, its concrete motives, social organization and psychic mainspring? How many psychoanalysts have had the good (or bad) fortune to encounter a genuine terrorist in their consultation rooms? One week after the day when the world stood still, and with his tongue firmly in cheek, Jacques-Alain Miller wrote a short piece, 'The Tenderness of Terrorists', which stood out from the stream of psychoanalytic interpretations of political terrorism and religious fundamentalism for its splendid critique of *intellectual* terrorism and *psychoanalytic* fundamentalism: 'From the moment psychoanalysis is at stake, through what an analysand or an analyst says about it, the question is: is this beautiful lie actually true? Go and find out! It concerns a structural defect. It is the lack of truth about truth, as Lacan designates it so nicely. This lack is everywhere in language and it is laid bare in psychoanalysis' (Miller 2002a: 143). Should this statement be true in itself, should its 'half-saying' that makes the factual reality appear through a mendacious structure of fiction still be sufficiently acceptable, would that imply that all those who claim to be able to tell the truth about 9/11, through their knowledge of psychoanalysis, do not only fool themselves and others, but also reject, perhaps foreclose, the central principles of psychoanalytic epistemology? If Žižek is indeed a genius in spotting and pointing out other people's stupidities, and if most of us from time to time enjoy his humorous exposure of the world's nonsense, then we still need to realize that we are probably enticed and enthralled by our own complicity with the superior master figure. But it is a complicity that is not innocuous, for it can blind us to our own stupidities and we might very well end up as 'stupid' followers of our allegedly demystifying and enlightening genius. It bears repeating that the psychoanalyst does not point out stupidities, if only because this type of act can proceed only from a position of intellectual mastery and a refusal of the inherent limits of knowledge.

Tempting as it may be to work one's way through a highly dramatic situation such as the terrorist attacks on the USA with the theoretical machinery of psychoanalytic knowledge, the outcome of this intellectual exercise, is less than promising. What does it matter if the Americans finally got what they fantasized about for many years in the products of their movie industry? What does it matter if the Twin Towers were destroyed as an object of jouissance or as a symbol of prosperity? If it might still matter for the psychoanalyst working with those whose relatives lost their lives in the disaster, the treatment setting is probably the environment where psychoanalysts will be the most unlikely professionals to intervene, in light of the contemporary discrediting of psychoanalysis as a clinical discipline. Yet even if they were called upon to deal with those clients whose distress originates in or has been exacerbated by the lethal effects of mass terrorism, how can we expect them to direct the treatment effectively if their attitude transpires an ardent desire to substantiate the knowledge they have constructed elsewhere, previously, under different circumstances and in a non-political context?

Returning to Derrida's assertion that it is the responsibility of politics (but also of ethics and law) to take stock of psychoanalytic knowledge, it seems that this may very well be a duty for political scientists, but that it can never be a task to which psychoanalysts should commit themselves. Working through politics or, for that matter, the undermining of political constellations, by means of psychoanalytic knowledge cannot feature on the political agenda of psychoanalysis. Reconstructing the destruction of the Twin Towers in terms of the fantasy, the signifier and the object *a*, working through the rubble of a skyscraper in search of the lost object or the phallus, cannot be part of the psychoanalytic menu, at least not inasmuch as it is designed by and for psychoanalysts. Does that imply that psychoanalysts should refrain from interpreting, discussing, indeed analysing socio-political circumstances? Does it entail that the psychoanalyst ought to resist being drawn into wider debates on political, ethical and legal issues? Does the analyst need to restrict him- or herself to the clinical realm out of which the theory emerged and in relation to which it developed? Absolutely not. The interdisciplinary confrontation between psychoanalysis and other areas of research within the so-called natural and human sciences, as well as the psychoanalyst's engagement with socio-political events, constitutes a crucial opportunity for theoretical advancement and epistemological reflection. Yet confrontation and engagement will contribute to theoretical advancement and epistemological reflection only if they follow a path that is substantially different from the applied route described above. In addition, the path may be approached from two different angles, depending on whether it is psychoanalysis or one of the other disciplines that benefits from the encounter.

Let us start with the discipline of psychoanalysis. How can Freud's ideas benefit from a confrontation with other disciplines, if the confrontation does not involve the simple application and extension of psychoanalytic knowledge? In order to address this question, we may reconsider Freud's rather peculiar notion of 'working-through' (*Durcharbeitung*). This term appears on no more than three separate occasions in Freud's entire oeuvre (Freud and Breuer 1895d: 288, 291; Freud 1914g: 155–156, 1926d [1925]: 159), an observation which has prompted some historians of psychoanalysis to argue that the notion and the process have no conceptual status in Freudian theory (Roudinesco and Plon 1997). Freud's minimal glosses on the nature and function of working-through are all the more remarkable given the fact that he himself regarded it as the most important aspect of psychoanalytic labour—a process bringing about the greatest transformation of the client's state of mind, guaranteeing psychoanalytic effects beyond those obtained through the power of suggestion (Freud 1914g: 155–156), and epitomizing the only effective response to the infernal resistance of the Id, that is, the compulsion to repeat (Freud 1926d [1925]: 159). The only indications Freud gives as to how exactly we need to understand the mechanism of working-through relate to the analysand's necessary immersion in the radius of psychical resistance in order to discover the drive on which this resistance is feeding. Working-through requires the most intensive of labours and its operation can be neither anticipated nor accelerated. 'One must allow the patient time' (Freud 1914g: 155) and the psychoanalyst can only wait. If working-through is a mental test for the analyst's patients, it is therefore simultaneously a test of endurance for the analyst's patience (ibid.: 155).

Rather than taking on board one of the numerous, often contradictory interpretations of Freud's term that have been advanced since the 1950s, we prefer to focus on a minute comment concerning working-through by Lacan in the final session of his *Seminar XI*. Lacan underscores that the end of analysis occurs 'after the mapping of the subject in relation to the *a*, [when] the experience of the fundamental phantasy becomes the drive' (Lacan 1994a [1964]: 273). This statement is immediately followed by the idea of the traversal of the fantasy, which has gained ascendancy as the most significant of Lacan's contributions to a theory of the end of analysis. Yet Lacan launched this idea by means of an open-ended question—'How can a subject who has traversed the radical phantasy experience the drive?' (ibid.: 273)—and deplored the fact that it had been investigated only from the viewpoint of an analytic treatment with training effects. At this precise point, Lacan rekindled Freud's notion of working-through, which he employed to designate the process whereby an analysand runs through the cycle of analytic experience a sufficient amount of times for the fantasy to give way to the drive and to make possible the transition from analysand to analyst. Hence, in Lacan's reading of Freud, working-through coincides with the traversal of the fantasy, prefigures the emergence of the drive and precipitates the concurrent adoption of the position of psychoanalyst by the former analysand. During the late 1960s, Lacan did not hesitate to qualify this transition from analysand to psychoanalyst as a passage to the act (*passage à l'acte*) (Lacan 1990b [1966], 2001c [1967]), so that working-through may be conceived as the psychic force that clears the path for this very act. Similar to the process of *Bahnung* (facilitation), which Freud adduced in his famous 'Project for a Scientific Psychology' (Freud 1950a [1895]), working-through involves path clearing—not of the neurons, but of the mental logic of the fantasy, and in view of the crystallization of an act. The latter point is fully consistent with Freud's outlook in 'Remembering, Repeating and Working-Through', where the effect of working-through is compared to that of an 'abreaction' (*Abreagieren*) (Freud 1914g: 156).

What is the relevance of this conceptual digression to the issues that concern us here? It seems that for all their enthusiasm in working their way through adjacent fields with the knowledge of psychoanalysis, psychoanalysts may benefit more from employing the most challenging aspects of these fields in order to work their way through their own body of knowledge. Rather than interpreting and working-through socio-political events from a constituted body of knowledge, psychoanalysis ought to take advantage of these events as intrinsically challenging interpretations in their own right, pushing established knowledge to the point where it reaches its limit in the radical hole of knowledge and where a path is being cleared for something new. Put differently, the eagerness of psychoanalysis to (re)confirm itself as a powerful and inviolate body of knowledge in the (re)configuration of the social field is but a reflection of its unwillingness to (re)configure its own enterprise, that is to say, a reflection of the resistance to traverse the pervasive fantasy of its

own mission as an explanatory superpower. This is exactly why
Lacan, when asked to contribute to a special journal issue on literature and psychoanalysis in the early 1970s, refused to detail the principles of applied psychoanalysis. Instead he argued that the direction
of the application should be inverted: '[F]ar from compromising
myself in this literary smoochy-woochy [*frotti-frotta*] with which
the psychoanalyst who is short of ingenuity denotes himself, I bear
witness there [in the *Écrits*] to the inevitable attempt at demonstrating the unevenness of his practice to motivate the least literary
judgement' (Lacan 2001e [1971]: 12).

Psychoanalysis, as Lacan portrays it here, is not equal to the
task of judging (psychoanalytically) what is happening within fields
outside its own modus operandi. Yet, the 'unevenness' of psychoanalysis to formulate literary (and other) judgements does not
exclude the possibility of psychoanalysis judging itself. On the contrary, this self-reflexive act may be the most ethically advanced task
befalling the theory and practice of psychoanalysis, a task which is
all the more denied as more psychoanalytic judgements are being
extended beyond the boundaries of psychoanalysis. What Lacan
designated as 'the ethics of psychoanalysis' thus also, and perhaps
primarily, concerns not only a judgement on the nature of psychoanalytic action in view of the goals and the end of the treatment, but
also a judgement on the nature and function of knowledge within
the general theory and practice of psychoanalysis. This judgement
can emerge only on the basis of an extensive and constant working-
through, aimed at the progressive dismantling of the unconscious
fantasy governing the epistemological status of psychoanalysis.
The judgement in itself can involve only an acknowledgement of the
limits of psychoanalytic knowledge, and will inevitably open the
door to something new, beyond the compulsion to repeat and therefore beyond the 'beyond of the pleasure principle'. This is also what
Lacan surmised when redressing the stakes of his famous 'Seminar
on "The Purloined Letter" ', some fifteen years after its initial publication: '[I]f I propose to psychoanalysis the letter as in abeyance [in
his 'Seminar on "The Purloined Letter" '], it is because [psycho-
analysis] shows its failure there. And it is through this that I illuminate
[psychoanalysis]: when I invoke in this way the Enlightenment [at the
end of the *Écrits*], it is to demonstrate where [psychoanalysis] constitutes a *hole*' (ibid.: 13). This demonstration does not represent
the radical failure of psychoanalytic knowledge, but rather intends
to propose that psychoanalysis can operate only by virtue of a

knowledge 'in failure' or 'in check' (*savoir en échec*). In other words, psychoanalysis incorporates a 'checked knowledge', a knowledge traversed by a rigorous hole, whose constitutive function needs to be acknowledged and conceptualized in view of the possible emergence of a new beginning. The latter process deserves to be called a 'psychoanalytic act' insofar as it constitutes a founding, creative moment which leaves behind all the time-honoured thoughts of the past and takes the risk of entering an uncertain terrain whose (lack of) solidity will be revealed only in retrospect.

If this is how psychoanalysis can take advantage of its encounter with other disciplines and its confrontation with socio-political events, the benefit is not merely on the side of psychoanalysis. Indeed, if psychoanalysis, as a theory of a specific clinical practice, is geared to the acknowledgement of the fundamental fissure residing at the heart of its own body of knowledge, this process of working-through and its ensuing ethical judgement on the nature of psychoanalytic action may inspire representatives of other disciplines to reassess their own relationship with the knowledge that supports their research. In many disciplines, labour is currently undertaken as an ongoing reflection upon the existing knowledge and the accepted methodologies, either with a view of building new and better knowledge (the accumulative strategy) or tailored to exposing the inadequacy of the available constructs (the sacrificial strategy), and sometimes with combined sacrificial and accumulative goals. However, within a properly psychoanalytic economy of labour, working-through implies neither the institutionalization nor the evacuation, neither the hierarchization nor the destruction of knowledge, but its recognition as an edifice built on the foundations of ignorance, a fantasmatic construct designed to control the stupidity of the drive. The corollary of this recognition is that psychoanalysis cannot be employed as a fully finished doctrine, either within or outside the treatment. And if the psychoanalyst needs to learn that 'his knowledge is but a symptom of his own ignorance', as Lacan put it (Lacan 1966c [1955]: 358), other disciplines may use their confrontation with psychoanalysis to adopt a similar stance vis-à-vis their own knowledge and methodologies. '[I]f literary criticism could effectively renew itself,' Lacan writes, 'it would be because psychoanalysis is there for the texts to measure themselves against it, the enigma being on its side' (Lacan 2001e [1971]: 13). If there is anything to be learnt from psychoanalysis, it is that the most advanced form of learning is learning how to acknowledge the unknown dimension of one's own knowledge.

Notes

1 From the perspective of the dynamic unconscious, Freud's opposition is of course less exclusive. For if we accept, as Freud argued throughout his work, that unconscious representations remain active and that repression is synonymous with the return of the repressed, then the renunciation of the passions in the pursuit and realization of 'full knowledge' must inevitably encounter the ineluctable reappearance of love and hatred, in symptomatic form, within the 'state of knowledge' and the research process (the desire to know) that is supporting it.

2 Throughout his work, Freud defined psychoanalysis (much like everything else) in a threefold way: psychoanalysis is first of all a specific treatment method for resolving all kinds of mental and bodily symptoms; apart from this, it is also a theory on the dynamic relationships in the mind, encompassing descriptive (qualities of mental representations), economic (energetic relations between representations) and topographical (systematic) perspectives; finally, psychoanalysis is a method of investigation that can be used for unravelling the unconscious motives that are at work in all aspects of human cultural and social activity. See, for example, Freud (1924f [1923], 1926f). This threefold distinction is of course slightly artificial because each of the three components relies on the others for its implementation and development. The psychoanalytic treatment is based on a set of theoretical ideas about how the mind works, and the application of these ideas follows a certain strategy. Likewise, the psychoanalytic theory of the mind is rooted in what takes place during the treatment process, and the investigative strategy is modified as a result of specific clinical problems. However, Freud's tripartite definition of psychoanalysis demonstrates that research is not something psychoanalysis should try to integrate within its realm of action. Studying research within psychoanalysis essentially comes down to explaining the nature of the psychoanalytic process as such. A phrase such as 'psychoanalytic research' is therefore not only tautological, but also misleading, since it seems to suggest that there is a type of psychoanalysis that involves research and another type that does away with it.

3 Lacan's concept of '*le sujet supposé savoir*', which informed his theory of

transference from the early 1960s, is usually translated as 'the subject supposed to know'. In choosing to render it as 'the supposed subject of knowing', we have followed Stuart Schneiderman's suggestion (Schneiderman 1993 [1980]: vii), because it conveys more accurately Lacan's idea of the supposition of a subject of knowledge (as opposed to a subject supposing knowledge).

4 Whenever we use the term 'non-knowledge' in this book, the reader should avoid interpreting it along the lines of Bataille's Nietzschean reversal of the Socratic 'know thyself' (Bataille 2001b [1973–88]). In our argumentation, non-knowledge does not refer to an inner experience of self-dissolution but to an inwardly divided reason. As such, non-knowledge is not tantamount to the absence of knowledge (thought, reason) but to moments of rational inversion, when thought suddenly runs into its unthought and unthinkable Other, when thought loses its meaningful, communicative function and strands into nonsensicality and meaninglessness.

5 The hackneyed words of St Francis were of course readily embraced by Margaret Thatcher on the day she became Britain's prime minister, but then the era of Thatcherism was one of the most successful for the promotion of a knowledge economy.

6 As we shall see in Chapter 4, psychoanalytic organizations have always found it extraordinarily difficult to guarantee their own knowledge domain, so much so that state interference with psychoanalytic practice and its training principles has constantly threatened the autonomy of the psychoanalytic community.

7 Lacan argued that a person's demand for analysis on the grounds of wanting to be an analyst is also a symptom, so that the difference between a 'regular' analysis and a 'training analysis' is superfluous. See Lacan (1966c [1955]: 358). For additional comments on this issue, see Forrester (1990: 221–242) and Libbrecht (1998).

8 Freud has of course often been vilified for indoctrinating his patients, especially the Rat Man (Freud 1909d) and the Wolf Man (Freud 1918b [1914]), with his own dubious, pan-sexualist ideology and the equally suspect mystification of the Oedipus complex. Yet in both these cases, Freud's ostensible intellectualist intervention has all the qualities of an analytic construction which, as we shall argue in the second part of our book, aims at the fall of knowledge rather than its authoritarian replacement and concurrent accumulation in the service of an economy of goods.

9 For a detailed exploration of the epistemological implications of Freud's 'conjunction' (*Junktim*), see Dreher (2000: 37–64).

10 On this point, see Lacan's opening statements of *Seminar XX* (Lacan 1998b [1972–73]: 1–2).

11 In his *Seminar VII, The Ethics of Psychoanalysis*, Lacan criticized the popular image of the analyst as a stoic figure who sustains the analysand's demands and abstains from direct intervention, because this type of ethics allows the analysand to direct the treatment and thus to become complicit with the tyranny of the desire for knowledge. See Lacan (1992 [1959–60]: 320–321).

12 Cardinal Nicholas of Cusa (Nicholas Cusanus) (1401–1464) gained notoriety for repudiating the mediaeval conception of the cosmos as a system which revolves around the central axis of the Earth and its inhabitants, because the latter have been created by God. Descartes interpreted Cusanus' cosmology as the first attempt to describe the universe as an infinite system, yet Koyré (1957) has argued that Cusanus' refusal to accept the world's finitude, and its closure by the celestial spheres, does not imply his simultaneous attribution of infinity to the universe. Koyré points out that only God is infinite in Cusanus' cosmology and that the universe is *interminatum*, meaning that it lacks precise determination in its constitutive components, and implying that it can never be captured by a totalizing science but can only be approximated by conjectural knowledge. Much like God, but for a different reason, the universe escapes our apprehension: we 'know that' God and the universe exist but we cannot 'know' them. Knowing (*connaître*) God and the universe must inevitably fail, despite our knowledge (*savoir*) of them. Hence, Cusanus acknowledges also with regard to the universe the essentially partial state of our knowledge, which is one of the crucial aspects of *docta ignorantia*. For detailed accounts of Cusanus' cosmology and his conception of ignorance, see Koestler (1989 [1959]: 209–210) and Martin (1985: 24–42). For Cusanus' eponymous treatise on *docta ignorantia*, see Cusanus (1985 [1440]). Much as Lacan's knowledge of Hegel was to a large extent derived from Kojève's seminars of the mid-1930s (Kojève 1969 [1933–39]), his knowledge of Cusanus stemmed from a year-long seminar conducted by Koyré in 1932.

13 It is unclear whether Lacan attended Bataille's four lectures on non-knowledge at the Collège philosophique during the early 1950s, but his definition of non-knowledge in this passage is clearly at odds with the inner experience of self-dissolution that Bataille endeavoured to theorize. Lacan only once explicitly referred to Bataille's lectures on non-knowledge, notably in his seminar on 'the knowledge of the psychoanalyst' (Lacan 1971–72: session of 4 November 1971), where he talked rather condescendingly about a lecture in which Bataille did not utter a single word, 'not a bad way to display non-knowledge'.

14 We may assume that Freud used the bizarre expression, 'before I had any opportunity of hearing about psychoanalysis', because he did not want his own identity to be revealed. In submitting his study anonymously, he thus presented the readers of *Imago* with a puzzle not dissimilar to the ones which Morelli had managed to solve with his revolutionary (analytic) procedure.

15 For this reason, Lester Luborsky's famous 'core conflictual relationship theme' method (CCRT method) for 'measuring' transference, which concentrates on the identification of key narrative episodes in the verbatim protocols of a patient's sessions, contravenes one of the central principles of Freudian research. See Luborsky and Crits-Christoph (1990).

16 Let us recall, here, that one of Freud's first interventions in the case of Little Hans involved his definition of Hans's horse phobia as a *Dummheit* (a stupidity, a piece of nonsense): 'I arranged with Hans's father that he should tell the boy that all this business about horses was a piece of

nonsense and nothing more' (Freud 1909b: 28). The father complied with Freud's request and soon after *Dummheit* became the new name of Hans's phobia.

17 Any remaining doubts that stupidity has a history will be taken away if one has a look at the highly entertaining volumes by Tabori (1993 [1959]) and van Boxsel (2003).

18 In the second part of this book we shall demonstrate how Freud eventually distanced himself from the 'archaeological metaphor', and how this departure revolved around a crucial aspect of psychoanalytic epistemology.

19 The significance of Poe's story 'The Purloined Letter', and Lacan's interpretation of it, will be discussed at length in Chapters 6 and 7.

20 For an interesting discussion of the importance of sound (the sonic boom) in analytic interpretation, see Shingu (2004 [1995]: 44–46).

21 The classic example here is the *Meno* 'dialogue', in which Socrates' interlocutor, after having asked the question of whether virtue can be taught, settles into mere expressions of approval and agreement. See Plato (1986). For the term 'endopsychic knowledge', see Kofman (1988 [1970]).

Chapter 2

1 The status of psychoanalytic knowledge, the discourse of the analyst and the function of psychoanalytic knowledge within the treatment will be dealt with at length in the second part of our book.

2 See also the first sentence of Lacan's 'Subversion of the Subject': 'A structure is constitutive of the praxis known as psychoanalysis' (Lacan 2002f [1960]: 281).

3 Coined by Gaston Bachelard, the notion of the 'epistemological break' became a staple of French philosophical discourse during the 1960s, figuring prominently in the works of Althusser and Foucault, amongst others.

4 Lacan's original sentence reads: '*A tout cela nous paraît être radicale une modification dans notre position de sujet, au double sens: qu'elle y est inaugurale et que la science la renforce toujours plus*' (Lacan 1966g [1965]: 856). The English translation of this phrase—'In this situation what seems radical to me is the modification in our subject position, in both senses of the term, for that position is inaugural therein, and science continues to strengthen it ever further' (Lacan 1989b [1965]: 5)—does not really make sense because it is unclear what the two senses of the term 'subject position' would be. Here, as further in the text, when Lacan discusses Freud's adage *Wo Es war, soll Ich werden*, the French word *sens* is likely to mean 'direction' instead of 'meaning'.

5 'Scientism' is often used as a term of abuse to denigrate the practice of those who are convinced that the research methods of the natural sciences (physics, chemistry, biology) ought to inform all types of scientific investigation because the only forces purportedly at work within human and non-human organisms are physico-chemical ones. The notion 'scientism' is generally traced back to an oath pledged between Ernst Brücke and Emil Du Bois-Reymond in 1842, yet they themselves never used the

term. In 'Science and Truth' Lacan does not seem to employ 'scientism' in a derogatory fashion, as an attitude which represents the nemesis of psychoanalysis, but as the central stake of Freud's entire itinerary. For a recent critical reading of Freud's position vis-à-vis 'scientism', see Leader (2000: 11–48).

6   The importance of game theory for the epistemology of psychoanalysis will be discussed in detail in the second part of our book.

7   Sheridan's translation of the first italicized sentence has been modified, because Lacan expressly avoided the 'I think', by using '*de penser*' instead of '*que je pense*', which Sheridan reintroduced by rendering '*de penser*' as 'that I think', obviously generating confusion as to why Lacan would subsequently say that he prefers a formula 'which will save us from getting caught up in the *cogito*, the *I think*'.

8   Throughout his career, the peculiar grammatical form of Freud's *Wo Es war, soll Ich werden* exercised a strange fascination on Lacan. In his 1955 text 'The Freudian Thing', he undertook a meticulous dissection of its structure, surmising that Freud would not have omitted the definite article *das*, as it had appeared previously in the title of his book *Das Ich und das Es* (*The Ego and the Id*) without good reason (Lacan 2002b [1955]: 120–121). In this paper Lacan also proposed to translate Freud's formula as '*Là où c'était, c'est mon devoir que je vienne à être*', 'There where it was, it is my duty that I come to being' (ibid.: 121). Some two years later, in 'The Instance of the Letter in the Unconscious', he suggested the alternative '*Là où fut ça, il me faut advenir*', 'There where that was, it is necessary for me to happen' (Lacan 2002c [1957]: 162, translation modified), eventually settling on '*Là où c'était, là comme sujet dois-je advenir*' during the early 1960s.

9   The English translation of Lacan's text is problematic here, inasmuch as '*d'en renverser le sens*' has been rendered as 'in reversing its meaning'. We believe that Lacan's argument is not about changing the meaning of Freud's motto, and it is unclear how that would be possible in the first place, but only about changing the direction in which it should be read.

10 When saying that the cause should be considered as causing the whole effect, Lacan echoed Heidegger's stance on causality in 'The Question Concerning Technology', in which he had insisted that the effect always comprises both the end of a process and the means to achieve it (Heidegger 1977 [1953]: 6).

11 Between the first part of 'Science and Truth' (on the subject of science in psychoanalysis) and the second part of the text (on the truth as material cause), Lacan brought to mind his provocative attempt in 'The Freudian Thing' at conjuring up the truth by means of identifying with it ('I, truth, will speak'), a so-called prosopopoeia which convinced neither his Viennese audience the first time he did it, nor the more familiar group of attendants at his own seminar some six weeks later (Lacan 1993 [1955–56]: 83–84). The text 'The Freudian Thing' in Lacan's *Écrits* (Lacan 2002b [1955]) emanated from his second presentation at his seminar in Paris, the first presentation being no more than a free improvisation based on a set of notes (Lacan 1987–88 [1955]).

Chapter 3

1 The notion of 'the meaning of meaning' of course also refers here to the extremely influential eponymous treatise by Ogden and Richards (1946 [1923]), originally published in 1923 but going through numerous new editions until after World War II. On a number of occasions Lacan distanced himself explicitly from the logico-positivistic inspiration of their work. See Lacan (1964–65: session of 12 May 1965, 1970–71: session of 17 February 1971, 1973–74: session of 2 November 1973).

2 For those who had been attending Lacan's weekly seminars during the 1950s, the sudden appearance of '*Che vuoi?*' ('What do you want?') in 'Subversion of the Subject' would not have been as bewildering as it is to the contemporary reader, for Lacan had explained in his *Seminar IV* how struck he was by this 'fundamental interrogation' coming from the camel's mouth in *Le Diable amoureux* by Jacques Cazotte, and how it constituted the most captivating exemplification of the Superego. See Lacan (1994c [1956–57]: 169).

3 It would definitely be worthwhile to compare the 'internally excluded', 'extimate' position of the stranger to that of the analyst, for which one could take as a starting point the first part of Theodor Reik's magnificent *Listening with the Third Ear*, entitled 'I Am a Stranger Here Myself'. See Reik (1949).

4 Needless to say, James Strachey had no qualms translating it as 'instinct'. The French term *dérive* could be translated into English as 'drift'.

5 As Turkle has pointed out, many of Lacan's patients did not seem to be enthralled by the humour of Weyergans' novel, but scoured it for recognizable details of their analytic experience with Lacan. See Turkle (1992: 200–201). To the best of our knowledge, Lacan never compared the analyst to the court jester, but the latter's licence to turn common discourse upside down and to express 'truth' as the inherent stupidity of official knowledge comes very close to the analytic position.

6 For an excellent exploration of the linguistic intricacies of this seminar, see Chadwick (2002).

7 It has become standard practice amongst Anglo-American scholars to translate Lacan's term *lalangue* as 'llanguage', partly by virtue of the success of Slavoj Žižek's works, in which he makes extensive use of the notion. The first time Žižek uses 'llanguage', in the third chapter of *For They Know Not What They Do*, he refers the reader to Russell Grigg's translation of Lacan's 'Geneva Lecture on the Symptom' (Lacan 1989c [1975]) for arguments supporting this translation, yet nowhere does Grigg point out in his translation why he decided to render *lalangue* as 'llanguage' instead of 'thelanguage', for example (Žižek 2002: 138, n. 11). Throughout this book we will continue to use 'llanguage', yet add Lacan's term *lalangue* in order to maintain the conceptual origin of the term.

8 '*Les non-dupes errent*' stands for 'The non-duped err'—those who do not want to be duped are in error and forced to wander—but the signifier '*Les non-dupes errent*' is strictly homophonic with '*Les Noms du Père*' (The Names of the Father). Only in the transition from speech to writing does it become clear which of the two signifieds Lacan has in mind.

9 For the reader who is unfamiliar with the wonder of 'mondegreens', we are happy to mention that the notion was introduced by the writer Sylvia Wright on the basis of a personal experience. As a child, Wright heard the Scottish ballad 'The Bonny Earl of Murray' and believed one of its stanzas was: 'Ye Highlands and ye Lowlands, Oh where hae you been? They hae slay the Earl of Murray and Lady Mondegreen'. Much later she discovered that what had actually happened was quite different and did not involve a lady: 'They hae slay the Earl of Murray and laid him on the Green'. To commemorate the tragic death of Lady Mondegreen, Wright then decided to immortalize her as the patroness of all accidental mishearings.

10 It is rather unlikely that Lacan scholars and students of Lacanese, which of course also include Lacanian psychoanalysts in training, will be strongly affected by the threat of mondegreens because they are likely to read Lacan rather than listen to his voice. Yet with the bulk of his work now being made up of transcriptions of his lectures, the question is to what extent these transcriptions have not already 'mondegreened' the master's discourse. As some clever readers of one of Lacan's earlier seminars revealed, shortly after its first transcription and publication in French, the transcript of this relatively non-homophonic series of lectures already contained a substantial number of mondegreens, for which Lacan's stenographer is as much to blame as his editor; this does not look promising for the transcriptions of the later lectures. See École Lacanienne de Psychanalyse (1991).

11 *Apophansis* is a declarative discourse. An apophantic statement is an assertion that does not reveal and does not hide, but merely points in a certain direction. See Lacan (1998b [1972–73]: 114).

12 We will return to the analytic value of misdirected interpretations in the second part of our book.

Chapter 4

1 It is extraordinarily difficult to get an accurate view of the circumstances leading up to the 'dissolution'. First-hand accounts differ substantially depending on the institutional position of the 'reporter', and the extraordinary complexity of Lacan's institutional 'endgame' makes it extremely awkward for an outsider to identify and appreciate all the variables at play. For a general overview of the state and players of the École freudienne de Paris during the last years of Lacan's life, the reader may profit from the situational analyses provided by Roudinesco (1997 [1993]: 399–409) and especially Turkle (1992: 251–302), but must bear in mind that both these books focus on personal and institutional matters rather than intellectual politics.

2 At the end of her biography of Lacan, originally published in 1993, Roudinesco listed some twenty different psychoanalytic organizations in France, the majority with roots in Lacan's teaching. If she were to make a new count in 2005, the number would probably be around thirty or forty, again with the majority having developed out of the Lacanian tradition. See Roudinesco (1997 [1993]: 450–451).

3 Once again, interested parties will be able to bite off more than they can chew from the two exceedingly detailed, if sometimes largely overstated books by Roudinesco (1990 [1986], 1997 [1993]) and the absorbing study by Turkle (1992), not to mention the numerous critical accounts that are available in French.

4 As it happens, the translation here already silently reduces some of the semantic ambiguities in the original French version of Lacan's paper by adding the adjective 'analytic' to the terms 'technique' and 'experience'. For some, this in itself might constitute a sufficient reason for saying that after the dehumanization of Freud's soul at the hands of Strachey (Bettelheim 1983) the Anglo-Americans now also 'own' a more streamlined, less equivocal variety of Lacanian knowledge, and rumour has it that this is precisely what Lacan's literary executor perceives as a potential threat in the English translations of Lacan's works. As was especially clear in the English translation of Lacan's *Seminar XX* (Lacan 1998b [1972–73]), Miller's desire to preserve the purity of Lacan's discourse in his French editions of the *Seminars* has not prevented the officially sanctioned translators from adding extensive explanatory footnotes to their translations. Quite unexpectedly, Miller himself recently expressed a willingness to negotiate other French versions of the *Seminars*. See Miller (2002a: 165–181).

5 Interestingly, Lacan's Zen-inspired image of the teacher as someone who 'supplies an answer when the students are on the verge of finding it' chimes with one of Freud's 'technical recommendations' in 'On Beginning the Treatment': 'Even in the later stages of analysis one must be careful not to give a patient the solution of a symptom or the translation of a wish until he is already so close to it that he has only one short step more to make in order to get hold of the explanation for himself' (Freud 1913c: 140). In 'Lecture 27' of the *Introductory Lectures on Psycho-Analysis*, on the topic of transference, Freud also embraced a version of this principle in order to avoid the *ex cathedra* position: 'You only want to know in the most general way the method by which psychoanalytic therapy operates and what, roughly, it accomplishes. And you have an indisputable right to learn this. I shall not, however, tell it to you but shall insist on your discovering it for yourselves' (Freud 1916–17a [1915–17]: 431).

6 Leonardo da Vinci introduced the distinction between *per via de porre* (by way of adding) and *per via de levare* (by way of subtracting) in order to differentiate between the (additive) practice of painting and the (subtractive) practice of sculpting. Freud adopted the distinction in 'On Psychotherapy' in order to explain the difference between psychoanalysis and suggestion. See Freud (1905a [1904]: 260–261).

7 For the notion of 'wild analysis' see Freud (1910k).

8 Lacan's argument here follows his analysis of the 'prisoner's sophism' (Lacan 1988a [1945]), to which we shall return in Chapter 6 of this book.

9 Although it did not prevent Lacan's analysands from subsequently climbing the hierarchical ladder within non-Lacanian institutions. Daniel Widlöcher, the current president of the International Psychoanalytic Association, is a former analysand of Lacan's.

10 On one of the very few occasions when Freud discussed the matter, in his defence of lay analysis, he remained quite ambivalent as to which course to follow: 'I have no intention of making proposals which are based on the decision as to whether legal control or letting things go is to be preferred in the matter of analysis. . . . I have already set out what seems to me to speak in favour of a policy of *laissez faire*. If the other decision is taken—for a policy of active intervention—then it seems to me that in any case a lame and unjust measure of ruthlessly forbidding analysis by non-doctors will be an insufficient outcome' (Freud 1926e: 237–238).

11 Again, the circumstances surrounding the events are complex and difficult to assess. For a general discussion of Accoyer's amendment and its impli cations, see Maleval (2003) and Miller (2004). For Miller's direct response to the amendment, see Miller (2005), and for an interesting exchange on 'evaluation and its discontents', see Miller and Milner (2004). Finally, for a thought-provoking reflection upon the place and status of psycho-analysis within our Western market ideology, see Clément (2004) and for a general discussion of the interrelationships between the state, the patient and the health-care professional, see Roudinesco (2004).

12 Lacan also points out that if application can take place at all in the interface between psychoanalysis and literature, it is literature that should be applied to psychoanalysis. For interesting reflections on this kind of project (and its own limitations), see Bayard (2004).

Chapter 5

1 Russell Grigg is currently completing a full translation of Lacan's *Seminar XVII* and was kind enough to give us access to a draft of his work in progress. All subsequent translated passages from *Seminar XVII* have been taken from this draft, with page numbers referring to the official French version (Lacan 1991 [1969–70]).

2 The term 'topography' (*topischer Gesichtspunkt*) is intended to express the division of the unity of consciousness into distinct agencies or sys-tems that are not mapped onto the anatomy of the brain. See Freud (1925d [1924]: 32).

3 In a paper that was first delivered at Lacan's invitation during his sem-inar of 15 May 1979, Juan-David Nasio made the following observation: 'Unlike the S_1, the One of the gap, S_2 designates all other signifiers. . . . Where do we get this idea that all the other signifiers form a chain? Why do we suppose that these other signifiers are arranged in a knowing manner? I said earlier that the signifier is not to be known, but the signifiers taken together are a knowledge, they form a knowledge, they know' (Nasio 1996 [1992]: 40).

4 In *Seminar XI* Lacan famously compared the unconscious signifiers to a menu written in Chinese whose translation does not make the hungry subject any wiser (Lacan 1994a [1964]: 269).

5 See also our discussion of Roustang's interpretation of Lacan's language in Chapter 3.

6 For detailed discussions of the four discourses, see Bracher *et al.* (1994), Quackelbeen (1994), Fink (1995a) and Verhaeghe (1995).

7 The gist of this idea is already present in Lacan's work from the 1950s. See Lacan (1998a [1957–58], 2002e [1958]).

8 We will return to the issue of timely intervention in the following chapter. For the moment, it is sufficient to note that the use of knowledge as a machine for the production of belief opposes the intervention that divides the field of knowledge.

9 *L'Envers de la psychanalyse* ('The Other Side of Psychoanalysis') is actually the title given by Jacques-Alain Miller. As Lacan pointed out in the first lesson, he himself decided to call his Seminar *La Psychanalyse à l'envers* ('Psychoanalysis Upside Down') (Lacan 1991 [1969–70]: 10).

10 For a rigorous didactic explanation of the changing 'paradigms of jouissance' in Lacan's oeuvre, see Miller (2000).

11 As we argued in Chapter 4, analysts (and especially Lacanian analysts) have not provided any evidence that they are better equipped, by virtue of their analytic training, to legitimize their knowledge domain than other professionals.

12 More recently, Ian Parker (2001) has leavened applied Lacanian discourse theory with the element of impossibility, but still with rather confusing results: 'Lacan's account helps us to explore implications for epistemology in psychology of the role of discourse in the production of distance from the real and from experience at the very same moment that it fabricates our image of what lies outside representation' (Parker 2001: 75).

13 The four volumes of Sage's 'Modernity and Political Thought' series under discussion were Connolly (1993), Flathman (1993), Dallmayr (1993) and Schapiro (1993). For more recent examples of this tendency to use Lacan's four discourses as a labour-saving device, see Houtman (2003) and Campbell (2004). Houtman employs the discourses in order to forge a relationship between 'the subject of discourse (the author or authors) and their speech act (the film or novel text)'. Campbell, on the other hand, sees Lacan's discourse theory as an 'epistemological metatheory', whereby she completely disregards (inevitably, perhaps) the headless, acephalic knowledge of the unconscious, whose subject is barred. In her interpretation, the divided subject is a knowing subject, as a result of which Lacan's formulas are being reduced to structural types of intersubjective communication.

Chapter 6

1 In *Jokes and Their Relation to the Unconscious* Freud takes on board Lichtenberg's comment on Hamlet's famous statement, 'There are more things in heaven and earth . . . / Than are dreamt of in your philosophy'. For Lichtenberg, Hamlet's critique is by no means trenchant enough, since there is also much in philosophy that is not to be found in heaven and earth. Philosophy 'compensates' for its insufficiencies by multiplying its categories, but this solution only makes things worse. See Freud (1905c: 72).

2 For a detailed discussion of Freud's ambivalent relationship with philosophy and its representatives, see Assoun (1995).

3 For additional comments on Lacan's text, see Fink (1996), Roudinesco (1997 [1993]: 176–178) and Nobus (2000: 80–82).

4 Lacan's aforementioned definition of the 'aim of the game' as the reduction of 'the moment of concluding the time for comprehending so as to last but the instant of the glance' could also be seen as a formula which legitimizes the compression of the analytic session, whereas Roudinesco tends to interpret the short session simply as a session that is shorter than it should be, or that 'short-changes' the analysand in some way.

5 The notion of a 'game beneath the game' will be discussed more extensively in the next chapter.

6 Wilhelm Wundt (1832–1920) is generally recognized as one of the founders of experimental psychology. Wundt placed special emphasis on the empirical analysis of sensory processes, the immediate content of conscious experience and psychophysical parallelisms.

7 For similar statements about the difference between the psychoanalytic and the philosophical unconscious, see Freud (1900a: 614–615, 1905a [1904]: 266, 1912g: 260, 1913: 178–179, 1925d [1924]: 31–32).

8 As we explained in Chapter 1, Lacan later portrayed the analyst as a saint, 'who doesn't command the respect that a halo sometimes gets for him', who abdicates 'personal brilliance' and whose business has nothing to do with charity but with acting as trash [déchet]; his business being trashitas [il décharite]' (Lacan 1990d [1974]: 15). Partly because of the analysand's right to waffle his way through the session, Lacan later also abandoned the distinction between 'empty speech' and 'full speech' (Lacan 2002a [1953]: 42, 1993 [1955–56]: 36–37), and the concurrent task of the analyst to curb emptiness into fullness.

9 Herschel and his co-writers provide a recipe for managing the conversion of tacit to abstract knowledge, emphasizing the desirability of a 'problem-solving', organizational culture linked to tangible rewards.

10 See Deflem (2000), who has made it his personal mission to denounce a 'technologically-based invasion of our profession that applies market principles in an area of society governed by fundamentally different standards. . . . Teaching is not a free entrepreneurial delivery of product.'

11 A list of Porter's lectures was accessed on the Yale University website, www.yale.edu on 8 August 2000.

Chapter 7

1 It is worth mentioning that when Lacan referred to 'applied psychoanalysis' in the 'Founding Act' of his own school, he used the term in order to designate the application of psychoanalytic techniques within 'therapeutics and clinical medicine' rather than the psychoanalytically inspired interpretation of art, literature and society. See Lacan (1990a [1964]: 99).

2 It is precisely the critical power of artifice in the construction of the 'pure game' that links Lacan's ideas in *The Ethics of Psychoanalysis* (Lacan 1992 [1959–60]) to Deleuze's arguments in *The Logic of Sense* (Deleuze 2001 [1969]), although Lacan's conception of the game is much more indebted to economic and mathematical game theory (Von Neumann

and Morgenstern 1944; Williams 1954) than Deleuze's, which draws extensively on the work of the highly underrated Greek philosopher Kostas Axelos (1964, 1969a, 1969b). For Deleuze's reading of Axelos' search for 'planetary thought', see Deleuze (2004 [1970]).

3 Sometimes Roudinesco is not content with modelling Lacan's theories on his own history, and so she models them on the social history of France! Witness, for example, the following passage, pertaining to Lacan's theory of freedom circa 1964: 'This then was Lacan's new theory on human freedom: man is only free through his desire for freedom (Spinoza), which gives him the freedom to die (Antigone) but also forces him to submit to a society in which good and evil are organized in terms of one and the same imperative (Bion/Kant/Sade). Thus did Lacan—a theorist of truth in his teaching but a sophist and dissimulator in his life, an admirer of Mazarin in politics, and one who hadn't chosen to die, as Cavaillès did, for a desire for freedom—come to pay tribute to the regicides of the year II . . .' (Roudinesco 1997 [1993]: 314).

4 Noam Chomsky, to whom Lacan addressed the previously mentioned statement that he was thinking with his feet (and sometimes with his forehead), recalled his encounter with the psychoanalyst during the mid-1970s as follows: 'In the case of Lacan, for example, it's going to sound unkind—my frank opinion is that he was a self-conscious charlatan, and was simply playing games with the Paris intellectual community to see how much absurdity he could produce and still be taken seriously. I mean that quite literally. I knew him' (Chomsky 1989: 32).

5 In the last lesson of *The Ethics of Psychoanalysis* Lacan first formulated three propositions and then added a fourth. The first proposition is 'the only thing one can be guilty of is giving ground relative to one's desire'; the second is 'a hero is someone who may be betrayed with impunity'; the third concerns the ethical act in response to this betrayal: 'For the ordinary man the betrayal that almost always occurs sends him back to the service of goods, but with a proviso that he will never again find that factor which restores a sense of direction to that service.' In other words, a hero is someone who follows the logic of his inevitable betrayal 'to the death', whereas the ordinary man, lost in the world of goods, pretends that this same betrayal never happened, and in so doing, loses his aim. See Lacan (1992 [1959–60]: 311–325).

6 Adam Smith's 'invisible hand' of the market offers a famously utopian interpretation of this phenomenon, but we owe our current conception of the effect to the American sociologist Robert K. Merton (1936). Merton was interested in the effect of ignorance, error, vested interest, value systems and self-fulfilling prophecies on the unforeseen outcomes of strategic decision making. He also detected an epistemological dimension to the problem, noting that a lack of adequate knowledge in the decision-making process arises because 'Our classifications of acts and situations never involve completely homogeneous categories nor even categories whose approximate degree of homogeneity is sufficient for the prediction of particular events' (Merton 1936: 898). Merton is certain that unanticipated consequences will occur, but can establish no rules for linking 'acts' to their 'situations'.

7 The epistemological status of this comparison, and of Freud's 'archaeological metaphor' in general, will be dealt with at greater length in the next chapter.

8 To clarify the difference a bit more, it may be useful to focus on the single trope of comparison, if only because Žižek sometimes seems to have a patent on its intellectual value. In *Did Somebody Say Totalitarianism?* (Žižek 2001b), he employs the following mode of evaluation: 'As such, the Khmer Rouge regime was a kind of political equivalent to the famous publicity description of the utterly evil Linda Fiorentino *femme fatale* character from John Dahl's neo-noir film *The Last Seduction*: "Most people have a dark side . . . She had nothing else" In the same way, while most political regimes have a dark side of obscene secret rituals and apparatuses, the Khmer Rouge regime had nothing else . . .' (Žižek 2001b: 98). Although many readers may appreciate this passage for its 'brilliant insightfulness', and the Žižek fan club has built itself on the grounds of this type of reasoning, comparing an oppressive regime to a fragment of advertising copy may be stretching the content of a judgement quite far and, more importantly, does nothing to affect the contract between the writer and the reader—in the end, the idea that is being communicated is quite clear. In *Maldoror*, however, Ducasse/Lautréamont experiments directly with the reader's own ability to make a comparison. Witness the following passage: 'Two columns that it was not difficult and yet less possible to take for two baobab trees appeared in the valley, larger than two pins. As a matter of fact they were two enormous towers. And although two baobab trees do not resemble at the first glance two pins, or even two towers, nevertheless . . . it may be affirmed without fear of error . . . that a baobab tree does differ so very much from a column that the comparison should be forbidden between these two architectural forms . . . or geometric forms . . . or the one or the other . . . or neither the one nor the other . . . or rather, massive and elevated forms' (Lautréamont 1987 [1868–69]: 166). This is the kind of direct experimentation Lacan is referring to when he describes the reader's loss of bearings in contact with Sade and Lautréamont.

9 Key texts of the 'Science Wars' include Bloom (1987), Kimball (1990), Anderson (1992) and D'Souza (1992).

10 See Quinn (2002: 268–271).

11 Glynos and Stavrakakis write, for example: 'This backlash is epitomized by a kind of pathological reaction against the likes of Lacan . . . dismissive opinions about a person's work are taken seriously even if expressed by those *who admit to their ignorance* regarding that person's discipline' (Glynos and Stavrakakis 2002: 224).

12 Paul Devatour and his partner Yoon Ya have assumed the identity of curators and critics of 'artists' who produce work in a variety of styles, yet this whole art-world ensemble is produced by themselves. It can be argued that in 'assuming the power' of art-world institutions, Devatour and Yoon Ya are merely repeating it. See Zahn (1991).

13 In an interview with Terry Eagleton, Bourdieu reflected upon his intellectual trajectory as follows: 'My trajectory may be described as miraculous, I suppose—an ascension to a place where I don't belong . . . And so

to be able to live in a world that is not mine I must understand both things: what it means to have an academic mind—how such is created [*sic*]—and at the same time what is lost in acquiring it' (Bourdieu and Eagleton 1994: 272).

Chapter 8

1 Freud's earliest references to archaeology appear in *Studies on Hysteria* (Freud and Breuer 1895d: 139), in which he compares psychoanalytic technique to the excavation of a buried city. Thereafter references to archaeological knowledge and technique occur in his preface to the 'Dora' case (Freud 1905e [1901]: 12–13); his study of Jensen's *Gradiva*, with its central character of the young archaeologist Norbert Hanold (Freud 1907a [1906]); the case of the 'Rat Man' (1909d: 176); *Civilization and its Discontents* (1930a [1929]: 69–72); and, of course, 'Constructions in Analysis', which contains Freud's most thorough and inspired treatment of archaeological knowledge (1937d: 259–260). In a judicious essay on the archaeological metaphor, Reinhard (1996) has argued that the critical potency of Freud's interest in archaeological knowledge is greatly obscured by the idea that archaeology is merely a more or less adequate analogy for psychoanalytic technique. This more or less adequate analogy has nonetheless inspired a plethora of scholars to delve into Freud's work and reconstruct the architecture of the archaeological metaphor. See, for example, Cassirer Bernfeld (1952), Wolf and Nebel (1978), Jacobsen and Steele (1979), Larsen (1987), Cotter (1989), Kuspit (1989), Petrella (1990), Corcoran (1991), Bowdler (1996), Verene (1997), Montserrat (2001), Schmidt (2001) and Wachtel (2003).
2 In translating Lacan's phrase as 'reducing the non-meaning of the signifiers', Alan Sheridan has given it exactly the opposite sense, making it virtually impossible for the Anglophone reader to follow Lacan's argument in this section of the seminar.
3 Peter Gay quotes Freud as saying to his physician, Max Schur, that his partiality for the prehistoric was 'an addiction second in intensity only to his nicotine addiction' (Gay 1988: 170).
4 As de Duve has noted, 'after the first exhibition of 1917, which was a great success, never again would the Society of Independent Artists, which remained in existence until 1944, produce an event worthy of remaining in the history books of modern art' (de Duve 1998: 100).
5 *The Game of War, Taking into Account Successive Positions of all Forces During a Game* is the title of a book by Guy Debord and Alice Becker-Ho (Debord and Becker-Ho 1987). The phrase has also been used by Andrew Hussey to describe the activities of the Situationist International and their part in the student action at the University of Strasbourg in 1966, as well as the Paris riots of 1968, which began with disturbances at the University of Nanterre. Hussey lists the situationist 'military objectives' in 1968 as follows: 'The occupation of factories. Power to the workers' councils. Abolition of the society of classes. Down with the society of mercantile spectacle. Abolition of alienation. End of the university' (Hussey 2001: 237).

6 See also Roudinesco (1997 [1993]: 342–343).

7 Compton (1980) gives the following details in the appendix to his study of Broodthaers' work: 'Marcel Broodthaers, "Section des Figures (Der Adler vom Oligozän bis Heute)", Städtische Kunsthalle, Dusseldorf, 16 May–9 July 1972'.

8 The various essays and commentaries collected in *The Philistine Controversy* have their origin in articles that Beech and Roberts published in *New Left Review* and elsewhere between 1996 and 1998.

9 For a discussion of how this phenomenon is a persistent characteristic of the operations of archaeological knowledge, see Quinn (1999).

References

Allouch, J. (1998) *Allô, Lacan?—Certainement pas*, Paris: E.P.E.L.

Al Marashi, I. (2002) 'Iraq's Security and Intelligence Network: A Guide and Analysis', *Middle East Review of International Affairs*, 6(3), pp. 1–13.

Anderson, M. (1992) *Impostures in the Temple: American Intellectuals are Destroying our Universities and Cheating our Students of Their Future*, New York: Simon and Schuster.

André, S. (2003) *Devenir psychanalyste . . . et le rester*, Marseille: Que.

Aristotle (1996) *Physics*, trans. Robin Waterfield, Oxford: Oxford University Press.

Assoun, P.-L. (1995) *Freud, la philosophie et les philosophes*, Paris: Quadrige/ PUF.

Atkins, P. (1995) 'Science as Truth', *History of the Human Sciences*, 8(2), pp. 97–102.

Axelos, K. (1964) *Vers la pensée planétaire*, Paris: Minuit.

Axelos, K. (1969a) *Arguments d'une recherche*, Paris: Minuit.

Axelos, K. (1969b) *Le Jeu du monde*, Paris: Minuit.

Bataille, G. (2001a [1942]) 'Socratic College', in Stuart Kendall (ed.) *The Unfinished System of Nonknowledge*, trans. Michelle Kendall and Stuart Kendall, Minneapolis, MN: University of Minnesota Press, pp. 5–17.

Bataille, G. (2001b [1973–88]) *The Unfinished System of Nonknowledge*, ed. Stuart Kendall, trans. Michelle Kendall and Stuart Kendall, Minneapolis, MN: University of Minnesota Press.

Bayard, P. (2004) *Peut-on appliquer la littérature à la psychanalyse?*, Paris: Minuit.

Beech, D. and Roberts, J. (eds) (2002) *The Philistine Controversy*, London– New York: Verso.

Bénabou, M., Cornaz, L., De Liège, D. and Pélissier, Y. (2002) *789 Néologismes de Jacques Lacan*, Paris: EPEL.

Bettelheim, B. (1983) *Freud and Man's Soul*, New York: Alfred A. Knopf.

Bloom, A. (1987) *The Closing of the American Mind*, New York: Simon and Schuster.

Bonaparte, M. (1934) *Introduction à la théorie des instincts*, Paris: Denoël et Steele.

Borch-Jacobsen, M. (1997) 'Basta così!: Mikkel Borch-Jacobsen on Psycho-analysis and Philosophy—Interview by Chris Oakley', in T. Dufresne (ed.) *Returns of the 'French Freud': Freud, Lacan, and Beyond*, New York–London: Routledge, pp. 209–227.

Borch-Jacobsen, M. (2000) 'How a Fabrication Differs from a Lie', *London Review of Books*, 22(8), pp. 3–7.

Bourdieu, P. (2000 [1997]) *Pascalian Meditations*, trans. Richard Nice, Cambridge: Polity Press.

Bourdieu, P. and Eagleton, T. (1994) 'Doxa and Common Life: An Inter-view', in S. Žižek (ed.) *Mapping Ideology*, London–New York: Verso, pp. 265–277.

Bowdler, S. (1996) 'Freud and Archaeology', *Anthropological Forum*, 3, pp. 419–483.

Bracher, M. (1994) 'On the Psychological and Social Functions of Language: Lacan's Theory of the Four Discourses', in Bracher, M., Alcorn M.W., Jr., Corthell, R.J and Massardier-Kenney, F. (eds) *Lacanian Theory of Discourse: Subject, Structure and Society*, New York–London: New York University Press, pp. 107–128.

Bracher, M., Alcorn, M.W., Jr., Corthell, R.J. and Massardier-Kenney, F. (eds) (1994) *Lacanian Theory of Discourse: Subject, Structure and Society*, New York–London: New York University Press.

Brook, A. (2003) 'Kant and Freud', in M. Cheung Chung and C. Feltham (eds) *Psychoanalytic Knowledge*, Basingstoke–New York: Palgrave Macmillan, pp. 20–39.

Bulhack, A. (1996a) *Postmodernism Generator*, www.csse.monash.edu.au/cgi-bin/postmodern, accessed on 6 June 2003.

Bulhack, A. (1996b) *Dada Engine Manual*, www.zikzak.net/~acb/dada/manual-1.0/dada.html#SEC1, accessed on 12 August 2003.

Bulhack, A. (1996c) *On the Simulation of Postmodernism and Mental De-bility using Recursive Transition Networks*, www.csse.monash.edu.au/publications/1996/tr-cs96-264-abs.html, accessed on 12 August 2003.

Campbell, K. (2004) *Jacques Lacan and Feminist Epistemology*, London–New York: Routledge.

Cassirer Bernfeld, S. (1952) 'Freud and Archaeology', *The Yearbook of Psychoanalysis*, 8, pp. 39–55.

Castoriadis-Aulagnier, P., Perrier, F. and Valabrega, J.-P. (1970) 'Lettre à l'adresse du Directeur', *Scilicet*, 2/3, pp. 51–52.

Cavell, M. (1993) *The Psychoanalytic Mind: From Freud to Philosophy*, Cambridge, MA–London: Harvard University Press.

Cavell, S. (1988 [1986]) 'The Uncanniness of the Ordinary', in *In Quest of the Ordinary: Lines of Skepticism and Romanticism*, Chicago–London: University of Chicago Press, pp. 153–178.

Chadwick, T. (2002) 'Escroquerie? That'll Give Them Something to Chew On!', *Analysis*, 11, pp. 26–34.

Chapsal, M. (1984) *Envoyez la petite musique . . .*, Paris: Grasset.

Cheung Chung, M. and Feltham, C. (eds) (2003) *Psychoanalytic Knowledge*, Basingstoke–New York: Palgrave Macmillan.

Chomsky, N. (1957) *Syntactic Structures*, The Hague: Mouton.

Chomsky, N. (1989) 'Noam Chomsky: An Interview', *Radical Philosophy*, 53, pp. 31–40.

Cioffi, F. (1998) *Freud and the Question of Pseudoscience*, Chicago: Open Court.

Clément, C. (1983 [1981]) *The Lives and Legends of Jacques Lacan*, trans. Arthur Goldhammer, New York: Columbia University Press.

Clément, C. (2004) 'Perte et recréation du sens humain', *Magazine littéraire*, 428, pp. 22–24.

Compton, M. (1980) *Marcel Broodthaers*, London: Tate Gallery.

Connolly, W.E. (1993) *The Augustinian Imperative*, Newbury Park, CA–London: Sage.

Corcoran, L. (1991) 'Exploring the Archaeological Metaphor: The Egypt of Freud's Imagination', *Annual of Psychoanalysis*, 19, pp. 19–32.

Cotter, J.L. (1989) 'Freud's Magnificent Obsession', *Archaeology*, 42, p. 84.

Crews, F. (1997) *The Memory Wars: Freud's Legacy in Dispute*, London: Granta.

Culler, J. (1988) 'The Call of the Phoneme: Introduction', in J. Culler (ed.) *On Puns: The Foundation of Letters*, Oxford: Basil Blackwell, pp. 1–16.

Cusanus, N. (1985 [1440]) *On Learned Ignorance*, trans. Jasper Hopkins, Minneapolis, MN: Arthur J. Banning Press.

Dallmayr, F.R. (1993) *G.W.F. Hegel: Modernity and Politics*, Newbury Park, CA–London: Sage.

Deacon, A.B. (1927) 'The Regulation of Marriage in Ambrym', *Journal of the Royal Anthropological Institute*, 57, pp. 325–342.

Debord, G. and Becker-Ho, A. (1987) *Le 'Jeu de la guerre', relevé des positions successives de toutes les forces au cours d'une partie*, Paris: Gérard Lebovici.

de Duve, T. (1998) *Kant After Duchamp*, Cambridge, MA–London: MIT Press.

Deflem, M. (2000) 'A Brief History of Online Notes Companies', available online at www.sla.purdue.edu/people/soc/mdeflem/znotesicaaup.htm, accessed on 6 August 2003.

Delabastita, D. (ed.) (1997) *Traductio: Essays on Punning and Translation*, Manchester: St Jerome Publishing.

Deleuze, G. (2001 [1969]) *The Logic of Sense*, ed. Constantin V. Boundas, trans. Mark Lester with Charles Stivale, London–New York: Continuum.

Deleuze, G. (2004 [1970]) 'The Fissure of Anaxagoras and the Local Fires of Heraclitus', in David Lapoujade (ed.) *Desert Islands and Other Texts 1953–1974*, trans. Michael Taormina, New York: Semiotext(e), pp. 156–161.

Derrida, J. (1986) 'Proverb: "He that would pun . . ." ', in J.P. Leavey, Jr. (ed.) *Glassary*, Lincoln, NE–London: University of Nebraska Press, pp. 17–20.

Derrida, J. (1998 [1996]) *Resistances of Psychoanalysis*, trans. Peggy Kamuf, Pascale-Anne Brault and Michael Naas, Stanford, CA: Stanford University Press.

Derrida, J. (2000 [1997]) *Of Hospitality: Anne Dufourmantelle Invites Jacques Derrida to Respond*, trans. Rachel Bowlby, Stanford, CA: Stanford University Press.

Derrida, J. (2002 [2000]) 'Psychoanalysis Searches the States of its Soul: The Impossible Beyond of a Sovereign Cruelty', in *Without Alibi*, trans. Peggy Kamuf, Stanford, CA: Stanford University Press, pp. 238–280.

Descartes, R. (1984 [1638–1640]) 'Meditations on First Philosophy', *The Philosophical Writings of Descartes*, Vol. II, trans. J. Cottingham, R. Stoothoff and D. Murdoch, Cambridge: Cambridge University Press, pp. 1–62.

Descartes, R. (1985 [1637]) 'Discourse on the Method', *The Philosophical Writings of Descartes*, Vol. I, trans. J. Cottingham, R. Stoothoff and D. Murdoch, Cambridge: Cambridge University Press, pp. 111–151.

Diatkine, G. (1997) *Jacques Lacan*, Paris: Presses Universitaires de France.

Diatkine, G. (2001) 'Les Lacanismes, les analystes français et l'Association Psychanalytique Internationale', in A. Green (ed.) *Courants de la psychanalyse contemporaine* (Revue française de psychanalyse-numéro hors-série), Paris: Presses Universitaires de France, pp. 389–400.

Donald, J. (1991) 'On the Threshold: Psychoanalysis and Cultural Studies', in J. Donald (ed.) *Psychoanalysis and Cultural Theory: Thresholds*, London: Macmillan, pp. 1–10.

Dreher, A.U. (2000) *Foundations for Conceptual Research in Psychoanalysis*, trans. Eva Ristl, London–New York: Karnac Books.

D'Souza, D. (1992) *Illiberal Education: The Politics of Race and Sex on Campus*, New York: Random House.

Dufresne, T. (ed.) (1997) *Returns of the 'French Freud': Freud, Lacan, and Beyond*, New York–London: Routledge.

École Lacanienne de Psychanalyse (ed.) (1991) *Le Transfert dans tous ses errata*, Paris: E.P.E.L.

Eissler, R.S. (ed.) (1954) '106th Bulletin of the International Psycho-Analytical Association', *International Journal of Psycho-Analysis*, 35(1), pp. 267–290.

Erasmus, D. (1993 [1509]) *The Praise of Folly*, trans. Betty Radice, Harmondsworth: Penguin.

Etchegoyen, R.H. and Miller, J.-A. (1996) *Silence brisé. Entretien sur le mouvement psychanalytique*, Paris: Agalma.

Eysenck, H.J. (1985) *Decline and Fall of the Freudian Empire*, New York: Viking-Penguin.

Fink, B. (1995a) *The Lacanian Subject: Between Language and Jouissance*, Princeton, NJ–London: Princeton University Press.

Fink, B. (1995b) 'Science and Psychoanalysis', in R. Feldstein, B. Fink and M. Jaanus (eds) *Reading Seminar XI: Lacan's Four Fundamental Concepts of Psychoanalysis*, Albany, NY: State University of New York Press, pp. 55–64.

Fink, B. (1996) 'Logical Time and the Precipitation of Subjectivity', in R. Feldstein, B. Fink and M. Jaanus (eds) *Reading Seminars I and II: Lacan's Return to Freud*, Albany, NY: State University of New York Press, pp. 356–386.

Fink, B. (2002) 'Knowledge and Science: Fantasies of the Whole', in J. Glynos and Y. Stavrakakis (eds) *Lacan and Science*, London–New York: Karnac Books, pp. 167–178.

Flathman, R.E. (1993) *Thomas Hobbes: Skepticism, Individuality and Chastened Politics*, Newbury Park, CA–London: Sage.

Forrester, J. (1990) *The Seductions of Psychoanalysis: Freud, Lacan and Derrida*, Cambridge: Cambridge University Press.

Freud, S. (1894a) 'The Neuro-Psychoses of Defence', *Standard Edition*, 3, pp. 45–61.

Freud, S. (1900a) *The Interpretation of Dreams, Standard Edition*, 4/5.

Freud, S. (1901b) *The Psychopathology of Everyday Life, Standard Edition*, 6.

Freud, S. (1905a [1904]) 'On Psychotherapy', *Standard Edition*, 7, pp. 257–268.

Freud, S. (1905c) *Jokes and Their Relation to the Unconscious, Standard Edition*, 8.

Freud, S. (1905e [1901]) 'Fragment of an Analysis of a Case of Hysteria', *Standard Edition*, 7, pp. 7–122.

Freud, S. (1907a [1906]) 'Delusions and Dreams in Jensen's *Gradiva*', *Standard Edition*, 9, pp. 1–95.

Freud, S. (1909b) 'Analysis of a Phobia in a Five-Year-Old Boy', *Standard Edition*, 10, pp. 5–147.

Freud, S. (1909d) 'Notes upon a Case of Obsessional Neurosis (the "Rat Man")', *Standard Edition*, 10, pp. 155–249.

Freud, S. (1910c) 'Leonardo da Vinci and a Memory of his Childhood', *Standard Edition*, 11, pp. 57–137.

Freud, S. (1910d) 'The Future Prospects of Psychoanalytic Therapy', *Standard Edition*, 11, pp. 139–151.

Freud, S. (1910k) ' "Wild" Psycho-Analysis', *Standard Edition*, 11, pp. 219–227.

Freud, S. (1911c [1910]) 'Psycho-Analytic Notes Upon an Autobiographical Account of a Case of Paranoia (Dementia Paranoides)', *Standard Edition*, 12, pp. 3–82.

Freud, S. (1912e) 'Recommendations to Physicians Practising Psycho-Analysis', *Standard Edition*, 12, 109–120.

Freud, S. (1912g) 'A Note on the Unconscious in Psychoanalysis', *Standard Edition*, 12, pp. 260–266.

Freud, S. (1912–13a) *Totem and Taboo*, *Standard Edition*, 13.

Freud, S. (1913c) 'On Beginning the Treatment (Further Recommendations on the Technique of Psycho-Analysis I)', *Standard Edition*, 12, 121–144.

Freud, S. (1913j) 'The Claims of Psycho-Analysis to Scientific Interest', *Standard Edition*, 13, pp. 163–190.

Freud, S. (1914b) 'The Moses of Michelangelo', *Standard Edition*, 13, pp. 209–236.

Freud, S. (1914g) 'Remembering, Repeating and Working-through (Further Recommendations on the Technique of Psycho-Analysis II)', *Standard Edition*, 12, pp. 145–156.

Freud, S. (1915a [1914]) 'Observations on Transference-Love (Further Recommendations on the Technique of Psycho-Analysis III)', *Standard Edition*, 12, pp. 159–171.

Freud, S. (1915b) 'Thoughts for the Times on War and Death', *Standard Edition*, 14, pp. 273–300.

Freud, S. (1915c) 'Instincts and Their Vicissitudes', *Standard Edition*, 14, pp. 109–140.

Freud, S. (1915d) 'Repression', *Standard Edition*, 14, pp. 141–158.

Freud, S. (1915e) 'The Unconscious', *Standard Edition*, 14, pp. 159–215.

Freud, S. (1916–17a [1915–17]) *Introductory Lectures on Psycho-Analysis*, *Standard Edition*, 15/16.

Freud, S. (1918b [1914]) 'From the History of an Infantile Neurosis (the "Wolf Man")', *Standard Edition*, 17, pp. 7–122.

Freud, S. (1920g) *Beyond the Pleasure Principle*, *Standard Edition*, 18, pp. 1–64.

Freud, S. (1923b) *The Ego and the Id*, *Standard Edition*, 19, pp. 1–66.

Freud, S. (1924f [1923]) 'A Short Account of Psycho-Analysis', *Standard Edition*, 19, pp. 189–209.

Freud, S. (1925d [1924]) *An Autobiographical Study*, *Standard Edition*, 20, pp. 1–74.

Freud, S. (1925e [1924]) 'The Resistances to Psycho-Analysis', *Standard Edition*, 19, pp. 211–222.

Freud, S. (1925f) 'Preface to Aichhorn's *Wayward Youth*', *Standard Edition*, 19, pp. 271–275.

Freud, S. (1925h) 'Negation', *Standard Edition*, 19, pp. 235–239.

Freud, S. (1926d [1925]) 'Inhibitions, Symptoms and Anxiety', *Standard Edition*, 20, pp. 75–175.

Freud, S. (1926e) 'The Question of Lay Analysis: Conversations with an Impartial Person', *Standard Edition*, 20, pp. 177–250.

Freud, S. (1926f) 'Psycho-Analysis', *Standard Edition*, 20, pp. 259–270.

Freud, S. (1927a) 'Postscript to "The Question of Lay Analysis"', *Standard Edition*, 20, pp. 251–258.

Freud, S. (1927e) 'Fetishism', *Standard Edition*, 21, pp. 152–157.

Freud, S. (1930a [1929]) *Civilization and its Discontents*, Standard Edition, 21, pp. 57–145.

Freud, S. (1933a [1932]) *New Introductory Lectures on Psycho-Analysis*, Standard Edition, 22, pp. 5–182.

Freud, S. (1937c) 'Analysis Terminable and Interminable', *Standard Edition*, 23, pp. 216–253.

Freud, S. (1937d) 'Constructions in Analysis', *Standard Edition*, 23, pp. 255–269.

Freud, S. (1940a [1938]) *An Outline of Psycho-Analysis*, Standard Edition, 23, pp. 144–207.

Freud, S. (1940b [1938]) 'Some Elementary Lessons in Psycho-Analysis', *Standard Edition*, 23, pp. 279–286.

Freud, S. (1940e [1938]) 'Splitting of the Ego in the Process of Defence', *Standard Edition*, 23, pp. 271–278.

Freud, S. (1950a [1895]) 'Project for a Scientific Psychology', *Standard Edition*, 1, pp. 281–397.

Freud, S. and Breuer, J. (1895d) *Studies on Hysteria, Standard Edition*, 2.

Galbraith, J.K. (1998 [1958]) *The Affluent Society*, 40th Anniversary Edition, Harmondsworth: Penguin.

Gay, P. (1988) *Freud: A Life for Our Time*, London: J.M. Dent.

Ginzburg, C. (1980) 'Morelli, Freud and Sherlock Holmes: Clues and Scientific Method', trans. Anna Davin, *History Workshop: A Journal of Socialist Historians*, 9, pp. 5–36.

Glynos, J. and Stavrakakis, Y. (2002) 'Postures and Impostures: On Lacan's Style and Use of Mathematical Science', in J. Glynos and Y. Stavrakakis (eds) *Lacan and Science*, London–New York: Karnac Books, pp. 207–229.

Godin, J.-G. (1990) *Jacques Lacan, 5, rue de Lille*, Paris: du Seuil.

Granoff, W. (1986) 'D'un fétiche en forme d'article', in M. Augé, M. David-Ménard, W. Granoff, J.-L. Lang and O. Mannoni (eds) *L'Objet en psychanalyse. Le Fétiche, le corps, l'enfant, la science*, Paris: Denoël, pp. 33–49.

Grigg, R. (1999) 'The Subject of Science', Paper presented at 'The Subject: Encore', conference organized by the American Lacanian Link (ALL), Los Angeles, CA, 7 March 1999, unpublished.

Gross, P.R. and Levitt, N. (1994) *Higher Superstition: The Academic Left and its Quarrels with Science*, Baltimore, MD–London: Johns Hopkins University Press.

Grünbaum, A. (1984) *The Foundations of Psychoanalysis: A Philosophical Critique*, Berkeley/Los Angeles, CA–London: University of California Press.

Grünbaum, A. (1993) *Validation in the Clinical Theory of Psychoanalysis: A Study in the Philosophy of Psychoanalysis*, Madison, CT: International Universities Press.

Grünbaum, A. (2004) 'Critique of Psychoanalysis', in A. Casement (ed.) *Who Owns Psychoanalysis?*, London–New York, NY: Karnac Books, pp. 263–305.

Haddad, G. (2002) *Le Jour où Lacan m'a adopté*, Paris: Bernard Grasset.

Hawker, P. (2002) 'Mind Fails to Equate', *The Age*, 7 March, www.theage.com.au/articles/2002/03/06/1015365716513.html, accessed on 1 July 2004.

Heidegger, M. (1977 [1953]) 'The Question Concerning Technology', in David Farrell Krell (ed.) *Basic Writings*, San Francisco, CA: Harper and Row, pp. 283–317.

Herschel, R.T., Nemati, H. and Steiger, D. (2001) 'Tacit to Explicit Knowledge Conversion: Knowledge Exchange Protocols', *Journal of Knowledge Management*, 5(1), pp. 107–116.

Hjelmslev, L. (1961 [1943]) *Prolegomena to a Theory of Language*, trans. Francis J. Whitfield, Madison, WI: University of Wisconsin Press.

Hofstadter, D.R. (1999 [1979]) *Gödel, Escher, Bach: An Eternal Golden Braid*, 20th Anniversary Edition, with a new preface, Harmondsworth: Penguin.

Houtman, C. (2003) 'Lacan's Theory of the Four Discourses and the Sixth Sense', *Journal for Cultural Research*, 7(3), pp. 277–296.

Hussey, A. (2001) *The Game of War: The Life and Death of Guy Debord*, London: Pimlico.

Jacobsen, P. and Steele, R. (1979) 'From the Present to the Past: Freudian Archaeology', *International Journal of Psychoanalysis*, 60(3), pp. 349–362.

Jakobson, R. (1963) *Essais de linguistique générale. I. Les Fondations du langage*, trans. Nicolas Ruwet, Paris: Minuit.

Jones, E. (1953–57) *The Life and Work of Sigmund Freud*, 3 vols, New York: Basic Books.

Joyce, J. (1961 [1922]) *Ulysses*, New York: Random House.

Joyce, J. (1992 [1939]) *Finnegans Wake*, Harmondsworth: Penguin.

Kaplan-Solms, K. and Solms, M. (2002) *Clinical Studies in Neuro-Psychoanalysis: Introduction to a Depth Neuropsychology*, 2nd Edition, London–New York: Karnac Books.

Kimball, B. (1990) *Tenured Radicals: How Politics Has Corrupted Higher Education*, New York: Harper and Row.

Klein, N. (2000) *No Logo*, London: Flamingo.

Koestler, A. (1989 [1959]) *The Sleepwalkers: A History of Man's Changing Vision of the Universe*, Harmondsworth: Penguin.

Kofman, S. (1988 [1970]) *The Childhood of Art: An Interpretation of Freud's Aesthetics*, trans. Winifred Woodhull, New York: Columbia University Press.

Kojève, A. (1969 [1933–39]) *Introduction to the Reading of Hegel*, ed. A. Bloom, trans. J.H. Nichols, Jr., New York–London: Basic Books.

Koyré, A. (1957) *From the Closed World to the Infinite Universe*, Baltimore, MD: Johns Hopkins Press.

Koyré, A. (1971 [1955]) 'De l'influence des conceptions philosophiques sur l'évolution des théories scientifiques', *Études d'histoire de la pensée philosophique*, Paris: Gallimard, pp. 253–269.

Kris, E. (1951) 'Ego Psychology and Interpretation in Psychoanalytic Therapy', *Psychoanalytic Quarterly*, 20, pp. 15–30.

Kuspit, D. (1989) 'A Mighty Metaphor: The Analogy of Archaeology and Psychoanalysis' in L. Gamwell and R. Wells (eds) *Sigmund Freud and Art: His Personal Collection of Antiquities*, New York: Abrams, pp. 133–151.

Lacan, J. (1958–59) *Le Séminaire VI, Le Désir et son interprétation*, unpublished.

Lacan, J. (1961–62) *Le Séminaire IX, L'Identification*, unpublished.

Lacan, J. (1964–65) *Le Séminaire XII, Problèmes cruciaux pour la psychanalyse*, unpublished.

Lacan, J. (1965–66) *Le Séminaire XIII, L'Objet de la psychanalyse*, unpublished.

Lacan, J. (1966a [1954]) 'Introduction au commentaire de Jean Hyppolite sur la "Verneinung" de Freud', *Écrits*, Paris: du Seuil, pp. 369–380.

Lacan, J. (1966b [1954]) 'Réponse au commentaire de Jean Hyppolite sur la "Verneinung" de Freud', *Écrits*, Paris: du Seuil, pp. 381–399.

Lacan, J. (1966c [1955]) 'Variantes de la cure-type', *Écrits*, Paris: du Seuil, pp. 323–362.

Lacan, J. (1966d [1957]) 'L'Instance de la lettre dans l'inconscient ou la raison depuis Freud', *Écrits*, Paris: du Seuil, pp. 493–528.

Lacan, J. (1966e [1964]) 'Position de l'inconscient', *Écrits*, Paris: du Seuil, pp. 829–850.

Lacan, J. (1966f [1965]) 'La Science et la vérité', *Cahiers pour l'analyse*, 1/2, pp. 5–28.

Lacan, J. (1966g [1965]) 'La Science et la vérité', *Écrits*, Paris: du Seuil, pp. 855–877.

Lacan, J. (1966–67) *Le Séminaire XIV, La Logique du fantasme*, unpublished.

Lacan, J. (1967 [1966]) 'Psychanalyse et médecine', *Lettres de l'École freudienne*, 1, pp. 34–51.

Lacan, J. (1967–68) *Le Séminaire XV, L'Acte psychanalytique*, unpublished.

Lacan, J. (1968a [1967]) 'De la psychanalyse dans ses rapports avec la réalité', *Scilicet*, 1, pp. 51–59.

Lacan, J. (1968b [1967]) 'La Méprise du sujet supposé savoir', *Scilicet*, 1, pp. 31–41.

Lacan, J. (1968c [1967]) 'De Rome 53 à Rome 67: La psychanalyse. Raison d'un échec', *Scilicet*, 1, pp. 42–50.

Lacan, J. (1968–69) *Le Séminaire XVI, D'un autre à l'autre*, unpublished.

Lacan, J. (1970–71) *Le Séminaire XVIII, D'un discours qui ne serait pas du semblant*, unpublished.

Lacan, J. (1971–72) *Le Séminaire XIX, . . . ou pire/Le Savoir du psychanalyste*, unpublished.

Lacan, J. (1972 [1956]) 'Seminar on "The Purloined Letter" ', trans. Jeffrey Mehlman, *Yale French Studies*, 48, pp. 38–72.

Lacan, J. (1973) 'Postface', in *Le Séminaire, Livre XI: Les Quatre Concepts fondamentaux de la psychanalyse*, texte établi par J.-A. Miller, Paris: du Seuil, pp. 251–254.

Lacan, J. (1973–74) *Le Séminaire XXI, Les Non-dupes errent*, unpublished.

Lacan, J. (1976–77 [1975–76]) 'Le Séminaire XXIII, Le Sinthome', *Ornicar?*, 6, pp. 3–20; 7, pp. 3–18; 8, pp. 6–20; 9, pp. 32–40; 10, pp. 5–12; 11, pp. 2–9.

Lacan, J. (1977a [1969]) 'Preface', in A. Lemaire, *Jacques Lacan*, trans. David Macey, London: Routledge and Kegan Paul, pp. vii–xv.

Lacan, J. (1977b) 'Ouverture de la section clinique', *Ornicar?*, 9, pp. 7–14.

Lacan, J. (1977–79 [1976–77]) 'Le Séminaire XXIV, L'Insu que sait de l'une-bévue s'aile à mourre', *Ornicar?*, 12/13, pp. 4–16; 14, pp. 4–9; 15, pp. 5–9; 16, pp. 7–13; 17/18, pp. 7–23.

Lacan, J. (1978a [1972]) 'Du discours psychanalytique', in G.B. Contri (ed.) *Lacan in Italia/En Italie Lacan (1953–1978)*, Milan: La Salamandra, pp. 32–55.

Lacan, J. (1978b [1973]) 'La Psychanalyse dans sa référence au rapport sexuel', in G.B. Contri (ed.) *Lacan in Italia/En Italie Lacan (1953–1978)*, Milan: La Salamandra, pp. 58–77.

Lacan, J. (1981 [1972]) 'La Mort est du domaine de la foi', *Quarto*, 3, pp. 5–20.

Lacan, J. (1983 [1967]) 'Interview donnée par Jacques Lacan à François Wahl à propos de la parution des *Écrits*', *Bulletin de l'Association freudienne*, 3, pp. 6–7.

Lacan, J. (1987–88 [1955]) 'Notes en allemand préparatoires à la conférence sur "La chose freudienne" ', trans. Geneviève Morel and Franz Kaltenbeck, *Ornicar?*, 42, pp. 7–11.

Lacan, J. (1988a [1945]) 'Logical Time and the Assertion of Anticipated Certainty: A New Sophism', trans. Marc Silver and Bruce Fink, *Newsletter of the Freudian Field*, 2(2), pp. 4–22.

Lacan, J. (1988b [1953–54]) *The Seminar. Book I: Freud's Papers on Technique*, ed. Jacques-Alain Miller, trans. with notes by John Forrester, Cambridge: Cambridge University Press.

Lacan, J. (1988c [1954–55]) *The Seminar. Book II: The Ego in Freud's Theory and in the Technique of Psychoanalysis*, ed. Jacques-Alain Miller, trans. Sylvana Tomaselli, with notes by John Forrester, Cambridge: Cambridge University Press.

Lacan, J. (1989a [1962]) 'Kant with Sade', trans. James B. Swenson, Jr., *October*, 51, pp. 55–75.

Lacan, J. (1989b [1965]) 'Science and Truth', trans. Bruce Fink, *Newsletter of the Freudian Field*, 3 (1/2), pp. 4–29.

Lacan, J. (1989c [1975]) 'Geneva Lecture on the Symptom', trans. Russell Grigg, *Analysis*, 1, pp. 7–26.

Lacan, J. (1990a [1964]) 'Founding Act', trans. Jeffrey Mehlman, in Joan Copjec (ed.) *Television/A Challenge to the Psychoanalytic Establishment*, New York: W.W. Norton, pp. 97–106.

Lacan, J. (1990b [1966]) 'Responses to Students of Philosophy Concerning the Object of Psychoanalysis', trans. Jeffrey Mehlman, in Joan Copjec (ed.) *Television/A Challenge to the Psychoanalytic Establishment*, New York: W.W. Norton, pp. 107–114.

Lacan, J. (1990c [1969]) 'Impromptu at Vincennes', trans. Jeffrey Mehlman, in Joan Copjec (ed.) *Television/A Challenge to the Psychoanalytic Establishment*, New York: W.W. Norton, pp. 117–128.

Lacan, J. (1990d [1974]) 'Television', trans. Denis Hollier, Rosalind Krauss and Annette Michelson, in Joan Copjec (ed.) *Television/A Challenge to the Psychoanalytic Establishment*, New York: W.W. Norton, pp. 1–46.

Lacan, J. (1990e [1980]) 'Letter of dissolution', trans. Jeffrey Mehlman, in Joan Copjec (ed.) *Television/A Challenge to the Psychoanalytic Establishment*, New York: W.W. Norton, pp. 128–130.

Lacan, J. (1991 [1969–70]) *Le Séminaire, Livre XVII, L'Envers de la psychanalyse*, texte établi par Jacques-Alain Miller, Paris: du Seuil.

Lacan, J. (1992 [1959–60]) *The Seminar. Book VII: The Ethics of Psychoanalysis*, ed. Jacques-Alain Miller, trans. with notes by Dennis Porter, New York: W.W. Norton.

Lacan, J. (1993 [1955–56]) *The Seminar. Book III: The Psychoses*, ed. Jacques-Alain Miller, trans. with notes by Russell Grigg, New York: W.W. Norton.

Lacan, J. (1994a [1964]) *The Four Fundamental Concepts of Psycho-Analysis*, ed. Jacques-Alain Miller, trans. Alan Sheridan, Harmondsworth: Penguin.

Lacan, J. (1994b [1976]) 'Preface to the English-Language Edition of *Seminar XI*', in Jacques-Alain Miller (ed.) *The Four Fundamental Concepts of Psycho-Analysis*, trans. Alan Sheridan, Harmondsworth: Penguin, pp. xxxix–xli.

Lacan, J. (1994c [1956–57]) *Le Séminaire. Livre IV: La Relation d'objet*, texte établi par J.-A. Miller, Paris: du Seuil.

Lacan, J. (1995a [1964]) 'Position of the Unconscious', trans. Bruce Fink, in Richard Feldstein, Bruce Fink and Maire Jaanus (eds) *Reading Seminar XI: Lacan's Four Fundamental Concepts of Psychoanalysis*, Albany, NY: State University of New York Press, pp. 259–282.

Lacan, J. (1995b [1967]) 'Proposition of 9 October 1967 on the Psychoanalyst of the School', trans. Russell Grigg, *Analysis*, 6, pp. 1–13.

Lacan, J. (1998a [1957–58]) *Le Séminaire, Livre V, Les Formations de l'inconscient*, texte établi par Jacques-Alain Miller, Paris: du Seuil.

Lacan, J. (1998b [1972–73]) *The Seminar. Book XX: On Feminine Sexuality, the Limits of Love and Knowledge (Encore)*, ed. Jacques-Alain Miller, trans. Bruce Fink, New York: W.W Norton.

Lacan, J. (2001a [1958]) 'La Psychanalyse vraie, et la fausse', in *Autres écrits*, Paris: du Seuil, pp. 165–174.

Lacan, J. (2001b [1960–61]) *Le Séminaire. Livre VIII: Le Transfert*, seconde édition corrigée, texte établi par J.-A. Miller, Paris: du Seuil.

Lacan, J. (2001c [1967]) 'Discours à l'École freudienne de Paris', in *Autres écrits*, Paris: du Seuil, pp. 261–281.

Lacan, J. (2001d [1969]) 'Adresse à l'École', in *Autres écrits*, Paris: du Seuil, pp. 293–295.

Lacan, J. (2001e [1971]) 'Lituraterre', in *Autres écrits*, Paris: du Seuil, pp. 11–20.

Lacan, J. (2001f [1972]) 'L'Étourdit', in *Autres écrits*, Paris: du Seuil, pp. 449–495.

Lacan, J. (2001g [1973]) 'Introduction à l'édition allemande d'un premier volume des *Écrits*', in *Autres Écrits*, Paris: du Seuil, pp. 553–559.

Lacan, J. (2001h [1975]) 'Joyce le Symptôme', in *Autres Écrits*, Paris: du Seuil, pp. 565–570.

Lacan, J. (2002a [1953]) 'The Function and Field of Speech and Language in Psychoanalysis', in *Écrits: A Selection*, trans. Bruce Fink, New York: W.W. Norton, pp. 31–106.

Lacan, J. (2002b [1955]) 'The Freudian Thing, or the Meaning of the Return to Freud in Psychoanalysis', in *Écrits: A Selection*, trans. Bruce Fink, New York: W.W. Norton, pp. 107–137.

Lacan, J. (2002c [1957]) 'The Instance of the Letter in the Unconscious or Reason since Freud', in *Écrits: A Selection*, trans. Bruce Fink. New York: W.W. Norton, pp. 138–168.

Lacan, J. (2002d [1958]) 'The Direction of the Treatment and the Principles of its Power', in *Écrits: A Selection*, trans. Bruce Fink, New York: W.W. Norton, pp. 215–270.

Lacan, J. (2002e [1958]) 'The Signification of the Phallus', in *Écrits: A Selection*, trans. Bruce Fink, New York: W.W. Norton, pp. 271–280.

Lacan, J. (2002f [1960]) 'The Subversion of the Subject and the Dialectic of Desire in the Freudian Unconscious', in *Écrits: A Selection*, trans. Bruce Fink, New York: W.W. Norton, pp. 281–312.

Lagache, D. (1949) *L'Unité de la psychologie*, Paris: Presses Universitaires de France.

Laplanche, J. and Leclaire, S. (1972 [1960]) 'The Unconscious: A Psychoanalytic Study', trans. Patrick Coleman, *Yale French Studies*, 48, pp. 118–175.

Larsen, S.F. (1987) 'Remembering and the Archaeological Metaphor', *Metaphor and Symbolic Activity*, 2(3), pp. 187–199.

Laurent, E. (1995 [1994]) 'Psychoanalysis and Science', trans. R. Klein,

Newsletter of the London Circle of the European School of Psychoanalysis, 3, pp. 4–10.

Lautréamont, Comte de (1987 [1868–69]) *Maldoror*, trans. A. Lyliard, New York: Schocken Books.

Leader, D. (2000) *Freud's Footnotes*, London: Faber & Faber.

Lear, J. (2003) *Therapeutic Action: An Earnest Plea for Irony*, London–New York: Karnac Books.

Leclaire, S. (1996) 'Proposition pour une instance ordinale des psychanalystes', in *Écrits pour la psychanalyse, Vol. 1: Demeures de l'ailleurs (1954–1993)*, Paris: Arcanes, pp. 327–348.

Lévi-Strauss, C. (1966 [1962]) *The Savage Mind (La Pensée sauvage)*, London: Weidenfeld and Nicolson.

Lévi-Strauss, C. (1968a [1949]) 'The Effectiveness of Symbols', *Structural Anthropology*, trans. Claire Jacobson and Brooke Grundfest Schoepf, London: Allen Lane/Penguin Press, pp. 186–205.

Lévi-Strauss, C. (1968b [1949]) 'The Sorcerer and his Magic', *Structural Anthropology*, trans. Claire Jacobson and Brooke Grundfest Schoepf, London: Allen Lane/Penguin Press, pp. 167–185.

Lévi-Strauss, C. (1968c [1952]) 'Social Structure', *Structural Anthropology*, trans. Claire Jacobson and Brooke Grundfest Schoepf, London: Allen Lane/Penguin Press, pp. 277–323.

Lévi-Strauss, C. (1969 [1949]) *The Elementary Structures of Kinship*, trans. J.H. Bell and J.R. von Sturmer, ed. Rodney Needham, London: Eyre and Spottiswoode.

Lévi-Strauss, C. (1978) *Myth and Meaning*, London–New York: Routledge and Kegan Paul.

Lévi-Strauss, C. (1983 [1964]) *The Raw and the Cooked: Mythologiques*, vol. 1, trans. John and Doreen Weightman, Chicago–London: University of Chicago Press.

Libbrecht, K. (1998) 'The Original Sin of Psychoanalysis: On the Desire of the Analyst', in D. Nobus (ed.) *Key Concepts of Lacanian Psychoanalysis*, London: Rebus Press, pp. 75–100.

Livingstone Smith, D. (2003) ' "Some Unimaginable Substratum": A Contemporary Introduction to Freud's Philosophy of Mind', in M. Cheung Chung and C. Feltham (eds) *Psychoanalytic Knowledge*, Basingstoke–New York: Palgrave Macmillan, pp. 54–75.

Luborsky, L. and Crits-Christoph, P. (1990) *Understanding Transference: The Core Conflictual Relationship Theme Method*, New York: Basic Books.

Lyotard, J.-F. (1984 [1979]) *The Postmodern Condition: A Report on Knowledge*, trans. Geoff Bennington and Brian Massumi, Minneapolis, MN: University of Minnesota Press.

Maier, C. (2003) *Le Lacan dira-t-on: Guide français-lacanien*. Paris: Mots & Cie.

Maleval, J.-C. (2003) 'Des vides juridiques aux évaluations', *Le Nouvel Âne*, 1, pp. 6–7.

Martin, A. (1985) *The Knowledge of Ignorance: From Genesis to Jules Verne*, Cambridge: Cambridge University Press.

Masson, J.M. (ed.) (1985) *The Complete Letters of Sigmund Freud to Wilhelm Flieβ (1887–1904)*, Cambridge, MA–London: Belknap Press of Harvard University Press.

Mehlman, J. (1972) 'French Freud . . .', *Yale French Studies*, 48, pp. 5–9.

Meltzer, F. (1988) 'Eat your *Dasein*: Lacan's Self-Consuming Puns', in J. Culler (ed.) *On Puns: The Foundation of Letters*, Oxford: Basil Blackwell, pp. 156–163.

Merton, R.K. (1936) 'The Unanticipated Consequences of Purposive Social Action', *American Sociological Review*, 1(6), pp. 894–904.

Mill, J.S. (2003 [1869]) *On Liberty*, ed. David Bromwich and George Kateb, New Haven, CT–London: Yale University Press.

Miller, J.-A. (ed.) (1976) *La Scission de 1953. La Communauté psychanalytique en France—1*, Paris: Navarin.

Miller, J.-A. (ed.) (1977) *L'Excommunication. La Communauté psychanalytique en France—2*, Paris: Navarin.

Miller, J.-A. (1985) *Entretien sur Le Séminaire avec François Ansermet*, Paris: Navarin.

Miller, J.-A. (1990a) 'Entretien sur la cause analytique avec Jacques-Alain Miller', *l'Âne*, 42, pp. 26–30.

Miller, J.-A. (1990b) 'A Reading of Some Details in Television in Dialogue with the Audience', *Newsletter of the Freudian Field*, 4(1/2), pp. 4–30.

Miller, J.-A. (1994) 'La Passe de la psychanalyse vers la science: le désir de savoir', *Quarto*, 56, pp. 36–43.

Miller, J.-A. (1996) 'Le Monologue de *l'apparole*', *La Cause freudienne*, 34, pp. 7–18.

Miller, J.-A. (2000) 'Paradigms of *jouissance*', trans. Jorge Jauregui, *Lacanian Ink*, 17, pp. 10–47.

Miller, J.-A. (2002a) *Lettres à l'opinion éclairée*, Paris: du Seuil.

Miller, J.-A. (2002b) 'Le Mot juste', unpublished lecture held in Paris on 9 November.

Miller, J.-A. (2003) 'Entretien avec Bernard Accoyer et Jacques-Alain Miller, par Jean-Pierre Elkabbach', radio broadcast, Europe 1, 31 October 2003, 8:30 am.

Miller, J.-A. (2004) 'Allilaire et le clan des palotins', *Le Nouvel Âne*, 3, pp. 4–5.

Miller, J.-A. (2005) *The Pathology of Democracy*, London–New York: Karnac Books.

Miller, J.-A. and Milner, J.-C. (2004) *Voulez-vous être évalué? Entretiens sur une machine d'imposture*, Paris: Grasset.

Milner, J.-C. (1978) *L'Amour de la langue*, Paris: du Seuil.

Milner, J.-C. (1991) 'Lacan and the Ideal of Science', in Alexandre Leupin (ed.) *Lacan and the Human Sciences*, Lincoln, NE–London: University of Nebraska Press, pp. 27–43.

Milner, J.-C. (1995) *L'Œuvre claire. Lacan, la science, la philosophie*, Paris: du Seuil.

Milner, J.-C. (1997) 'Lacan and Modern Science', *Journal of European Psychoanalysis*, 3/4, pp. 105–132.

Milner, J.-C. (2000) 'The Doctrine of Science', trans. Oliver Feltham, *Umbr@*, 3, pp. 33–63.

Montserrat, D. (2001) 'Freud and the Archaeology of Aspiration', *Apollo*, 153(473), pp. 27–34.

Morris, M. (1988) 'Banality in Cultural Studies', *Discourse*, 10(2), pp. 3–29.

Muller, J.P and Richardson, W.J. (eds) (1988) *The Purloined Poe: Lacan, Derrida and Psychoanalytic Reading*, Baltimore, MD–London: Johns Hopkins University Press.

Nasar, S. (1998) *A Beautiful Mind*, London: Faber and Faber.

Nasio, J.-D. (1996 [1992]) 'The Concept of the Subject of the Unconscious', trans. Boris Belay, in David Pettigrew and François Raffoul (eds) *Disseminating Lacan*, Albany, NY: State University of New York Press, pp. 23–42.

Nobus, D. (2000) *Jacques Lacan and the Freudian Practice of Psychoanalysis*, London–Philadelphia, PA: Brunner-Routledge.

Nobus, D. (2001) 'Littorical Reading: Lacan, Derrida and the Analytic Production of Chaff', *JPCS: Journal for the Psychoanalysis of Culture and Society*, 6(2), pp. 279–288.

Ogden, C.K. and Richards, I.A. (1946 [1923]) *The Meaning of Meaning: A Study of the Influence of Language upon Thought and of the Science of Symbolism*, London: Kegan Paul, Trench, Trubner & Co.

Parker, I. (2001) 'Lacan, Psychology and the Discourse of the University', *Psychoanalytic Studies*, 3(1), pp. 67–77.

Peirce, C.S. (1934 [1903]) *The Collected Papers of Charles Sanders Peirce*, Vol. V, ed. Charles Hartshorne and Paul Wei, Cambridge, MA–London: Harvard University Press.

Perrier, F. (1985) *Voyages extraordinaires en Translacanie*, Paris: Lieu Commun.

Petrella, F. (1990) 'Analytical Archaeology in Freud's Latter Phase', *Rivista di Psicoanalisi*, 36(4), pp. 956–971.

Plato (1986) *Protagoras and Meno*, trans. W.K.C. Guthrie, Harmondsworth: Penguin.

Pluth, E. (2004) 'How Acts Use Signifiers', *Journal for Lacanian Studies*, 2(1), pp. 18–33.

Poe, E.A. (1988 [1844]) 'The Purloined Letter', in *The Complete Illustrated Stories and Poems of Edgar Allan Poe*, London: Chancellor Press, pp. 319–333.

Porter, B. (2000) 'Take Note', *Guardian Education*, 7 March, pp. 12–13.

Quackelbeen, J. (1994) 'The Psychoanalytic Discourse Theory of Jacques Lacan: Introduction and Application', *Studies in Psychoanalytic Theory*, 3(1), pp. 21–43.

Quine, W.V.O (1969) *Ontological Relativity and Other Essays*, New York–London: Columbia University Press.

Quinn, M. (1999) 'The Séance of 27 August 1889 and the Problem of Historical Consciousness', in P.P.A. Funari, M. Hall and S. Jones (eds) *Historical Archaeology: Back from the Edge*, London–New York: Routledge, pp. 85–96.

Quinn, M. (2002) 'The Legions of the Blind: the Philistine and Cultural Studies', in D. Beech and J. Roberts (eds) *The Philistine Controversy*, London–New York: Verso, pp. 255–271.

Radin, M.J. (1996) *Contested Commodities*, Cambridge, MA–London: Harvard University Press.

Regnault, F. (1985) *Dieu est inconscient*, Paris: Navarin.

Reik, T. (1949) *Listening with the Third Ear: The Inner Experience of a Psychoanalyst*, New York: Farrar, Straus and Company.

Reinhard, K. (1996) 'The Freudian Things: Construction and the Archaeological Metaphor', in S. Barker (ed.) *Excavations and Their Objects: Freud's Collection of Antiquity*, Albany, NY: State University of New York Press, pp. 57–79.

Rey, P. (1989) *Une saison chez Lacan*, Paris: Robert Laffont.

Ricoeur, P. (1970 [1965]) *Freud and Philosophy: An Essay on Interpretation*, trans. Denis Savage, New Haven, CT–London: Yale University Press.

Ronell, A. (2002) *Stupidity*, Urbana/Chicago, IL: University of Illinois Press.

Rorty, R. (1979) *Philosophy and the Mirror of Nature*, Princeton, NJ: Princeton University Press.

Roudinesco, E. (1990 [1986]) *Jacques Lacan & Co.: A History of Psychoanalysis in France, 1925–1985*, trans. Jeffrey Mehlman, Chicago: University of Chicago Press.

Roudinesco, E. (1997 [1993]) *Jacques Lacan*, trans. Barbara Bray, Cambridge: Polity Press.

Roudinesco, E. (2004) *Le Patient, le thérapeute et l'état*, Paris: Fayard.

Roudinesco, E. and Plon, M. (1997) *Dictionnaire de la psychanalyse*, Paris: Fayard.

Roustang, F. (1990 [1986]) *The Lacanian Delusion*, trans. Greg Sims, Oxford–New York: Oxford University Press.

Rubenstein, D. (1994) 'The Four Discourses and the Four Volumes', *Journal of Politics*, 56(4), pp. 1119–1132.

Rubin, B. (2004) 'British Government Plagiarizes MERIA Journal: Our Response', http://meria.idc.ac.il/british-govt-plagiarizes-meria.html, accessed on 5 July 2004.

Schapiro, M.J. (1993) *Reading 'Adam Smith': Desire, History and Value*, Newbury Park, CA–London: Sage.

Schmidt, D. (2001) 'Refuse Archaeology: Virchow–Schliemann–Freud', *Perspectives on Science*, 9(2), pp. 210–232.

Schneiderman, S. (1983) *Jacques Lacan: The Death of an Intellectual Hero*, Cambridge, MA–London: Harvard University Press.

Schneiderman, S. (ed.) (1993 [1980]) *How Lacan's Ideas are Used in Clinical Practice*, Northvale, NJ–London: Jason Aronson.

Shapin, S. (2003) 'Ivory Trade', *London Review of Books*, 25(17), pp. 15–19.

Shepherd, M. (1985) *Sherlock Holmes and the Case of Dr Freud*, London–New York: Tavistock.

Shingu, K. (2004 [1995]) *Being Irrational: Lacan, the Object a and the Golden Mean*, trans. Michael Radich, Tokyo: Gakuju Shoin.

Simmel, G. (1971 [1908]) 'The Stranger', trans. Donald N. Levine, in Donald N. Levine (ed.) *On Individuality and Social Forms*, Chicago–London: University of Chicago Press, pp. 143–149.

Snow, C.P. (1993 [1964]) *The Two Cultures*, Cambridge: Cambridge University Press.

Sokal, A. (1996) 'Transgressing the Boundaries: Toward a Transformative Hermeneutics of Quantum Gravity', *Social Text*, 46/47, pp. 217–252.

Sokal, A. and Bricmont, J. (1998) *Intellectual Impostures*, London: Profile Books.

Soler, C., Soler, L., Adam, J. and Silvestre, D. (2000) *La Psychanalyse, pas la pensée unique. Histoire d'une crise singulière*, Paris: Éditions du Champ Lacanien.

Solms, M. and Turnbull, O. (2002) *The Brain and the Inner World: An Introduction to the Neuroscience of Subjective Experience*, London–New York: Karnac Books.

Strauss, M. (1994) 'Psychanalyse et science', *Quarto*, 56, pp. 23–30.

Sulloway, F. (1992) *Freud, Biologist of the Mind: Beyond the Psychoanalytic Legend*, Cambridge, MA–London: Harvard University Press.

Tabori, P. (1993 [1959]) *The Natural History of Stupidity*, New York: Barnes & Noble Books.

Taylor, C. (1989) *Sources of the Self*, Cambridge, MA–London: Harvard University Press.

Thatcher, M. (1987) 'Interview', *Woman's Own*, 31 October.

Torney, P. (1994) 'Freud, Religion and the Oedipus Complex: Some Reflections on the Infantile Origins of Religious Experience', in R. Ekins and R. Freeman (eds) *Centres and Peripheries of Psychoanalysis: An Introduction to Psychoanalytic Studies*, London: Karnac Books, pp. 143–168.

Turkle, S. (1992) *Psychoanalytic Politics: Jacques Lacan and Freud's French Revolution*, 2nd Edition, London: Free Association Books.

van Boxsel, M. (2003) *The Encyclopaedia of Stupidity*, London: Reaktion Books.

Verene, D.P. (1997) 'Freud's Consulting Room Archaeology and Vico's

Principles of Humanity: A Communication', *British Journal of Psychotherapy*, 13(4), pp. 499–505.

Verhaeghe, P. (1994) 'La Psychanalyse et la science: une question de causalité', *Quarto*, 56, pp. 73–76.

Verhaeghe, P. (1995) 'From Impossibility to Inability: Lacan's Theory of the Four Discourses', *The Letter: Lacanian Perspectives on Psychoanalysis*, 4, pp. 76–99.

Verhaeghe, P. (2002) 'Causality in Science and Psychoanalysis', in J. Glynos and Y. Stavrakakis (eds) *Lacan and Science*, London–New York: Karnac Books, pp. 119–145.

von Hartmann, E. (1931 [1869]) *Philosophy of the Unconscious: Speculative Results According to the Inductive Method of Physical Science*, New York: Harcourt, Brace.

Von Neumann, J. and Morgenstern, O. (1944) *Theory of Games and Economic Behavior*, Princeton, NJ: Princeton University Press.

Wachtel, P.L. (2003) 'The Surface and the Depths: The Metaphor of Depth in Psychoanalysis and the Ways in Which it Can Mislead', *Contemporary Psychoanalysis*, 39(1), pp. 5–26.

Weyergans, F. (1974) *Le Pitre*, Paris: NRF-Gallimard.

Williams, J.D. (1954) *The Compleat Strategyst, Being a Primer on the Theory of Games of Strategy*, New York–Toronto–London: McGraw-Hill.

Wolf, E. and Nebel, S. (1978) 'Psychoanalytical Excavations: The Structure of Freud's Cosmography', *American Imago*, 35, pp. 178–202.

Zahn, O. (1991) 'Yoon Ya and Paul Devatour: Sylvana Lorenz Galerie Beaubourg', *Artforum*, September, pp. 144–145.

Žižek, S. (1989) *The Sublime Object of Ideology*, London–New York: Verso.

Žižek, S. (1998) 'The Seven Veils of Fantasy', in D. Nobus (ed.) *Key Concepts of Lacanian Psychoanalysis*, London: Rebus Press, pp. 190–218.

Žižek, S. (2000) 'Holding the Place', in J. Butler, E. Laclau and S. Žižek (eds) *Contingency, Hegemony, Universality: Contemporary Dialogues on the Left*, London–New York: Verso, pp. 308–329.

Žižek, S. (2001a) *The Fright of Real Tears: Krzystof Kiéslowski Between Theory and Post-Theory*, London: BFI.

Žižek, S. (2001b) *Did Somebody Say Totalitarianism?*, London–New York: Verso.

Žižek, S. (2002) *For They Know Not What They Do: Enjoyment as a Political Factor*, 2nd edition, London–New York: Verso.

Index